EU–US Relations

Also by Nikos Kotzias

GOALS AND TACTICS IN THE IGC OF THE EUROPEAN UNION 1996–1997 (*co-author with St. Perrakis*)

INTER-GOVERNMENTAL CONFERENCE (in Greek) (*with Ch. Rozakis, G. Papadimitrou, N. Skandamis, S. Perrakis and A. Pliakos*)

THE EEC: a Second Degree State of an Emerging System – the National State and the Procedure for Political Unification in the European Union Community (in Greek)

GLOBAL COMPETITION: the Comparison of Ethnocratic Systems (in Greek)

THE INTELLIGENTSIA IN GREECE: Social Position and Ideology (in Greek) (*with G. Diamantis, A. Thersiotis, Th. Ioannou, G. Konstantinidis and T. Symeonidis*)

DER AUTONOME INTELLECKT (*with P. Brand, H.J. Sandkuehler, F. Schumacher, W. Von Haren and M. Wilmes*)

THE DIALECTIC OF THE STATE: Theories on the State and Greek Political Parties on the State (in Greek)

GREECE ON THE THRESHOLD OF 2000 (in Greek) (*with A. Adrianopoulos and G. Papadakos*)

PASOK'S THIRD WAY (in Greek)

A DISCUSSION THAT NEVER TOOK PLACE

ART AND SOCIETY (in Greek)

THE COALITION OF THE LEFT: Politics and Society (in Greek)

CONSCIOUS AND SPONTANEOUS (in Greek)

Also by Petros Liacouras

INTERNATIONAL LAW AND THE USE OF OCEAN FLOOR FOR MILITARY PURPOSES

(*et al.*) NATIONAL AND EUROPEAN SECURITY (in Greek)

EU–US Relations

Repairing the Transatlantic Rift

Kastellorizo Papers

Foreword by

George A. Papandreou
President of the Pan-Hellenic Socialist Party (PASOK)
President of the Socialist International

Edited by

Nikos Kotzias
Senior Expert
Ministry of Foreign Affairs, Greece

and

Petros Liacouras
Lecturer in International Law
Department of International and European Studies
University of Piraeus, Greece

First published 2006 by
PALGRAVE MACMILLAN
Houndmills, Basingstoke, Hampshire RG21 6XS and
175 Fifth Avenue, New York, N.Y. 10010
Companies and representatives throughout the world

PALGRAVE MACMILLAN is the global academic imprint of the Palgrave
Macmillan division of St. Martin's Press, LLC and of Palgrave Macmillan Ltd.
Macmillan® is a registered trademark in the United States, United Kingdom
and other countries. Palgrave is a registered trademark in the European
Union and other countries.

ISBN 13: 978–1–4039–3520–5   hardback
ISBN 10: 1–4039–3520–3   hardback
ISBN 13: 978–1–4039–3521–2   paperback
ISBN 10: 1–4039–3521–1   paperback

This book is printed on paper suitable for recycling and made from fully
managed and sustained forest sources.

A catalogue record for this book is available from the British Library.

Library of Congress Cataloging-in-Publication Data

EU-US relations : repairing the transatlantic rift / edited by Nikos Kotzias
and Petros Liacouras.
    p. cm.
    Includes bibliographical references and index.
    Contents: The nature of transatlantic disagreements : duration and
progress – The long-term character of the EU-US disagreements –
Differences and mutual completion – Short-term causes – The
recommendations – The studies and their recommendations.
    ISBN 1–4039–3520–3 (cloth) – ISBN 1–4039–3521–1 (paper)
      1. European Union countries – Foreign relations – United States.
    2. United States – Foreign relations – European Union countries. I. Title:
European Union-United States relations. II. Kotzias, Nikos. III. Liakouras,
Petros El.

D2025.5.U64E8 2006
341.242'20973–dc22   2005058267

10   9   8   7   6   5   4   3   2   1
15   14   13   12   11   10   09   08   07   06

Printed and bound in Great Britain by
Antony Rowe Ltd, Chippenham and Eastbourne

Contents

Foreword: the Importance of Transatlantic Relations and Dialogue

George A. Papandreou
President of the Pan-Hellenic Socialist Party (PASOK)

New opportunities and challenges for humankind

The end of the Cold War marked a major turning point in modern history. With the end of polarization between East and West, many believed that humankind might now focus its attention on tackling real global problems such as poverty, inequality, illiteracy and environmental degradation. Others spoke of the end of history – the end of grand ideologies and great conflicts. But their expectations were belied by the events that followed 1989. Globalization became a new political and ideological battleground. The breakup of the Soviet Union and Yugoslavia, the collapse of failed African states, and growing social inequity in the West all indicated that history had, in fact, not come to an end. On the contrary, old problems were taking on a heightened intensity as new problems began to surface.

Today, these problems continue to plague our planet. As we enter the twenty-first century, new dangers have emerged which pose a real threat to humanity's prospects for a brighter future – and indeed to our very survival. These are the problems on which wealthy, developed countries like the United States and organizations such as the European Union should focus both their attention and resources. Instead of using our powers creatively, all too often we use them to generate new threats to ourselves and our environment. Now we must gather the resources we need to meet the challenges of our age. We must act with the requisite wisdom and resoluteness to confront threats. At the same time, we should be aware of the new opportunities at our disposal – the new possibilities, means and channels to solve problems that in the past seemed insurmountable, in ways that will benefit all our peoples. We must look to the future with optimism and vision, and we must learn from the past without becoming the prisoner of history.

The international community has a moral obligation to try to solve the world's problems. In order to meet these challenges, we must first reach a democratic consensus about our global goals. We must convince our citizens that the provision of funds and means to combat global problems will not detract from their prosperity but on the contrary will create a safer environment that allows for the greater prosperity of all. Second, those countries capable of rising to such a challenge must engage in close cooperation, while respecting those states and regions that suffer most, precisely because they do not have the means to combat complex problems single-handedly. Third, we must be resolute in fighting any forces that threaten our commitment to democracy, freedom, and respect for diversity.

But in our efforts to achieve these objectives, we are likely to confront a series of obstacles, especially regarding transatlantic relations. While I am optimistic that these can be overcome, an identification and analysis of the difficulties that lie ahead will help us move faster towards lasting solutions.

The implications of terrorism for collective security

Security – and, by extension, terrorism – has become the primary focus of transatlantic relations. New types of horizontal or asymmetrical warfare have become a source of friction between the US and a number of European states. This hampers the resolution of long-standing transatlantic disputes over related questions of international law, environmental protection, global trade and world poverty.

Transnational terrorism and other types of 'new' conflict do not, as a rule, involve a power struggle between two or more states, nor are they confined to battles between armies. Their perpetrators subscribe to the logic of war for war's sake because they thrive on the ideological fanaticism that is the justification for war, the material means obtained in its name, and the power secured as a result. Terrorism offers an apparent opportunity – albeit one that is ultimately catastrophic – to a large section of the population who cannot imagine a better future for themselves. At the same time, it gives these people the false impression that they are extremely powerful. Terrorism can strike anywhere in the world, whenever and wherever it chooses – a capacity once possessed only by very powerful nations like the United States. As 11 September 2001 demonstrated, a supranational, terrorist network such as al-Qaeda can strike a serious blow at the most powerful country in the world.

In many ways, terrorism represents the dark side of globalization. New technologies enable terrorist networks to operate and access funds internationally. This undermines the power of the nation-state. In fact, the organizational and technological capacities of many states and international institutions are developing at a slower pace than transnational terrorism. The more geographic and virtual space terrorism occupies, the more dangerous it becomes. When terrorist groups are allowed to flourish by complicit countries, as was the case in Afghanistan, the combination is even more explosive, for it allows them to develop more advanced means and increases the danger of terrorists gaining access to weapons of mass destruction.

In seeking effective policies to confront terrorism, we must ask ourselves: Should we try to fight violence with force, or should we fight terror with other means? Should we take pre-emptive measures? If so, should they be military or social? Is it enough to simply deal with the consequences of terrorism, or must we attempt to eradicate its root causes? The latter is clearly most likely to succeed, because as long as its causes continue to exist, terrorism will continue to flourish, like a mythical Hydra that is all too real. And we cannot wait for some new Hercules to slay it for us. Given that today's complex security threats are not only military in nature, a military machine – no matter how powerful – will never be enough to defeat terrorism alone. Similarly, unilateral actions will never achieve lasting results. Defeating the underlying causes of terrorism requires greater assistance and cooperation towards the less fortunate peoples of our planet. Developed countries must provide as much aid as possible, to be applied and distributed as effectively as possible.

At the same time, we must not delude ourselves into thinking that a long-term policy of tackling global social problems will immediately eliminate terrorism. Global problems may give terrorists an added justification for their cause, but terrorists are not necessarily poor, deprived or illiterate. In order to combat both the social causes that provoke terrorism and its impact on global security, the world's most powerful forces must take concerted action. We need to establish global mechanisms to systematically gather intelligence, monitor the flow of capital, and enhance international customs cooperation. The weakest states, who suffer the consequences of terrorism most acutely, must be included in this process.

Iraq: a watershed for transatlantic relations

Paradoxically, since the collapse of the former Soviet bloc in 1989, transatlantic approaches to tactical problems have tended towards divergence rather than convergence. The terrorist attacks on the United

States in 2001 triggered a wave of solidarity with the United States. Americans and Europeans joined forces to fight the oppressive Taliban regime in Afghanistan. But shortly afterwards, differing views on how best to deal with Saddam Hussein's regime in Iraq led to a dangerous cooling of transatlantic relations.

The war in Iraq demonstrated that our long-standing transatlantic partnership can no longer be taken for granted. We must now ensure that this vital partnership is reshaped and adapted to the current global reality. We must ask ourselves whether the differences between the US and many Europeans are fundamental or strategic. Are these differences likely to be permanent, or is there a way to overcome them? As the United States and its allies prepared for the war in Iraq, I spent a long time considering this problem. As Greece held the Presidency of the European Union at the time, I travelled to most of the capitals involved to try to broker a peaceful settlement. I debated the issue repeatedly with my colleagues at the United Nations Security Council. And I was invited to address the Arab League, the first time a non-Arab politician has done so. My desire for peace was compounded by a determination not to allow differences of opinion to harden into transatlantic conflicts that might in future have disastrous implications for world peace and stability.

The war in Iraq not only tested the cohesion and strategic orientation of the European Union, it also put a real strain on transatlantic relations, which had been deteriorating for some time. Many citizens on both sides of the Atlantic had become distrustful of one another because the US administration insisted on adopting unilateral policies that it called upon all its allies to support without question. Europe, on the other hand, was and is in the process of defining a more prominent role for itself in the global arena. In the European Union, our strategic alliance of nation-states functions through a joint evaluation of problems and risks, consensus on how best to confront them, followed by collective action. The United States has a tendency to interpret this policy of compromise and consensus as a sign of weakness or inaction. When it wishes to protect its own interests, international laws and institutions like the United Nations are now of secondary importance for the United States. The debate about whether Europe should participate in the United States-led campaign in Iraq developed into a political dispute over whether the European Union should allow the United States to act unilaterally.

At the same time, deeper divisions between those Western European nations who were more or less pro-US began to surface. The Greek

Presidency did its utmost to achieve consensus among EU member states and managed to broker agreement on a series of decisions. But it became increasingly clear that there was an urgent need for a frank and far-reaching discussion among all EU partners regarding our security and defence policy, and an even more urgent need to engage in a meaningful EU–US dialogue. Greece therefore put these issues at the top of the agenda for the Informal Council of EU Foreign Ministers in Kastellorizo in May, 2003. Because the Informal Council is traditionally a relaxed meeting of a small group of foreign ministers and their closest aides, where no formal conclusions are issued, it presented an ideal opportunity to air our grievances and share our views. Kastellorizo, the southernmost of the Dodecanese islands, was a symbolic choice of location as it lies between Greece and Cyprus, only a few miles from the coast of Turkey. Our message was that peoples with a painful history of tensions and conflicts, like Greece and Turkey, can overcome their differences and live in peace.

It was my belief that our discussions should neither be constrained by official texts, nor take place in a vacuum. Therefore I concluded that the best course would be to solicit the opinions of specialists in transatlantic relations on the problems brought to a head by the war in Iraq. I asked a number of politicians and academics of international prominence to consider how we might identify and tackle our differences, without losing sight of the values and interests that unite us. How could we avoid a damaging dispute within the EU and instead identify the methods and tools to strengthen the EU's role in the world? How might we increase our influence within the United States by promoting mutual understanding and cooperation? How could we breathe new life into a multipolar, multilateral, multilevel system of global governance, founded on international laws and institutions, so that it might truly respond to the problems and challenges of today's interdependent world?

The papers contained in this volume played a decisive role in the extensive discussion of these issues that took place on Kastellorizo. These contributions helped us to reconsider both the problems and potential of transatlantic relations in a constructive, forward-looking manner. The different views and perspectives, from both sides of the Atlantic, across a wide range of expertise, acted as a springboard for taking concrete initiatives and developing news tools and networks to improve transatlantic ties. The outcome of the Kastellorizo meeting was a decisive step for the European Union: the launching of the first ever European Security Strategy, which will be submitted for adoption by the European Council in December 2003. This will allow the Union to strengthen its defensive capabilities and tackle global security threats in a more strategic manner.

We also agreed on various measures to strengthen dialogue between the citizens and institutions of the European Union and the United States. With hindsight, it is clear that the Kastellorizo meeting was the right moment to begin a far-reaching dialogue on the future of transatlantic relations. Our discussions were not conclusive, but they were an important point of departure.

During our talks, I set out a number of positions that were met with general acceptance by my counterparts: First, there are undeniably differences between the EU and the US, especially but not exclusively, on issues of defence and security policy. We do prioritize and tackle certain problems differently, particularly environmental issues (witness the US's refusal to sign the Kyoto Protocol) and the interpretation of international law (witness the non-participation of the United States in the International Criminal Court). But our relationship is by no means limited to or defined by differences of opinion. The European Union and the United States share common values and a common commitment to democracy. The European peace project could not have developed after the Second World War and during the Cold War without the security guarantee provided by the US. Our far-reaching cooperation on issues that go far beyond security should not be underestimated.

To this end, we all agreed that we must not allow the tendency to underestimate Europe, prevalent in certain circles in the United States, to gain ground. This misguided perception of Europe as a 'soft power' is based on a one-sided view of international relations that gives undue emphasis to military power. Europe might not be as strong as we could and should be in terms of our defence capabilities and military power, but in other areas – economic, political, and diplomatic – we are just as powerful as the US, if not more so. Our recent experience building democracies in southeastern Europe is unique and could be very useful in formulating, together with the United States, an effective global conflict prevention and resolution strategy. Rebuilding nations in the aftermath of war is a critical factor in security and defence policy, as the United States is learning the hard way in Iraq. Without European peacekeeping and crisis management experience, American military power will not be effective in maintaining security and building lasting peace. We therefore concluded that relations between Europe and the United States should become more of a partnership of equals, because both sides need each other in equal measure. Lasting alliances are not based on one party blindly subordinating itself to the will of the other. True partners must be able to engage in a frank and open dialogue. We must not allow the narrow ideology espoused by a minority in the US that 'you are either with us or against us' to prevail.

A strategy for bridging the transatlantic divide

In Europe, we have a highly developed sense of our responsibility in an increasingly complex world. But in order to tackle global problems more effectively, I believe our strategy should develop in two directions. First, we must strengthen those areas where the European Union remains weak. We must correct the imbalance with the United States regarding the Union's ability to influence international affairs. The new European Constitution is a decisive step forward in this respect. We are taking the necessary institutional measures to strengthen our common foreign and security policy by developing new strategies and committing increased finances to protect our common interests, both within and beyond the frontiers of Europe. At the same time, in tackling issues as diverse as terrorism and sustainable development, we must remain true to our vision of a democratic, multicultural Union, and show greater political commitment and coherence in our 'Wider Europe' policy.

We must also systematically deepen transatlantic cooperation in areas of mutual interest and concern. Our common objectives should be to improve prosperity, reduce inequality, and encourage the spread of democracy worldwide. We should develop economic cooperation in a way that will facilitate, not hinder, development in the rest of the world. We must implement measures to facilitate mutual understanding across the Atlantic – particularly concerning the fears and motives that drive US foreign policy. And we must make more of an effort to exert a positive influence on the US by communicating European positions systematically and clearly to all players in the United States, from the federal and local government to non-governmental institutions and the American public. We need to improve the existing framework for transatlantic dialogue at the level of legislators, businesspeople, consumers, trade unions, environmental organizations and other civil movements. The prevalent view in the United States favouring a division of responsibilities – with one side waging war, while the other tries to make peace – has been proven flawed. Both sides must choose cooperation over conflict.

Our top priority should be a constructive debate on more effective forms of global governance. We need to develop more systematic cooperation in multilateral institutions so that we can formulate viable solutions to major socio-political problems, such as AIDS, famine, poverty and illiteracy. We must promote transnational solutions to new global security threats such as organized crime, illegal immigration and weapons of mass destruction. And we must work together in the fields of research, education and training to promote and protect democracy, development and human rights. In order to make real progress in all these areas, we need to further our cooperation at all institutional levels, from closer links between the European Parliament and the US Congress to exchange programmes between youth groups and young leaders. We might also establish a transatlantic council of experts from both sides of the Atlantic, who would formulate the strategies and tools for sustainable development and democratic global governance – an Atlantic Charter for the twenty-first century.

Good governance in a global society

Whether we are dealing with poverty, inequality, human rights violations, terrorism, pollution or weapons of mass destruction, people expect a new type of global governance which will transform today's insecurity into tomorrow's opportunities. Global public opinion increasingly demands the strengthening of international institutions such as the United Nations. But if we are to convince the powerful that unilateralism does not pay, we need to prove that multilateralism is effective. We need to achieve realistic targets and tangible results. We need to convince those who espouse narrow self-interest that sustainable development can bring sustainable peace.

Today, our challenge is to examine whether our current international system of governance is truly democratic. We need to re-evaluate the role of international institutions so they are more financially and politically viable. We must ensure that our institutions derive their legitimacy not only from the actions we take and the decisions we make, but also from the fact that they are truly representative – as far as possible – of a global consensus. This requires the courage to undertake far-reaching reforms and open up a sincere dialogue between citizens, countries, continents and civilizations.

Greece has placed great emphasis on engaging in a meaningful dialogue of cultures which can heal the deepening rifts regarding how different cultures view our changing world. Otherwise, our democracies will always be prey to extremist forces that resort to violence, exploiting the sense of exclusion from prosperity and human rights felt by many citizens.

In terms of effective global governance, much can be learned from the experiences of the European Union. In Europe, we have come to realize that matters of war and peace are so important for humanity that they cannot be left simply to leaders, no matter how great they may be. They cannot be left to negotiators, no matter how skilful they may be. They cannot be left to earthquakes, apocalypses or inspirations, however momentous they may be. What is needed is a sustainable environment of shared values, international law, accepted practice and common purpose. Within this secure environment, we can create effective and representative institutions, equipped with credible tools for the peaceful resolution of conflict.

Developing and deepening transatlantic relations in such a way that they promote peaceful cooperation and sustainable security will benefit all the peoples of the world. Such policies will no doubt be rewarded with the support of communities, institutions and citizens on both sides of the Atlantic. I would like to thank all those who contributed to this publication for sharing their experience and expertise and helping to shape this debate on the future of transatlantic relations.

List of Contributors

Gilles Andréani: former Head of Policy Planning in the French Foreign Ministry and Adjunct Professor at Paris II University. Fellow of the IISS, France.

David Andrews: Senior Research Fellow in Transatlantic Relations, Robert Schumann Centre for Advanced Studies, European University Institute, Florence, Italy.

Emilios Avgouleas is a Lecturer in International Business Transactions, University of Piraeus. He has researched, taught and published widely in the area of Law and Economics, International Trade and Investment, International and European Financial Market Regulation and International Economic Organizations, Greece.

Scott Barrett is Professor of Environmental Economics and International Political Economy, at the School of Advanced International Studies, Johns Hopkins University, Washington, DC, USA. His book *Environment and Statecraft*, was published in 2003.

Dick Benschop was State Secretary for Foreign Affairs for the Netherlands from 1998–2002. He joined the Royal Dutch/Shell Group in 2003, where he is Vice-President for Shell Energy Europe.

Tom Bentley: President of Demos, UK.

Christoph Bertram: Director of SWP, the German Institute for International Politics and Security, Berlin, Germany. From 1974 to 1982 he headed the International Institute for Strategic Studies in London.

Jan Dirk Blaauw: Political and Economic Consultant, EWPPP, Netherlands.

Elmar Brok: Chairman of the Committee of Foreign Affairs of the European Parliament. He was EPP Coordinator in the European Convention and EP representative at the 2000 and 2004 Inter-Governmental Conferences: He is also a long-standing member of the EP Delegation for relations with the United States.

John Bruton: former Prime Minister of Ireland, and the European Union's ambassador to the US.

Ted Galen Carpenter is Vice-President for Foreign Policy and Defence Studies, Cato Institute, Washington, DC, USA, and is the author or editor of 15 books on international affairs including *Peace & Freedom: Foreign Policy for a Constitutional Republic* (2002).

Dimitri Constas: Professor of International Relations and Director, Institute of International Relations, Panteion University, Athens, Greece.

Theodore A. Couloumbis, Professor Emeritus of International Relations, Athens University and Director General of the Hellenic Foundation for Defence and Foreign Policy (ELIAMEP), Greece.

Kemal Dervis, is a Member of the Turkish Parliament (Republican Peoples' Party). He has served as Minister for Economic Affairs, as a member of the European Convention and Vice-President of the World Bank. He has taught at Princeton.

A.A. Fatouros: Professor Emeritus of International Economic Law, University of Athens, Greece.

Timothy Garton Ash: Director, European Studies Centre, St Antony's College, Oxford University, UK.

Bronislaw Geremek is a Historian and Politician. He is a former Minister of Foreign Affairs of the Republic of Poland (period of Poland's accession to NATO), member and co-founder of the Union of Freedom and founding member of Solidarity's Independent Self-Governing Trade Union. He is the Head of the Chair of European Civilization at the College of Europe, Natolin Campus (Warsaw).

Misha Glenny is an author and award-winning journalist. His books include *The Balkans: Nationalism, War and the Great Powers, 1804–1999*, and *The Fall of Yugoslavia*. He is currently working as a political consultant in South East Europe.

Alan K. Henrikson: Professor of International Relations and Director, The Fletcher Roundtable, The Fletcher School of Law and Diplomacy, Tufts University, Massachusetts, USA.

Christopher Hill: Professor of International Relations, University of Cambridge, UK; Burton Professor of International Relations, LSE, Royal Institute of International Affairs; Woodrow Wilson International Center for Scholars, Washington DC; Department of Government, Dartmouth College, New Hampshire; European University Institute, Florence; Università di Catania; Universitat Autònoma de Barcelona; University of California at San Diego; Università di Siena.

Stanley Hoffmann is the Paul and Catherine Buttenwieser University Professor, Harvard University, USA, where he has taught, since 1955: French intellectual and political history. American foreign policy, the sociology of war, international politics, ethics and world affairs, modern political ideologies, the development of the modern state, and the history of Europe since 1945.

Nikos Kotzias: Senior Expert Counsel, Hellenic Foreign Ministry, formerly member of the Hellenic National Council for Foreign Policy; author of numerous books; Visiting Professor at the Department of International and European Studies, University of Piraeus, Greece.

F. Stephen Larrabee is a Senior Research Fellow at the Rand Corporation, visiting the John F. Kennedy School of Government, Cambridge, MA, USA.

Petros Liacouras: Lecturer in Public International Law, Department of International and European Studies of the University of Piraeus, member of the Advisory Legal Board of the Greek Foreign Ministry, Greece.

Jonathan Lipkin is a Research Fellow at the European Research Institute, University of Birmingham, UK.

Margarita Mathiopoulos: Professor for US Foreign Policy and International Security at the University of Potsdam; Founding and Executive Director of the Potsdam Centre for Transatlantic Security and Military Affairs, Potsdam, Germany.

Anand Menon: Professor of European Politics, University of Birmingham, Director of the European Research Institute, Birmingham, UK.

Kalypso Nicolaidis: University Lecturer, St Antony's College, Oxford University, UK; formerly Assistant Professor at Harvard University.

Joseph Nye: Professor, Dean of the Kennedy School of Government, Harvard University, Cambridge, Massachusetts, USA, and author of *The Paradox of American Power: Why the World's only Superpower can't go it Alone* (2002).

George A. Papandreou: President of the Pan-Hellenic Socialist Party (PASOK). Currently, President of the Socialist International as of 2006. A former Minister of Foreign Affairs, Greece.

Georgios Papastamkos: Professor of EU Institutions and Politics, University of Piraeus, Greece, and a member of the European Parliament.

William Pfaff is a Columnist for the *International Herald Tribune*, the Los Angeles Times Syndicate, USA.

Friedbert Pflüger: Chairman of the German Bundestag's Committee on EU Affairs; member (CDU) of the Bundestag, Germany.

Scherle R. Schwenninger is a Senior Fellow at the World Policy Institute at the New School University and Co-Director of the Global Economic Policy Program at the New America Foundation, USA.

George Soros is a well-known active philanthropist since 1979 and Chairman of the Soros Fund Management LLC. He is the author of eight books including *The Bubble of American Supremacy* (2004). He founded the Central European University, with its primary campus in Budapest.

Joseph Stiglitz: University Professor of Economics. He teaches at Columbia University, Graduate Business School (Department of Economics) and the School of International and Public Affairs. He is the Co-founder and Executive Director of the Initiative for Policy Dialogue (IPD). He was a Nobel Prize winner in Economics in 2001, USA.

Hellen Wallace: Professor, Robert Schuman Centre for Advanced Studies, European University Institute, Florence, Italy.

Part I

The Nature of Transatlantic Disagreements: Duration and Progress

1
Introduction: Rupture and Continuity in Transatlantic Relations

Nikos Kotzias and Petros Liacouras

1. Analysing transatlantic relations: the fundamental questions

The answer to the question 'how to understand the nature and evolution of US–EU relations' is a key to interpreting the flowing situation of the contemporary world (Featherstone and Ginsberg, 1996:34). The relations between the two sides of the Atlantic Ocean (the United Kingdom having an intermediate role – see Black, 2003, and in more detail Gamble, 2003) remain significant in world affairs, even after the end of the Cold War. They also remain significant in the context of the 'survival' of the West, whether these questions are real or only rhetorical.

In the era of globalization, transatlantic relations are undergoing a process of transformation. They retain elements of the past. However, continuity is increasingly accompanied by discontinuity. The certainties of yesterday become today's fundamental questions. Uncertainty about the future of EU–US relations leads to wildly divergent assessments. 'Pessimists maintain that differences in power, threat perceptions, and values, are forcing an inexorable divergence in European and American interests', while 'optimists see recent troubles as the product of rigid ideologies, domestic politics, and missed diplomatic opportunities' (Moravcsik, 2003:75).

All the contributors to the present volume agree that the analysis of transatlantic relations is of paramount political significance, and that such analyses must revolve around the following critical questions: What is to be done about transatlantic relations? Should the two sides seek to compete with each other, or should they seek interdependence? Should such interdependence be equal or hierarchical? Could competition result in conflict, which would be costly for both

3

sides and others? Even if a policy of interdependence is pursued, is it certain that an equal balance between the two sides can be restored? It is possible that the side that enjoys superiority in one field [a+] (such as defence) will determine the manner in which the other side uses and applies its strong points in another field [n+].

Until now, relations between the US and the EU were typified by a clear division of labour and mutually complementary activities. This division developed, to a degree only, spontaneously (Keens-Soper, 1999). In this context, until recently the US first identified the opposition/enemy/target, and then invited its European allies to join its assessment. This kind of division has made many Europeans feel uncomfortable. To that end, some of the allies of the United States intensely demand that the 'aims of the West' should jointly be determined. From his point of view, Robert Kagan (2003) interprets this kind of demand as a claim that the foreign policy of the USA should be formed by others. To paraphrase, the Lilliputians (EU), wish to dictate how Gulliver (the USA) employs its power. Kagan speaks for that segment of the US administration which believes that there exist issues of global security, and of US security only, that need to be dealt with directly, even unilaterally, if that is deemed necessary. Or otherwise, as formulated by the current president of the USA himself, 'the course' of the USA, 'can not depend on the decisions of others' (George W. Bush, 2003). On the other side, the Europeans cannot admit that the definition of global security and how to frame it should solely depend on the national interests of the USA (Bahr, 2003).

2. Prioritizing the stages – differentiation in structures

Currently, the more powerful side in transatlantic relations (the USA) is not willing to subject its power to the consent of the less powerful side (the EU). Such behaviour, however, may well prevent the stronger party from applying the full extent of its power, through failure to exploit alliances that would increase the power it already enjoys, through missed chances in complementing its own power with that of friends and allies, and through overstretching its capabilities and capacity (regarding the USA, Ferguson and Kotlikoff, 2003; for a more general view with a historical perspective, even though it contains certain absolute statements, see Kennedy, 1987). The weaker side, on the other hand, runs the risk of overestimating its capabilities and perhaps becoming involved in a sterile confrontation with the stronger party. If it chooses not to take matters to breaking point, it may be forced to retreat from its positions. Playing with fire is dangerous. If the fire is alive, you can get burned. If it has been extinguished, you can get dirty from the ashes.

In the case of fighting terrorism and the war in Iraq, considerable differences between the US and Europe emerged. These differences assumed the form of the 'reasoning' described above. The US evaluated global terrorism as a much more acute problem than did the EU. From the beginning, the Americans indicated their intention to lead an international campaign against terrorism and against whomever they considered, fairly or arbitrarily, a supporter or protector of terrorists. It was considered more important to be imminently occupied with the problem itself than to form an alliance that would 'lose time' by discussing the lawfulness (or not) of the actions to be undertaken in order to suppress terrorism (Rivkin and Casey, 2003). The European allies of the USA, on the other hand, worried that this campaign aimed at determining the internal structures of the West by invoking a common enemy, as had occurred during the Cold War, in order to establish American hegemony.

In the case of Afghanistan, the US was able to form an alliance on its own terms. In this, it was aided by the fact that the terrorist strikes of 11 September 2001 were a sufficiently convincing argument to provoke its European allies to follow along without much discussion. Later, during the war in Iraq, where there emerged a divergence of interests with the EU, the Americans considered that there was no need to 'wait' for the Europeans and lose time in discussions. The US, at Britain's behest, did 'wait' for the Europeans. The US reportedly was ready to invade six months earlier but was convinced by Britain to hold off. The US and Britain then worked hard to get the Europeans and the UN onboard. But France made it clear that they would veto any UN resolution explicitly sanctioning an invasion. They also thought that even if their campaign against Baghdad was for the most part a unilateral action, so was the French veto in the UN Security Council. But they considered the former unilateral action 'necessary', and the latter 'hostile'.

An important issue in EU–US relations is whether the world can and must be uni-polar or bi-polar. This is a fundamental question in politics, which is also addressed by many of the contributions in this volume. It is an issue that emerges in every decision-making process, and it has tangible practical repercussions. It arises in institutions, especially political parties, and can be a cause of their fragmentation. It arises especially in the process of globalization. The dilemma of whether one wishes to control 100 per cent of the actions to be taken (uni-polarity), even if the chances of success are reduced by 50 per cent, or control at most 50 per cent of such actions (multi-polarity) and increase the chances of success up to 100 per cent, is fundamental to every decision-making process. Naturally, if one party considers that having 100 per cent control ensures an 80 per cent chance of success, while giving away 50 per cent of control would increase the chance of success by only 5 per cent, it is likely they would choose the former strategy, as the US did in the case of Iraq.

A second supposition is that the US thought it would combine a uni-polar course (100 per cent +n) in the war, with the participation of Western allies under conditions (a multi-polar approach) in the 'second stage of the war', the stage of building peace. In this second stage, however, the participation of the potential multi-polar allies would require an acceptance on their part of the *faits accomplis* and the fears (Barber, 2003) created in the first stage. In the name of multi-polarity in the second stage, the Europeans demanded its application in the first. In other words, the US wanted the structure of the first stage to predetermine the manner of applying multi-polarity in the second, while some Europeans sought, by invoking multi-polarity in the second stage, to prevent the sway of uni-polarity of the first stage.

3. The Cold War and current structures: three interpretative approaches

During the Cold War era, in the context of the transatlantic alliance, a community of ideas, values, and aims was formulated, which for the most part remains current. In our opinion, the process of formulating joint values and aims was accompanied by the undoubted development of a hierarchy of dominance in relations between the USA and Western Europe, which has remained in force to this day. These relations were institutionalized as normative and structural power in several international organizations and regimes (Krasner, 1983) and by extension in the shaping of the global governance system (Rosenau and Czempiel, 1992; Rosenau, 1997; Rhodes, 1996; Pierre, 2000; Brandt et al., 2000). It is not coincidental that certain contributors to this volume consider that the current divergence of views and pronounced disagreements between the US and the EU run deep and are long-term, while others consider them transient and defined by the specific historic juncture. Often, these differing assessments are linked to the authors' evaluation of the nature of the Cold War and the significance of disputes within the Western camp during that period. Such assessments can be classified under three approaches:

The first approach considers that the Cold War was exclusively about the conflict of the Western world with applied socialism, and especially its conflict with the USSR. The realistic school interprets the essence and the outcome of the Cold War as a power struggle between the US and the former USSR (Cox, 1990; Mearsheimer, 1994/5; Lebow and Risse-Kappen, 1995; Lebow, 1999). Others, mostly from the liberalists' camp, believe that the conflict was limited to the purely ideological level (Fukuyama, 1992; Peterson, 1992). Even more typically, H. Kissinger (1999) describes the entire post-war foreign policy of the US as an effort to contain the USSR. In the context of the same one-dimensional approach, L. Gaddis (1993:7–9), while referring to ten factors that in his opinion led to and sustained the Cold War, does not record even one concerning the internal structure of the Western system. In general, this first approach considers that while 'the Cold War is over, there is no consensus on what has replaced it' (Dunne, Cox and Booth, 1999: xiii).

According to the second approach regarding the Cold War, which is closely linked to the first in its methodology, it is argued that after 1989 appeared conditions for universal 'dramatic changes in world affairs'. These changes were considered by some as being so dramatic as to mark the end of any necessity for wide-ranging interpretative systems (Richardson, 2000; George, 2000).

The third approach provides a different viewpoint: During the Cold War there were noted developments not only in the conflict between the two systems, but also within the internal structures of each. In this framework, it is argued either that the current situation represents a continuity without breaks, since 'the American policy had not changed since Vietnam' (Pilger, 2001:13–14), or – a view that in our opinion is more accurate – that there exists a dialectic of relative continuity (retention of several pre-Cold War structures) and discontinuity (emergence of new factors). Several contributions to this volume adopt this third view, though they differ as to the significance they lend to one or the other (continuity or discontinuity) and their specific factors.

4. Today's power structure: a product of the Cold War

During the Cold War, the US continued to manage its dominance over its Western allies in a manner that would safeguard both the security and the stability of the Western camp (Walter, 1993), as this was understood by the US, and its economic growth (Webb and Krasner, 1989:195; Wyatt-Walter, 1999:127). The US contributed decisively to the establishment of international law and international institutions (World Bank, International Monetary Fund, NATO, and, to a degree, the UN). Its policy during the Cold War allowed the countries of Western Europe to participate in this system and obtain benefits, but also created a framework ensuring the ongoing primacy of the US. The US, in the role of a stabilizer, accepted that there are rules of the game, though it considered acceptable only those rules which had been determined to a large extent by the US itself, through the policies it applied. The US knew that attempts to co-operate with third parties might entail difficulties, but that such difficulties were contained within the strict limits of consent and the context of American hegemony. In particular, during the Cold War, the US dismissed the idea of a dominant role that would be imposed within the West by direct, unmediated military power (Halliday, 2001), as it tends to do today, according to the findings of most contributions to this volume.

The structure and framework of the Euro-Atlantic alliance prior to 1989 was mainly determined by the conditions and necessities of the Cold War, but – in our opinion – not by them alone. As noted by G.J. Ikenberrry, 'the basic logic of order among the Western world was set in place before the Cold War and it was a logic that addressed problems internal to Western capitalism'. It is not a coincidence that since the 'absolute' dominance of capitalism after 1989, this state of affairs 'has become more firmly embedded in the wider structures of politics and society'. In other words, 'the Cold War bi-polarity gave the US added hegemonic leverage at critical moments in the management of Western order' forcing even friendly powers to consent to the 'grand Strategy' of the US 'for building order within the Western World'. The result is that, even today, 'overall, American hegemony is reluctant, penetrated, and highly institutionalised' (Ikenberrry, 1999:124–7, 135–9; Ikenberrry and Kupchan, 1990:283–7; see also Brand et al., 2000, 89 et seq., and similarly Brzezinski, 1997: chapter 1). Seen from a certain point of view, it could be considered that a 'fundamental aspiration' of the US after the Second World War was to attach Japan and Germany 'by invoking the spectre of the risk posed by the Soviet Union, to a system of complex agreements and financial/military commitments, in which the role played by the US was decisive' (Volger, 1994:923).

Therefore the invocation of the threats posed by the Soviet Union during the Cold War also aimed at subjecting the Western allies of the

US to the latter's leadership ambitions. To a degree, the powerful in continental Europe realized this state of affairs. Thus, during the Cold War relations in the Western world regarding a common, solid foreign policy were sometimes directed or strained by mild or even rupture-threatening rifts, even regarding policy towards the Soviet Union. Typical examples are the French policy of defence autonomy vis-à-vis NATO, and later the Ost-Politik of the German government and the overall policy of appeasement against the USSR on the question of armaments.

As regards the evolution of transatlantic relations after the Cold War and in the current era, our position is that both continuity and discontinuity are present, with breaks in the historical continuity. The unification of Germany, the fall of the USSR and the collapse of Russia, changes in Eastern Europe and in parts of Asia, are all developments that have created a new, post-Cold War environment in which the relations between the US and (Western) Europe are now played out (Brandon, 1992; Cox, 1995). These changes were significant because they eliminated the common enemy of the West, i.e. those countries that belonged to the socialist camp. In addition, they speeded up and reinforced the globalization process, and in particular in the political process. Thus, the context within which the power of Western leading actors could be measured had changed, as had their respective positions and their interdependence. In light of the above, we may reach the conclusion that after 1989 there appears a very significant break in transatlantic relations – which also affects internal developments – while concurrently there also exists a continuity, based on the system of capitalist relations and on the political structures and institutions that had developed in the Western world during the Cold War 'within the system'.[1]

Today, the two main protagonists in the Western world are revisionary in their trends. The secondary disagreements regarding relations with the USSR have evolved into acute disagreements regarding policy to deal with global problems and new actors. Concurrently, each side seeks to restructure transatlantic relations in its own favour. Thus, most analysts consider that the USA and Europe are in a process of redetermining their relations in the wake of the Cold War (Keens-Soper, 1999). This redetermination is occurring despite the progress being made in developing and establishing a community of values, objectives and strategic choices between the socially dominant groups on the two sides of the Atlantic, and despite the fact that to a degree, their common action had increased before the second Gulf War in Iraq.[2]

It may be noted that contrary to the position maintained by some Western powers towards the war in Vietnam, in both the Yugoslav and Afghan campaigns the European states stood by US choices and policy orientations (Nye, 2000). This alignment occurred even though the US sought through these wars to influence even more the internal evolution of the EU (Gnesotto and Roper, 1992) by highlighting contradictions and certain *impasses* in the EU.[3] By contrast, in the 2003 war in Iraq, the US and the powers within the EU indicated their strong desire to review the internal structures of the Western world in the post-Cold War era (Watrin, 2003), which resulted in a change of their attitudes towards each other.

5. Competition, conflict, or cooperation?

This tendency to review transatlantic relations is to a large degree due to the new state of affairs that evolved after the Cold War – a proposition that reflects our position. From the angle of our analysis of the issue, the new reality is comprised of three main components (regarding the most important bibliography on transatlantic relations and developments in the US, see *Spiegel Special*, 2003).

The first component is the effort to restructure relations in the Western world. In particular, we refer here to the emergence of strong opposition internally, to the elimination of the old enemy and the 'necessity' of having a new one, and to the emergence of acute political clashes within the Western world.

The second component concerns the intensification of the process of European integration, but also the fact that this process has in many ways been more difficult than initially expected. The new EU member states from Central and Eastern Europe have acceded to the EU, while addressing their strategic security concerns against 'old enemies' by co-operating with the US (Viksnins, 2003).

The third component is the 'non-decline' of the US – a decline that many had predicted, and still expect, today. For example, E. Todd (2002), who considered that the American system was already on its last legs, has been proved wrong. He even claimed that 'the collapse of the American system might occur before the attack on Iraq' (Todd, 2003:10).[4]

If the US has to face the fundamental question of uni-polarity or multi-polarity, Europe has to decide whether it will take the course of close co-operation with the US or, on the contrary, whether it will seek a balance of political power. Currently, the former choice appears to have prevailed. But there are others in Europe who think the time has come to adopt the second course. They claim that since the US is not acting in accordance with the principles of international law and institutions, and is refusing to consult in a binding manner with its allies, the EU must speed up the process of integration in the military-defence field (Hoyer and Kaldrack, 2002; Reiter, Rummel and Schmidt, 2002).

Another view would posit that it is doubtful whether the EU can ultimately impose on the US respect for international law and global institutions by applying a conventional balance-of-power policy. It even claims that if the EU seeks to become unilaterally active in fields where the US prevails, it will be creating future problems in transatlantic relations, since such an aspiration would be driven by the spirit of competition. According to this view, such reasoning can distort the system itself. When the Athenians decided they wanted to have a power structure similar to Sparta's (Buckler, 2003; Schulz, 2003), they ended up by distorting their own system, which had several advantages as against Sparta. In other words, the Europeans certainly need to reinforce their defence structures, as noted in many of the contributions here, so that the US will take them more into account. If, however, they attempt to become a US in the place of the US, then this effort will not succeed. Its failure will be due to two main reasons: Firstly, the US knows better than anyone how to be itself; and secondly, in such a situation, the EU risks losing all the advantages it enjoys and which make it so successful in the current world, capable of attracting scores of other countries. In addition, by adopting such a course, the EU would lose its own orientation – an orientation that provides the capability to instil even in the US elements of the European social model. Otherwise, the EU will be 'forced' to choose between conflict and deference as against the US; both these alternatives are unacceptable.

Assuming that Europe selected a course of conflict with the US, it would have to structure its internal architecture correspondingly. In particular, it would have to reinforce its institutional system so as to allow centralization of authority in a single axis, such as the Paris–Berlin axis. It would also have to reinforce its defence capabilities and impose recognition and application of international law wherever it holds power. In this framework, there would develop a directory of powers supporting the advancement of the EU in a way that would strengthen it as fast as possible in the fields in which the US is superior. In such a scenario, the EU would not seek to attract other countries on the basis of its cultural and democratic advantages, but primarily by its power. In our opinion, however, such a course would neutralize the

EU's comparative advantages and would position Europe in a playing field in which the US is admittedly superior in know-how and skills.

If the EU made the choice to subject itself to the will of the US, the outcome would again be negative. In this case, too, many of the EU's advantages, such as its political and cultural resources, would remain unexploited. In following such a direction, the EU would inevitably be led to undertake several internal changes and, most significantly, abandon its efforts to contribute to the resolution of global problems of long-term significance that are not linked one-dimensionally nor limited to military security. A mutation of the EU into a small, illegitimate sibling of the US would undermine its internal cohesion. It would arrest the process of integration and unification, limiting its aspirations to pursue geographical expansion and a stronger presence in the global market.

A thoughtless adoption on the part of the Europeans of any and every position held by the US would not indicate friendship toward the Americans. And this is because friends speak the truth to one another and do not just say whatever will please the other. In other words, we would posit that the US should not consider any criticism of one or other of the US government's actions as anti-Americanism (Judt, 2003). On the other hand, it is clear that not all 'anti-Americanism' is democratic. Criticism generated on both sides of the Atlantic and which is typified by lack of civility, dialogue and tolerance, such as criticism originating from fundamentalist quarters, cannot be seen as a component of a democratic approach to transatlantic relations, nor as a component of a relationship aiming at resolving current world problems and dealing with current world risks. The former Greek Foreign Minister, George A. Papandreou, addresses such problems and risks in his Foreword to the present volume.

In the context of the future of transatlantic relations there is also a third course: that of co-operation between equal partners. Here, the end objective is that both sides contribute to building bridges between their institutions and peoples. Such an approach requires that both sides develop their respective advantages, but also respect each other and each other's advantages. In this framework, the Europeans would be called upon to respect the fears generated among Americans after 11 September. The Americans, on their part, must understand the European position and a fundamental element of EU culture, regarding respect for international law and international institutions, international rules and status quo. Concurrently, transatlantic relations, being a bridge between two capitalist sub-systems, must not exclude the rest of the planet from growth, prosperity, democracy and freedom.

In the framework of this third alternative, the EU can pursue increased democracy in transatlantic relations. At the same time, it can pursue a development of European affairs in a manner that will not end up subjecting the smaller EU member states to the will of their stronger partners. Undoubtedly, any context of subordination would create an internal problem within the EU and generate centrifugal forces within it. In addition, the two sides of the Atlantic must contribute to a rethinking of the global institutional system and the respect it must be shown. This is not an issue of how much power the US or the EU enjoys, but of how to exploit all available opportunities to bring stability to the global system and promote democratic governance worldwide. Such governance would not only normalize relations between the US and the EU, but would also enhance the role of other states in resolving the global problems faced by the world today, as outlined in many contributions to this compendium.

6. Preventive war and pre-emptive self-defence: politics and law

A major cause of transatlantic conflict is the development by the US of a new strategic security doctrine in response to the terrorist attack of 11 September 2001 and to Iraq's stance in early 2002. In the current American administration's view, contemporary threats require types of reaction proportional to the imminence of the threat or the anticipated armed attack – swifter and more flexible than before. As the US administration claims, this development could not have been foreseen when the UN Charter was adopted. In one of the most fundamental provisions of peremptory character of this Charter, the use of force and coercion in international relations is forbidden. However, the UN Charter equally provides for self-defence. This right of self-defence is of the same legal weight, and is an inherent right of any state which is under an unauthorized armed attack. This right has been extensively claimed in cases in which a state is under the threat or preparation of an armed attack, which has not yet developed. The US broadens and enshrines this claim of self-defence to include the recent types of terrorist threats, which could not have been predicted at the drafting stage of the UN Charter, in which the right of self-defence was prescribed and thus could not fall within the ambit of this right's scope. These threats come from the possible employment of weapons of mass destruction by the so-called failed states or other illicit organized groups and networks. The US is seeking to extend the meaning and application of self-defence, on the basis and within the framework of its new strategic doctrine, to include in its ambit pre-emptive reactions to acts that include or presage violence and destruction, even if these have not as yet occurred.

Currently, the US includes terrorism in the category of immediate and existing threats to its security. In this context, it demands a campaign against terrorism before it can account for new victims. For this purpose, the US also demands the 'timely' disarmament of terrorist pockets (whether states or supra-national networks) and pre-emptive strikes in the form of combating terrorism against them. It was exactly this new American doctrine of pre-emptive self-defence – as applied in Iraq and by the US's interventionist policy in general, which bypasses the UN – that met with strong international opposition in early 2003, by France primarily, but also by Russia, China, and Germany.

The recent US military intervention in Iraq led to an enrichment of the terminology in the field of international law. Formerly, we had become accustomed to the use of the term 'anticipatory self-defence' as a claimed right against imminent threats. It was first used in the Cuban Quarantine incident in 1962 to justify the blockade of part of the high seas by invoking the need to protect US national security against the upcoming, developing Soviet missile threat (McDougal, 1963; Shlei, 1962/2003). Justifying anticipatory self-defence, as invoked in practice up to now, depends more on demonstrating the existence of threat, whether imminent or prospectively destructive, and less on a constrained framework of principles. In other words, an imminent, tangible threat may be perceived as being equivalent to an attack, which would justify the recourse to defensive measures, including forceful means, by the state which claims to be a definite target or a prospective victim. Anticipatory self-defence was also claimed by Israel during the two wars in 1967 and 1973. It was then considered that the threat encountered was so imminent that no measures other than pre-emptive defence would be of any avail.

International practice has shown that anticipatory self-defence initially meets with strong opposition and disapproval, but is often justified with hindsight, when it emerges that the threat was indeed imminent, and that its non-anticipation would have resulted in casualties and heavier and much wider-ranging losses as well as innumerable human victims. A case in point is Israel's anticipatory air strike that destroyed the Iraqi nuclear reactor in 1981. Initially, most states condemned the Israeli action in the UN; but later many countries that now subscribe to the new American doctrine have invoked that action as a positive example. They consider that had Iraq been allowed to complete its nuclear programme and develop weapons of mass destruction, the restoration of Kuwait's sovereignty after the invasion of

2 August 1990 would have been attained at a much higher cost in human lives and other damages. Generally, the common denominator in demands for anticipatory self-defence is national security and territorial integrity and the possible prevention of ensuing casualties. We would like, however, to note here that according to the practice adhered to in the framework of bi-polarity, for such an invocation to be justified the state claiming it will be a prospective and potential victim of an armed aggression or other violent attack, and must first seek to persuade the competent UN-instituted organs, which are authorized to manage and have overall control of any reactive measures including the use of force, about the necessity, proportionality and discriminating kind of the anticipatory self-defence it is contemplating. As has been widely asserted, the UN-authorized organs that have been occupied with the international security preservation reserve the final and controlling authority and responsibility to determine whether any such anticipatory self-defence is lawfully claimed (Franck, 2002:107).

Lawyers and other analysts mainly from the US employ the new term of 'pre-emptive self-defence'. This term implies a dominant element of imminent, rapid action, and is wider in scope than the term 'anticipatory self-defence'. Pre-emptive self-defence is unilateral, without any prior authorization, and has the objective of arresting an incipient attack that is not yet operational. This is a strategy that suppresses the attack 'at birth' (Lippman, 2003). According to the definition given by the American Professor W.M. Reisman, pre-emptive self-defence is the unilateral use of force without prior international authorization aiming at alienating the means and weapons which are the components for the preparation of an aggressive action and effectively neutralizing the aggressive enemy. The logic behind this kind of rapid reaction is to prevent an aggressive act from developing, because if allowed to develop it would lead to a higher cost of reaction and definitely would most probably lead to accounting for innocent human victims and material damages. Pre-emptive self-defence aims at eliminating the potential threat or the occurrence of unforeseen events, contrary to anticipatory self-defence, which responds to a tangible, immediate threat (Reisman, 2003:87). Thus, the former is, in its historical practice, the extension of the latter. However, because the former requires power of a certain weight and has been advanced by the US since the end of the Cold War era, it is interpreted by those, who oppose the US, as an effort to achieve a targeted role of world hegemony. Thus, the Europeans are increasingly distrustful of the new US strategic security doctrine, and they increasingly and more systematically invoke the rules of international law.

Disputes on interpreting international law, particularly as to how older rules may be applied to new (assumed or real) threats, suggests a lively future for the interrelations among the Western countries. In contrast to this prospect, those who advance the need for mutually complementary policy and co-operation between the US and the EU suggest that the protagonists of the transatlantic relationship should seek to create a modern working framework of collective security, which would respond to any kind of contemporary threats. This kind of collective security implies that both sides would interrogate into the usefulness or even the necessity of military action or any other mode of proportional reaction in clearly delineated, extreme cases (Daalder, 2002:11). Such cases should constitute real and tangible threats, and any action to be taken should meet with as broad as possible consent of the main actors and obtain a clear signal of legitimacy through a UN resolution.

7. The contributions to this volume

7.1. A paradox

One of the paradoxes of the Cold War was the comparatively limited bibliography on transatlantic relations. Many publications could be found on both sides of the Atlantic concerning the internal structures and features of each side, but the number of references to the relations between them, particularly as regards their foreign policy toward each other, was much smaller. It should be mentioned that during the 1980s, only one noteworthy book concerning the European Union's foreign policy was published in the US. Most works published in the US about the EU discussed economic relations and security. The bibliography about foreign policy in transatlantic relations only started growing in the 1990s.

In contrast to the years before 1989, the main subject in the early 1990s was the competition for primacy in the post-Cold War world between the two Western centres. By the late 1990s, the bibliography was increasingly concerned with globalization and the stance maintained by the two centres as towards that process. A common trend throughout the 1990s was, and still is, research into the prospects of American hegemony (Rudolf and Wilzewski, 2000) and the extent to which it will continue in the twenty-first century.

The low productivity of the two sides, both on academic and on political research about the transatlantic relations during the Cold War era, probably indicates that some considered them self-evident and therefore not worthy of further study or research, while others (the majority) seemed reluctant to touch upon the real but thorny problems which they viewed as extremely sensitive. As has been shown in recent years, the truth is that problems in transatlantic relations have long been greater than those that are shown up, while the waves that could, and still can arise are varied in scope and intensity, as shown in detail in the contributions to this volume.

7.2. The nature of transatlantic disagreements: duration and progress

The present volume contains a Foreword and 34 contributions, of which two are studies and 32 are short essays by internationally renowned features of academia and politics. For the sake of presentation, we start with the essays and end up with the two lengthy studies. All contributions contain the views requested by the then Greek Foreign Minister, George A. Papandreou, in the context of preparing for the Kastellorizo informal meeting of EU foreign ministers in the first week of May 2003. These contributions constituted the informal input to the discussions among foreign ministers. This is the first concerted effort since 1989 with the objective of formulating a far-reaching, long-term European policy on transatlantic relations. The contributions include widely differing views on the future of such relations, encompassing both optimistic and pessimistic outlooks. Some consider the difficulties that have arisen as a long-term, others as transient. Some of the analyses and proposals consider that the EU is developing in competition with the US, others that it is following a complementary course. Some contributors suggest that relations should be reinforced, while others do not think that is necessary. All, however, agree that the EU must be strengthened, and its role and responsibility in transatlantic relations enhanced. Several courses are suggested on this subject, which is of particular interest to academics and politicians. The division of the contributions into categories (see sub-headings from 7.2.3 to 7.2.5.) is made on the basis of grouping articles emphasizing specific proposals rather than more general analysis, and vice versa. It is not an actual division, in the sense that all contributions contain proposals for the future of transatlantic relations.

7.2.1. The long-term character of EU–US disagreements

Several of the authors claim that the differences between the EU and the US are of a long-term character. They date from before the 2003 war in Iraq and will endure longer than the war's repercussions. They are therefore pessimistic regarding the future of transatlantic relations unless appropriate measures are taken, for which they submit several suggestions. Such suggestions often coincide with those of the optimists, who believe that the problem is short-term and will be short-lived.

The internationally acclaimed journalist **William Pfaff** considers that the differences between the US and Europe have historical depth and will not be easily overcome. He suggests that the Europeans should adopt a more systematic approach in influencing the US political-institutional system and US society to bring about a change in their current positions. In the same context, **Christoph Bertram**, director of the leading German Institute for International Relations and Security (SWP) in Berlin, believes that the break between Europe and the US is not a result of present circumstances alone, but of the fundamental differences between the two sides. He claims that the cause of such differences lies in the existence of differing interests and different views regarding history and the state of the contemporary world and its prospects. He considers that what is needed in order to restore relations is a systematic dialogue between the two sides. In this context, he suggests a stabilization of relations in fields where the two sides already co-operate, and stronger efforts on the part of the EU to influence US public opinion.

In the same spirit, **Scott Barrett**, professor at the Johns Hopkins University School of Advanced International Studies, considers that the tensions created because of the war in Iraq prove that the transatlantic and other supranational institutions developed up to now are unfit in the new global environment. For some European states, institutions such as the United Nations serve as a means to constrain American power. By contrast, for the US such institutions are noxious, especially when they are used to curb US dominance. According to S. Barrett's views, the way to restore the transatlantic relationship at the present juncture is to attain minor objectives in specific fields of common interest.

A similar pessimistic outlook, though differing from the above, is also given by the historian and former foreign minister of Poland, **Bronislaw Geremek**. In his view, a fundamental cause of current transatlantic problems is the fact that for the first time in decades, American policy is not reflecting sufficient positive interest in the process of European unification. He believes that the main objective should be to strengthen the EU, so as to convince the US that it is a powerful, reliable ally in global governance.

7.2.2. Differences and mutual completion

Some of the contributors who maintain the long-term nature of transatlantic differences point out, with some force, that despite their differences, each side can act in a manner complementing the other. **Gilles Andréani**, then Head of Policy planning staff, at the Ministry of Foreign Affairs of France and Advisor to the Foreign Minister, sees the differences in overall political culture at the root of transatlantic disagreements. He notes that the EU is more familiarized with negotiation and compromise processes as well as policies aimed at reaching consensus with other actors. The US, on the contrary, is more likely to resort to more coercive means. The author further notes, however, that such differences are not necessarily a cause of conflict. He expresses his hope that at the end of the road such differences may serve as mutually complementary attributes.

In the same vein as Gilles Andréani, but offering a different perspective, Professor **Joseph Stiglitz**, the Noble Prize winner in economics, considers co-operation between the US and the EU not as a possibility, but as a necessity. He believes that today's conflict between the US and the EU is due to the fact that the former currently tends to uni-polarity, while the latter to views of a multi-polar world. He notes, however, that despite their differences, their co-operation is necessary in the context of globalization and in the joint resolution of global problems. He further suggests that despite the difficulties, such co-operation might be developed by reinforcing non-governmental transatlantic relations, by shared action on issues of common concern to both sides, and by incorporating the EU–US relationship into a wider, international framework. The same issue of uni-polarity versus multi-polarity is addressed by **Dimitri Constas**, professor of international relations and head of the International and European Studies Department of the Panteion University of Athens. D. Constas considers that the Americans tend to uni-polarity, and that there are many indications that this trend will become even more pronounced, even when it is unnecessary. In order to prevent the establishment of uni-polarity, he suggests that the EU should regain Washington's respect as a collective international actor. He further notes that the EU is able to take care of its own backyard. European attention should also focus on America and its foreign policy elites, with the aim of expanding the 'New Transatlantic Agenda'.

The world-famous analyst **F. Stephen Larrabee**, senior fellow at the leading American research institute Rand, expresses his belief that, after the end of US military involvement in Iraq, there will be opportunities to restore transatlantic relations. He holds the view that if the EU aspires to 'put itself on the US radar screen', it must first identify the wider security problems that concern the US. He suggests that in order to improve relations there should be a dialogue process similar to that of the Transatlantic Agenda of 1995. Issues to be addressed may include a discussion of Turkey's future course and the reinforcement of co-operation with that country, the reconstruction of Iraq, peace in the Middle East, and suggestions about a resolution of the problems both the US and the EU countries face regarding North Korea, Iraq and Iran. He suggests further issues of international concern, such as addressing the problem of terrorism through multilateral co-operation in fields such as control of bank deposits and transfers, cross border control, as well as gathering and exchange of information and intelligence. This dialogue over these issues must be supported through closer relations with the American Congress. The author stresses the necessity of a 'division of labour' between the two sides. He believes, though, that security is indivisible, and considers disastrous a global division of security, with Europe under the auspices of the EU, and security of the remaining world under the auspices of the US.

Former Dutch foreign minister **Dirk Benschop** also believes relations between the two sides are not healthy because of choices made by the US. Even so, he believes that the EU should avoid defining itself as being in conflict with America. He stresses that the EU should further develop its positive attributes in a manner that will ultimately benefit transatlantic relations. As discussed in the same spirit by **Christopher Hill**, professor of international relations at the London School of Economics, the real issue confronting the EU is not whether it will maintain relations with the US, nor whether it will choose a course of conflict or subjection, but rather the terms of the relationship between the two. Regarding such terms, he notes that there are three possible courses, of which the most preferable is that of the European 'citizens' path' and the further evolution of the EU as a civilian superpower.

Timothy Garton Ash, director of the European Studies Centre of St Anthony's College, University of Oxford, widely known for his comprehensive studies on Europe, believes that if the former Soviet Union contributed to the unity of the West, it is indisputable that the Middle East now divides that unity. He therefore suggests that the EU and the US should embark on a (non-public) dialogue regarding the future of that region. He also says the EU must not define itself through a negative stance towards the US, and that the EU and US should instead pull together again. On the other hand, as he notes, the US must realize that the strengthening of the EU is in its interest. On this point it is worth repeating a similar view expressed by **Tom Bentley**, director of the United Kingdom's Demos Institute. T. Bentley suggests that the EU undertakes a division of competencies with the US, with the EU assuming a controlling role on issues such as cross-border crime, immigration, humanitarian assistance and the proliferation of weapons of mass destruction. Overall, he suggests that the EU should promote the image of a moderate (soft) power, tackling issues in which the US is not interested. Nevertheless, he adds that the Europeans should not develop a defensive identity opposing American power.

Joseph Nye, dean of the Kennedy School of Government at Harvard, considers Robert Kagan's view of an 'old Europe descended from Venus fighting a unilateral America descended from Mars' a short-sighted myth. Like Garton Ash, he notes that uni-polarity does not apply on all levels. Regarding military power, the world is indeed uni-polar and will remain so unless the Europeans decide to increase their defence expenditure. He claims, though, that regarding economic power, the international system may be seen as multi-polar, with the EU enjoying power that is absolutely necessary to the US in the context of international trade agreements. Regarding supranational issues, such as illegal immigration, contagious diseases, climate change and terrorism, he insists that international co-operation is necessary. Nye's proposals are in the same spirit as those of most authors in this volume. He suggests that the EU should develop its strengths so as to 'balance' US power, but also to exert influence on it.

Sherle Schwenninger, senior fellow of the World Policy Institute, in his note holds the opinion that Europe is currently a more important factor in international affairs than it used to be because it offers the world an alternative approach in its policy by championing a multilateral, global policy, serving the interests of all, even those of the US. In particular, the EU has much to offer by exporting democracy and economic restructuring, and in nation-building. According to Schwenninger, division of labour and allocation of competencies must form the basis of transatlantic co-operation. **Jan Dirk Blaauw**, president of the Assembly of the Western European Union (WEU), considers that there is no alternative to transatlantic co-operation. The EU can reinforce its defence and foreign policy in general, but this would make no sense and have no objective if undertaken in confrontation with the US. In order to reinforce US–NATO ties, Europeans must demonstrate a spirit of understanding concerning the security problem the US contends it faces, and convince US officials that it would be in their country's interests if they acted jointly through long established international institutions (such as the UN and NATO). The President of the WEU suggests that the EU must increase its defence expenditure and assume military actions in the context of a division of labour with the US. The US, on its side, needs to admit and give credit to the international role of the EU and show their confidence in Europeans. Such a course would be facilitated to the degree that co-operation between the national institutions of the two sides increases, especially through the establishment of a joint parliamentary committee on global security policy.

Kalypso Nicolaidis, lecturer in international relations at the University of Oxford, strikes a note of realism, suggesting that the US and the EU must learn to live with their differences. In her view, both the American approach of stressing military force exclusively, and the French approach that still sees the current world in a balance of power context, must be left behind. The EU, says Kalypso Nicolaidis, must evolve into a civilian power with military assets in pursuit of peacemaking efforts, overcome its internal differences and splits, and take advantage of its internal diversities as a factor of strength. In this way, she concludes, the EU will be able to act as more of an equal with the United States, with greater flexibility as a complementary but independent power.

7.2.3. Short-term causes

Some of the analysts included in this category of views suggest that the current deterioration of transatlantic relations can be attributed to the particular circumstances of a specific period, rather than to any longterm, insurmountable factors. **Stanley Hoffman**, the eminent professor of international relations at Harvard, submits the position that the tensions in transatlantic relations are due to recent changes in US foreign policy, rather than to pre-existing differences. The EU is worried about the US pursuit of pre-emptive war, its emphasis on fighting terrorism and the diminishing of the role it is willing to give to international institutions and international law.

Theodore Couloumbis, professor of international relations at the University of Athens and formerly at the American University considers that the US is indeed acting in a uni-polar manner at the present juncture, but that the elements of its system are more complex; he therefore calls that system 'uni-multi-polar'. He suggests that the USA's current behaviour indicates the characteristics of a declining power, and reminds us of history's lessons, according to which the great powers have every interest to conserve a state of affairs that perpetuates their position of prominence. The EU, however, must demonstrate that it is able to contribute to rebuilding a system of global order that is both equitable and economically sufficient and sustainable.

Arghyris Fatouros, a professor of international law at the University of Athens and formerly at the University of Indiana, proposes a strategy aimed at transforming the EU into a leading actor in global affairs, promoting international law and institutions. He believes that the current crisis in EU–US relations does not derive from the distant past. Rather, it is due to current factors, such as the present US administration and the still present situation of increasing European integration.

Georgios Papastamkos, professor of the University of Piraeus, considers that the framework of transatlantic relations should undergo political and institutional restructuring. Such a restructuring can be realized on the basis of three different scenarios concerning the future orientation of the ESDP (European Security and Defence Policy) and transatlantic co-operation. According to the first, static scenario, the new global challenges must be dealt with via a shared allocation of responsibilities. According to the second, dynamic scenario, the establishment of an independent ESDP is required. As regards the third scenario, that of a fragmented ESDP, there would be enhanced co-operation with certain EU member states only. G. Papastamkos also outlines a range of suggestions concerning the advancement of global governance, the incorporation of the EU's foreign policy into a single constitutional framework, the reform and restructuring of the United Nations and building bridges to enhance the transatlantic relationship. These suggestions aim at forming a more equitable world, and at rendering the EU even more appealing. The policy proposals of **Misha Glenny**, a journalist and historian specializing in the Balkans, are in the same spirit. In his view, the EU can advance an alternative foreign policy at this time, lending special emphasis to policies concerning the Balkans, the Middle East and immigration. Such policies need not compete with US policy. By adopting such a course, the EU will be in a position to handle crises like the one in Iraq more effectively, as an equal partner with the US.

7.2.4. The recommendations

All the contributors referred to above, irrespective of whether their views are optimistic or not, essentially share the view that the future of transatlantic relations will depend on the further strengthening of European integration, especially in the fields of defence, security and foreign policy. This would include a fuller presence of the UK in European processes and a greater commitment from France. The contribution by the **Transatlantic Policy Network** (TPN) includes suggestions on how to strengthen the EU and secure transatlantic relations. In the TPN essay it is claimed that a strong, effective transatlantic alliance can only be obtained in the framework of common interests at the global level, by encouraging political dialogue and mutual understanding. According to the TPN, the main points of European policy must be co-operation in sectors such as the economy and the increase of European expenditure on defence.

Elmar Brok, chairman of the Committee on Foreign Affairs, Human Rights, Common Security and Defence Policy of the European Parliament, outlines a systematic agenda for a new transatlantic relationship, examining the course of action to be taken by the EU. For E. Brok, the question is: How can Europe recover its dynamism and speed up the process of integration (particularly defensive integration), and concurrently restore its relations with the US? Brok considers reinforcing the Common Foreign and Security Policy (CFSP) and European Security and Defence Policy (ESDP) the best way of reinforcing NATO. What is needed, he claims citing very specific references, is to create a long-term collaborative framework and action plan for combating terrorism, while simultaneously promoting a 'transatlantic community of action'. A transatlantic marketplace should be formed, and the EU and the US should act together on other important global challenges. In order to formulate and realize such a course, there is a need to expand a dialogue in a renewed transatlantic partnership, and to define civil society as an anchor. Inter-parliamentary co-operation between the US and Europe should also be encouraged.

Charles Grant, director of the Centre for European Reform, who is not among the contributors of this volume, agrees with Nye's views (outlined in 7.2.2. above) regarding the importance of a 'soft power'. He believes that the lost honour of the US on the diplomatic level, i.e. its tarnished image as a soft power which attains its objectives by persuasion and attraction rather than by coercion, may be saved if the US collaborates with the Europeans on economic, institutional and restructuring issues. He attributes the blame for the rupture between the US and the EU to the US, but also to France. According to Grant, US President George W. Bush must demonstrate a more diplomatic stance and focus on the Middle East peace process. He further states that British Prime Minister Tony Blair must prove that his support for the US was not unlimited, but also had European interests at heart.

Regarding French President Jacques Chirac, he notes that the French President should admit the reality of EU expansion, and pursue friendship among Central and Eastern European countries. He should also stop seeing the objective of the EU as resisting the US. Grant suggests, on the contrary, that a strong West needs more countries enjoying more power, both soft and hard, on both sides of the Atlantic.

A similar evaluation is submitted by **Kemal Dervis**, former Turkish finance minister, who also believes that while inequalities in the power enjoyed by the EU and US do exist, the American superpower is forced to operate in an exceedingly complex international environment, a fact that imposes the need to co-operate with other powerful international actors, especially on economic issues. In addition, he notes that US actions require greater 'moral' and 'democratic' legitimacy. Kemal Dervis suggests enhanced European cohesion, institutional changes in the United Nations (such as the creation of an Economic and Social Security Council), a single (common) EU representation in the UN, reinforcement of European civil defence and security, and retaining NATO as the main forum of transatlantic relations, with wider objectives to include building bridges with the Islamic world.

Of similar importance are the views expressed by the former prime minister of Ireland, **John Bruton**, who argues for the further reinforcement of defence capabilities and integration within the EU. He suggests that in order for the EU to upgrade its position regarding transatlantic relations, it must adhere to and advocate respect for international law and global institutions, and seek to influence public opinion in the US. Concurrently, the EU must secure the development of its economic and cultural links with the US. John Bruton also maintains that there is need for formal, comprehensive talks between the EU and the US regarding three interconnected issues: pre-emptive wars; weapons of mass destruction; and international terrorism. The EU and the US should jointly develop – and not only on a governmental level – a new, intelligible and intellectually sustainable doctrine for dealing with the post-11 September world, including clear-cut rules regarding the crucial question of the lawfulness of resorting to use of force.

The issue of preventive war is also addressed by **Ted Galen Carpenter**, vice-president of the Cato Institute in the US. Ted Carpenter considers that at the root of the rupture in transatlantic relations lies the Bush strategic doctrine on pre-emptive war and the US interventionist policy in the Middle East. He considers that if Europe wishes to reject the role of a junior partner with limited participation and power, it must acquire a solid, cohesive security identity, and support it with reliable resources.

Friedbert Pflüger, a member of the Christian Democrat Party and chairman of the Foreign Affairs Committee of the German Bundestag, suggests instituting effective mechanisms of transatlantic co-operation and consultation, and a common global agenda. He believes that fuller co-operation is required not only in fighting terrorism, but also in stabilizing countries undermined by internal crises and break ups, unending ethnic conflicts, and dealing with the desperate and marginalized social groups that usually constitute the fighters and core of extreme irredentist or terrorist networks. On issues of common security (terrorism, non-proliferation of weapons of mass destruction), transatlantic co-operation must be solid and effective, so as to persuade countries in the Middle East and Central Asia that there is seamless co-operation and common action on both sides of the Atlantic. He also notes that other issues of common interest include contagious diseases, secured flow of supply of energy resources and issues surrounding digital economy.

Alan Henrikson, professor of international relations at the famous Fletcher School of Law and Diplomacy, recommends specific measures for building closer transatlantic ties. On the ideological level, he suggests focusing on the principles of universality. On the institutional level, he proposes that the transatlantic relationship be organized under a top-level group (a similar proposition, referred to as the 'steering group', had been made by H. Kissinger) representing the two pillars of the relationship, NATO and the EU. On the economic level, he promotes the idea of enhanced collaboration though the adoption of a comprehensive economic agreement to include the NAFTA partners. Finally, on the social and cultural level he proposes a global educational programme to include increased transatlantic exchanges and co-operation on distance learning in developing countries, such as those in the Middle East.

World-famous businessman and analyst **George Soros** believes the rift in EU–US relations is real. He suggests, however, that the two sides can agree on the need for pre-emptive action, if that action stops short of war. The two sides can, or rather they must, agree that the source of many evils in our contemporary world is bad government, and they must therefore undertake a whole range of joint actions, such as ensuring democratic elections. He also suggests that the two sides should agree on some common global objectives and co-operate in pursuing them. He cites greater transparency and accountability for revenues derived from natural resources, and the war against HIV-AIDS as examples of global issues that demand concerted action.

The contribution by **Emilios Avgouleas**, lecturer in international banking law and finance at the University of Piraeus, addresses co-operation in the fields of economic policy and relations with developing countries. He argues that the role the International Monetary Fund and the World Bank (the Bretton-Woods institutions) plays in the international economic landscape has not been given due prominence on the EU–US agenda. He then discusses the neo-liberal doctrine – usually called the 'Washington consensus' – that formulates the economic policies dictated by the Bretton-Woods institutions to borrower countries. Finally, he argues that rethinking and reconceptualizing the economic policies that both institutions dictate to the developing world is a very important issue and should take central stage in EU–US relations.

David Andrews, research fellow at the Robert Schuman Centre for Advanced Studies, European University Institute, whose contribution is co-authored by the director of the Institute, **Hellen Wallace**, also refers to EU–US economic relations. Their main position is that the immediate aim of European policy must be centred on keeping the economic relationship insulated from any political crisis in transatlantic relations. In their essay they suggest that the longer-term aim must focus on the use of the economic relationship as a lever to refashion a more positive political relationship between the EU and the US. The two academics also examine transatlantic relations in the light of the prospects of these relations for further development in the fields of trade, investment and growth. They conclude that the current accumulation of transatlantic problems should not be allowed to continue, since this would ultimately derail efforts to improve global stability.

7.2.5. The studies and their recommendations

At the end of the present volume, we present two lengthy studies, specially prepared for the informal council of foreign ministers in Kastellorizo. The studies address two different issues.

The first study, by the Potsdam Centre for Transatlantic Security and Military Affairs in Germany, has been prepared under the academic supervision of the acclaimed professor of international relations **Margarita Mathiopoulos**. This study analyses the conditions within which transatlantic relations are evolving, and it analyses their future prospects. She stresses the need for the US and EU to avoid retrogressing to a 'balance of power' logic, such as that which prevailed during the nineteenth century. A range of suggestions regarding how and where such relations must develop is presented clearly and concisely.

They include the creation of a 'European Academy', the creation of a 'Transatlantic Area', the institution of a European seat at the Security Council of the UN and the reform of international law. The study suggests that such changes must be compatible with retaining NATO's political and military role. In the study it is stressed that NATO must incorporate the ESDP and reinforce its Mediterranean dimension and mechanisms for dialogue, while also being prepared to undertake missions worldwide. A table is included, presenting the main positions of EU member states in terms of transatlantic relations and foreign policy in general. Considerable labour and considerable knowledge about the state of affairs in transatlantic relations have gone into preparing this table. It serves as a useful starting point for conceptualizing and rethinking the whole issue.

The study contains such a wide range of suggestions, that it is impossible to describe them all in detail in this introduction. Original and useful suggestions for anyone wishing to systematically study transatlantic relations and their prospects are included in this volume. May we suggest that readers take pen in hand, read through the Potsdam Institute study, and record their agreement and/or objections to the points that are raised. Readers' knowledge and views on transatlantic relations will no doubt be enriched by the experience – something that could also be said about all contributions presented in this volume.

The second study, prepared by the Centre for European Studies in Birmingham under the academic supervision of Professor **Anand Menon** and research fellow **Jonathan Lipkin**, presents the views expressed internationally just before and during the war in Iraq. The presentation is methodical, and highlights the political and academic conflicts that occurred during the war, regarding present and future transatlantic relations. Anyone who in the future wishes to study the atmospherics and attitudes regarding transatlantic relations before and during the war in Iraq, and understand the mechanisms that shape public opinion on issues of war and peace, will be well satisfied by reading the Menon–Lipkin essay.

We wish the reader a pleasant journey through the pages of this book. They have been written by eminent politicians and analysts of transatlantic relations, and contain the collected ideas, views, and suggestions of people from the most diverse backgrounds; people from many different countries who are active in many different fields, but who are all in pursuit of the same critical objective: how to shape a better world for tomorrow.

Notes

1. We should note here that during the Cold War there had emerged not only a common institutional global system, but also the main elements or tools of US foreign policy as against its allies. By applying such policy, the US tried to commit the Western European states (but also Japan) to a common position against third countries, on global economic and security issues (beyond the rivalry with the system of applied socialism), and regarding culture; further, it tried to commit its allies to a strategy of asymmetrical interconnection and interdependence with the US (Ikenberry, 1996; Doyle and Ikenberry, 1997).
2. In the military field for example, we should note that while the US entered the Second World War as an ally of the Western European states, it denied similar support during the Suez crisis in 1956 (one of the main reasons for the adjustment of UK policy in favour of closer ties with the EEC, the precursor of the EU). The European allies of the US acted in a similar manner as against the war in Vietnam, where they not only failed to display any marked willingness to lend support to the US, but also distanced themselves from US policy.
3. Developments similar to the above military campaigns in the last decade can also be identified in fighting organized crime and terrorism, and in dealing with regional powers that refuse to be subjected to the 'new order' as determined by Bush (Senior).
4. The assessment that 'this is as far as it goes' with the US and that the US is already in decline makes many within the EU feel that the European Union should redetermine to a considerable extent its relations with the US (Bahr, 2003; Jospin, 2002; Vedrine, 2001). This sentiment led in 2003 to increased collaboration between Germany and France regarding global security issues. As this collaboration became closer, it led France to an increasingly radicalized criticism of the US. In their turn, such radical sentiments brought pressure upon Germany and deepened the (internal) differences between those who believe Germany should share a global role with France – keeping a distance from US policy that would allow them to express criticism thereof – and those who believe Germany can assume alone a leading role in European affairs, as long as it enjoys 'the support of the global reach of the US'.

Bibliography

Adams, W.P. and Lösche, P. (Hrsg.) (1998, 3. Aktualisierte und neu bearbeitete Auflage) *Länderbericht USA. Geschichte – Politik – Geographie – Wirtschaft – Gesellschaft – Kultur*. Bonn: Bundeszentrale für politische Bildung.

Asmus, R.D. (1996) Double enlargement: redefining the Atlantic partnership after the Cold War, in Gompert, D.C. and Larrabee, F.S. (Eds) *America and Europe. A Partnership for a New Era*. Cambridge: Cambridge University Press, pp. 19–50.

Bahr, E. (2003) *Der deutsche Weg*. Munich: Blessing Verlag.

Barber, B.R. (2003) *Fear's Empire. War, Terrorism, and Democracy*. New York and London: W.W. Norton and Co.

Black, C. (2003) Counsel to Britain. How to stay independent and close to the United States at the same time. *National Interest* 73, Fall, 71–6.

Brand, U., Brunnengräber, A., Schrader, L., Stock, C. and Wahl, P. (2000) *Global Governance. Alternative zur neoliberalen Globalisierung*. Münster: Westfälisches Dampfboot.

Brandon, H. (Ed.) (1992) *In Search of a New World Order. The Future of US–European Relations*. Washington DC: The Brookings Institution.

Brezinski, Z. (1997) *Grand Chessboard: American Primacy and its Geostrategic Imperatives*. New York: Basic Books.

Buckler, J. (2003) *Aegean Greece in the Fourth Century BC*. Leiden, London, Boston: Brill Academic Publishers.

Bush, George W. (2003) State of the Union Address, 28 January 2003.

Butler J. (1999) Op-Ed Page, *The New York Times*, 20 March 1999.

Cox, M. (1990) From the Truman Doctrine to the Second Superpower Detente: the Rise and Fall of the Cold War, *Journal of Peace Research*, 27:1, 25–41.

Cox, M. (1995) *US Foreign Policy after the Cold War*. London: Chatham House Papers.

Cox, M., Booth, K. and Dunne, Tim (Eds) (1999) Introduction: the Interregnum. Controversies in World Politics 1989–1999, in: *The Interregnum. Controversies in World Politics 1989–1999*. Cambridge: Cambridge University Press, pp. 3–19.

Cumings, Bruce (1999) Still the American Century, in: *The Interregnum. Controversies in World Politics 1989–1999*. Cambridge: Cambridge University Press, pp. 271–99.

Czempiel, E-O. (2000) Nicht von gleich zu gleich? Die USA und die Europäische Union, Merkur, Sonderheft, Europa oder Amerika? *Zur Zukunft des Westens*, 9/10-2000, 617/8: 901–95.

Daalder, I. (2002) The Use of Force in a Changing World – US and European Perspectives, The Brookings Institution, Policy Brief, November 2002.

Doyle, W. and Ikenberry, G.J. (Eds.) (1997) *New Thinking in International Relations Theory*. Boulder CO: Westview Press.

Dunne, T., Cox, M. and Booth, K. (1999) Introduction: The Eighty Years' Crisis, in: Dunne, T., Cox, M. and Booth, K., *The Eighty Years' Crisis. International Relations 1919–1999*. Cambridge: Cambridge University Press, pp. xiii–xx.

Featherstone, K. and Ginsberg, Roy (1996) Introduction, in Featherstone, K. and Ginsberg, Roy, *The United States and the European Union in the 1990s* (2nd edition) Basingstoke: Macmillan – now Palgrave Macmillan, pp. 3–47.

Ferguson, N. and Kotlikoff, L.J. (2003) Going Critical, *National Interest* 73, Fall, 22–32.

Franck, T. (2002) *Recourse to Force: State Action against Threats and Armed Attacks*. Cambridge: Cambridge University Press.

Fukuyama, F. (1992) *The End of History and the Last Man*. New York: Free Press.

Gaddis, J.L. (1993) The Cold War, the Long Peace, and the Future, in: Lundestad, G. and Westad, O.A., *Beyond the Cold War: New Dimensions in International Relations*, 90th Anniversary Nobel Jubilee Symposium. Oslo: Scandinavian University Press, pp. 7–22.

Gamble, A. (2003) *Between Europe and America. The Future of British Politics*. Basingstoke: Palgrave Macmillan.

George, J. (2000) Back to the Future?, in Fry, G. and O'Hagan, J., *Contending Images of World Politics*, London-New York: Macmillan – now Palgrave Macmillan, pp. 33–47.

Gnesotto, N. and Roper, J. (Eds) (1992) *Western Europe and the Gulf. A Study of West European Reactions to the Gulf War*, Paris.

Halliday, F. (2001) *The World at 2000*. Basingstoke: Palgrave Macmillan.

Hoyer, W. and Kaldrack, G.F. (Eds) (2002) *Europäische Sicherheits- und Verteidigungspolitik (ESVP). Der Weg zu integrierten europäischen Streitkräften*. Baden-Baden: Nomos Verlagsgesellschaft.

Huntington, S.P. (1999) The Lonely Superpower, *Foreign Affairs*, 78:2, 39–40.

Ikenberry, G.J. (1996) *American Foreign Policy: Theoretical Essays*. New York: Harper Collins College Publishers.

Ikenberry, G.J. (1999) Liberal Hegemony and the Future of American Post-war Order, in, Paul, T.V. and Hall, J.A. *International Order and the Future of World Politics*. Cambridge: Cambridge University Press.

Ikenberry, J.G. and Kupchan, C.A. (1990) Socialization and Hegemonic Order. *International Organization* 44: 283–315.

Jospin, L. (2002) My Vision of Europe and Globalization. Edited by F. Michel, with an introduction by P. Mandelson and text from P. Lamy and J. Pisani, *The Europe We Want*. London: Polity: Policy Network.

Judt, T. (2003) Anti-Americans Abroad. *The New York Review*, 1 May 2003, 24–7.

Kagan, R. (2003) *Of Paradise and Power*. New York: Alfred A.Knopf.

Keens-Soper, M. (1999) *Europe in the World: the Persistence of Power Politics*. New York: St. Martin's Press – now Palgrave Macmillan.

Kennedy, P.M. (1987) *The Rise and the Fall of the Great Powers: Economic Change and Military Conflict from 1500 to 2000*. New York: Random House.

Keohane R. (1984) *After Hegemony*. Princeton, NJ.; Princeton University Press.

Kissinger, H.A. (1999) *Years of Renewal. The Concluding Volume of His Memoirs*. New York: Simon and Schuster (München 1999: C. Bertelsmann).

Kotzias N. (2001) Die Transatlantishce Beziehungen aus der Sicht der USA, in Bieling, H-J., Dörre, K., Steinhilber, J. and Urban, H-J. (Eds) *Flexibler Kapitalismus*. Hamburg: VSA, pp. 145–60.

Kotzias, N. (2003) The Relation between USA and Europe. Preface to the Greek edition of R. Kagan, *Of Paradise and Power*. Athens: Kastaniotis, pp. 7–22.

Krasner, S.D. (Ed.) (1983) *International Regimes*. Ithaca NY: Cornell University Press.

Lebow, R.N. (1999) The Rise and Fall of the Cold War in Comparative Perspective, in: *The Interregnum. Controversies In World Politics 1989–1999*. Cambridge: Cambridge University Press, pp. 21–39.

Lebow, R.N. and Risse-Kappen, T. (1995) *International Relations Theory and the End of the Cold War*. New York: Columbia University Press.

Lippman, M. (2003) The New Terrorism and International Law, *Tulsa Journal of Comparative and International Law* 10, 358–61.

McDougal, M.S. (1963) The Cuban Quarantine, 57 *A.J.I.L.* 597.

Mearsheimer, J.J. (1994–5) Back to the Future: Instability in Europe After the Cold War, *International Security*, 19 (Winter), 91–129.

Moravcsik, A. (2003) Striking a New Transatlantic Bargain, *Foreign Affairs*, July/August, 74–89.

Nye, J.S. Jr. (2000) *Understanding International Conflicts: an Introduction to Theory and History*. New York: Longman, third edition.

Peterson, T. (1992) *On Every Front: the Making and Unmaking of the Cold War*. New York: W.W. Norton.

Pierre, J. (Ed.) (2000) *Debating Governance. Authority, Steering and Democracy*. Oxford: Oxford University Press.

Pilger, J. (2001) US Foreign Policy Has Not Changed, *New Statesman*, 25 December 2000–1 January 2001, 13–14.

Reisman, M.W. (2003) Editorial Comment: Assessing Claims to Revise the Laws of War, 97 *A.J.I.L*, 82.

Reiter, E., Rummel, R. and Schmidt, P. (Eds) (2002) *Europas ferne Streitmacht, Changen und Schwirigkeiten der Europäischen Union beim Aufbau der ESVP*. Hamburg, Berlin, Bonn: Verlag E.S. Mittler & Sohn.

Rhodes, R.A.W. (1996) The New Governance: Governing without Government, *Political Studies* 44: 652–67.

Richardson, J.L. (2000), The 'End of History'? in Fry, G. and O'Hagan, J., *Contending Images of World Politics*. London-New York: Macmillan – now Palgrave Macmillan, pp. 21–32.

Rivkin, D.B. Jr. and Casey, L.A. (2003) Leashing the Dogs of War. *National Interest* 73, Fall, 57–70.

Rosenau, J. (1997) *Along the Domestic–Foreign Frontier: Exploring Governance in a Turbulent World*. Cambridge: Cambridge University Press.

Rosenau, J. and Czempiel, E.O. (Eds) (1992) *Governance without Government*. Cambridge: Cambridge University Press.

Rudolf, P. and Wilzewski, J. (Hrsg.) (2000) *Weltmacht ohne Gegner. Amerikanische Außenpolitik zu Beginn des 21. Jahrhunderts. Stiftung Wissenschaft und Politik / SWP*. Baden-Baden: Nomos Verlag.

Schulz, R. (2003) *Athen und Sparta*. Darmstadt: Wissenschaftliche Buchgesellschaft.

Shlei, N. (1962/2003) From the Bag: Anticipatory Self-Defence: A 1962 OLC Opinion on Lawful Alternatives for the US in the Cuban Missile Crisis, 6 *Green Bag* 2d, 195, 2003.

Shustov, V.V. (1990) A View on the Origins of the Cold War and Some Lessons Thereof, In: Lundestad, G. and Westad, O.A., *Beyond the Cold War: New Dimensions in International Relations*, 90th Anniversary Nobel Jubilee Symposium. Oslo: Scandinavian University Press, pp. 23–38.

Spiegel Special (2003) America – Der Schatten der Weltmacht.

Strange, S. (1987) The Persistent Myth of Lost Hegemony, *International Organization*, 41: 4, 5–16.

Strange, S. (1988) *States and Markets*. London and New York: Pinder, second edition 1994.

Strange, S. (1988) The Future of the American Empire, *Journal of International Affairs*, 42:1, 1–19.

Todd, E. (2002) *Apres l' empire. Essai sur la decomposition du systeme americain*. Paris: Gallimard.

Todd, E. (2003, 4th edn), *Weltmacht USA. Ein Nachruf*. Munich-Zürich: Piper.

Vedrine, H. with Moïsi, D. (2001) *France in an Age of Globalization*. Washington DC: The Brookings Institution.

Viksnins, G.F. (2003) New Europe, New Problems, *National Interest* 73, Fall, 85–92.

Virilio, P. (2000), *Information und Apokalypse*. Munich: Hanser.

Volger, von G. (1994) Partners in leadership? Über die deutsch-amerikanischen Beziehungen. Merkur Sonderheft: Deutschland in der Welt. *Über Außenpolitik und Nationalstaat*, Heft 9–10, Sept./Okt. 1994, 48.Jahrgang, ss.922–929.

Walter, A. (1993) *World Power and World Money: the Role of Hegemony and International Monetary Order*. Hemel Hempstead and New York: Pearson Higher Education.

Watrin, K. (2003) *Shock and Awe*. Munich: Olzog Verlag.

Webb, M.C. and Krasner, S.D. (1989) Hegemonic Stability Theory: an Empirical Assessment, *Review of International Studies*, 15: 183–98.

Weintraub, T. (Ed.) (1992) *Toward a History of Game Theory*. Durham and London: Duke University Press.

Wyatt-Walter, A. (1999) The United States and Western Europe: the Theory of Hegemonic Stability, in Woods, N., *Explaining International Relations Since 1945*. Oxford: Oxford University Press, pp. 126–54.

Part II

The Long-Term Character of EU–US Disagreements

2
Present and Future of the Tensed EU–US Relations

William Pfaff

I am responding to your invitation to contribute a note to the preparations for the EU foreign ministers meeting next week because I believe the policies of the European Union in coming months can have a crucial, and I would hope constructive, influence, not only on international society but on developments in the United States, which are a matter of concern to myself and to many American citizens.

There are fundamental differences of interest between this American administration and the EU, rooted in the fact that the Bush government is increasingly hostile to an alliance relationship other than one of implicit or explicit domination and subordination. This has been apparent in the Iraq war controversy, and follows from the Bush administration's radical new conception of American power and national mission.

An effort to deny or ignore the implications of this development will eventually produce malaise and division within the EU, while fuelling the most negative forces currently at work in the US and reducing the influence of those Americans who seek a return to constructive and cooperative transatlantic relations between equals.

I should add that I expect to repeat the substance of these remarks in a forthcoming column in the *International Herald Tribune* and other newspapers.

I will respond in sequence to the questions you have posed.

The EU on the US radar screen

Yes. The US is very much focused on Europe because Europe is its sole serious economic and political counterweight and potential rival. This American administration is particularly concerned by the implications

37

of European popular opposition as well as French, Belgian and German governmental resistance to American policy on Iraq, which it takes as a signal that a common European foreign policy might in the future become a serious constraint on US freedom of action. It will do all that it can to prevent this.

Philosophies and strategies

There are deep differences in fundamental policy assumptions and strategy between the Bush administration and, I would think, nearly all the EU's members, not only on most of the cited issues, but also philosophical differences concerning the nature of history, historical expectation, and the scope of legitimate national action, notably in the use of violence and the practice of pre-emptive war. This administration wishes to ensure permanent US global military predominance. It believes that the United States should be exempted from international law in selected areas, and that the role of existing international institutions must be restricted in matters that constrain US freedom of action.

I stress that I am talking about the current American administration. The Bush government has made a radical break from American foreign policy as it has existed since the Second World War. This has provoked much controversy inside the United States itself. The Bush government could disappear in 20 months, after the next presidential election. On the other hand, if Mr Bush is re-elected, the policies and practices inaugurated by his government are in my opinion likely to have a lasting and deleterious effect on the character of the American polity as well as on international relations.

Global priorities

My rough judgement is that current US government's foreign preoccupations are, in order, power predominance, rogue states, weapons of mass destruction (in the hands of certain countries), terrorism, Islamic fundamentalism, regional conflict, human rights, economic development as measured by globalization, education, environment, poverty, inequality.

Focus on the 'do-able'? Yes.

Expand dialogue? Yes, with much attention to communicating to Congress and the public in the United States. Both Congress and the American public are widely ignorant of European Union realities and policy positions.

Future of relations

The US outlook is uncertain. Areas of transatlantic conflict are well known, and their implications should not be minimized. In my opinion, the most important things the EU can do to affect transatlantic relations constructively are to nourish and develop European economic power and autonomy, and European high technology research and development on *autonomous terms*.

Technology and the economy are two areas of European actual or potential advantage, and together with diplomacy and political action they provide Europe with its most important levers for influencing US policy and international affairs generally. Certainly the current military disorder of Europe is scandalous, in view of the sums currently expended by the member states acting individually, and it should be remedied.[1] But the gross global military advantage of the US provides a very narrow form of power which is of limited utility in fundamentally influencing the evolution of relations among the major actors in modern industrial society.

Collaboration with US governmental and corporate projects concerning crucial technologies and research should be treated with great caution, because US security and proprietary restraints invariably place the European partner in a subordinate role, seriously limiting its share in the benefits of collaboration. This is particularly important with respect to technologies essential to projecting power (both hard power and soft).

Why I say this

My belief is that the current policy course of the US will increasingly provoke serious transatlantic tensions. This will reflect two aspects of what might be called the historic and political 'nature of things' – *la force des choses*. The first is that while the effort to acquire and exercise imperial or hegemonic power may be successful in the short term, it is ultimately vain because it automatically generates resistance, leading towards crises – sometimes bloody ones. The other is the reality that Europe's nations are too ancient and too powerful culturally as well as materially, to indefinitely accept domination by the US.

I am thus convinced that steps to place Europe in a position to exercise independent and autonomous power in international society, in defence of the principles of balance in international relations and of multilateral global 'governance' would provide an essential service to international order, as well as to the enduring interests of both the United States and Europe.

Notes

1. I would cite (in summary) Christoph Bertram. There are three reasons why Europe lacks strategic power: lack of military means (the least important); a profound incapacity for decision; and most important and most pre-occupant, the absence of any true ambition to play a strategic role (*Commentaire*, Paris, No. 101, Printemps 2003).

3

The EU and the Future of
Transatlantic Relations

Christoph Bertram

1. The falling-out between and among the members of what was the transatlantic community over the recent Iraq conflict is not an accident after which there can be a return to the old consensus. There is, of course, on both sides of the Atlantic, a need to limit the damage done, by demonstrating mutual respect and exercising rhetorical restraint and pragmatic cooperation. The common task of consolidating Iraq after the war offers a chance for putting this into practice. But this does not remove the deeper reason for the transatlantic rift: On the fundamental issue of how to promote international order in the twenty-first century, most if not all European countries no longer see eye-to-eye with their major security partner, the United States.

2. America has for long been the most powerful state in the modern world. But it basically accepted the international status quo as it had emerged after the Cold War. Under the impact of 11 September 2001, however, America has ceased to be a status quo power. Irrespective of the ideological inclination of the government in Washington, the US will now make use of its extraordinary military capability to address the new strategic challenges which 9/11 symbolizes: proliferating states, non-state actors with access to destructive weapons, and states which harbour them. This will not always mean the US will resort to war, but it will mean that a military threat will generally accompany any demand by the world's only superpower to get its way.

3. The European Union is not a status quo power on the European continent, where enlargement and integration are truly revolutionary concepts of how to provide stability and prosperity to a growing number of states. But beyond the boundaries of their Union, European governments either have no strategic ambition at all or are content with things as they are, seeking to encourage stability through inter-

national agreement and inclusion instead of military intervention and the outlawing of problem states. This is so by conviction, but also partly by indifference, lack of the means or the inability to take urgent strategic decisions at the Union level. Even if the European Convention should, as is to be hoped, produce more efficient decision-making procedures for the Union's international role, these will fall well short of those of a unitary state.

4. That is why the transatlantic rift over strategy is here to stay and why it will continue to endanger both transatlantic trust and transatlantic institutions. Perhaps one day the United States will rediscover the advantages of a firm transatlantic partnership with the Union, based on institutions which make its leadership both sustainable and acceptable. That day is not near. In the long interim, the answer of how to cope with the rift cannot, therefore, lie in attempting to paper over the disagreements. Instead it will be necessary to limit them by identifying and debating the differences, and trying to make sure that other areas of cooperation and consensus – of which there are many – are not poisoned by the differences.

5. Pursuing transatlantic cooperation while not hiding the disagreements will require two qualities from European political leaders: a high degree of mature pragmatism in dealing with the United States; and a major effort to instil in the respective publics support for the continued value of working with America on most issues, and respecting those areas where differences will persist.

4
The Future of Transatlantic Relations

Scott Barrett

Recent world events bear witness to a qualitative change not only in transatlantic relations but in international relations more generally. The trigger point for this change seems to have been the 11 September 2001 terrorist attacks. Also important were the collapse of the Soviet Union and the ascendance of US power in a new, unipolar world. Suddenly the institutions developed for a different world seem ill suited to the new one, and the strains are showing. Some European countries see institutions like the UN as serving to restrain US power. Precisely for this reason, however, some people in the US see these institutions as harmful to US interests. When forced to choose, the US, like any country, can be expected to put its own interests first.

Two examples: The Bush administration saw Iraq as a threat to US security. It was prepared to go to war to stop this threat, preferably with the support of other nations, but alone if necessary. It sought approval from the UN to enforce previous Security Council resolutions, and got this in Resolution 1441. But it failed to get a second resolution, and so acted 'minilaterally', with Britain and the support of some other European countries. I opposed this war on the basis that Iraq was not an imminent threat to the United States, that Iraq's use of weapons of mass destruction (WMD) against the US could be deterred, and that a policy of pre-emption was destabilizing (the aim of regime change coupled with the policy of pre-emption provides an incentive for countries like North Korea to acquire WMD in order to deter the US from attacking). However, it was plain that Iraq only allowed international inspectors to return after the US had amassed forces in the region. Ironically, unilateral action by the US (and Britain) impelled Iraq to take the UN seriously. In declining to support a second resolution, however, the Security Council weakened the UN threat of 'serious consequences'. It also failed to restrain the US (and Britain).

Though unhappy with certain aspects of the Kyoto Protocol, I opposed the reasons given by the US for rejecting this treaty. Even worse was the manner in which the US view was communicated. At the same time, however, European insistence on US acceptance of key provisions of this treaty made participation by the US almost impossible. Of course, George W. Bush never supported the agreement. But it is highly unlikely that even Al Gore could have convinced the US Senate to ratify this agreement. Again, an international institution was used to try to restrain US behaviour, and the effort succeeded only in alienating the US from the institution. This is bad for Europe. It is also bad for the US. A climate treaty without US participation is doomed to partial success at best.

I don't see these and other ruptures as foretelling US abandonment of multilateralism. There are numerous issues that require multilateral remedies, including the fight against terrorism, surveillance of diseases like SARS, controls on WMD proliferation and climate change mitigation. The US and Europe both gain from collective action in these areas, and progress in addressing these problems requires joint leadership by the US and Europe. It would be of great symbolic importance for the US and Europe to initiate agreement for a new multilateral framework which addresses a problem of common concern.

It might seem that Europe and the US have reached an impasse on climate change, but the choice is not between the Kyoto Protocol and unilateralism. There is much that both sides of the Atlantic can gain from collective research into new energy technologies, and such a programme would be compatible with both the Kyoto Protocol and the Bush administration's domestic climate policy. Progress on research and development may in turn lead to further cooperation. A successor to the Kyoto Protocol will need to be negotiated in the next few years, and it is essential that this effort be led jointly by the US and Europe.

That is how the transatlantic relationship should be repaired: by making small achievements in particular areas of common concern.

5
Note on the Transatlantic Bonds of the EU

Bronislaw Geremek

1. The actual crisis regarding the relationships between the United States and the European Union can be improved only by a coherent (and pragmatic rather than cordial) European Union policy aimed at restoring the friendship between the EU and the US, and by the assertion of the European Union's common foreign and security policy, known as CFSP.

The Greek presidency is presented, thanks to its relative neutrality in the recent controversies, with an important if not unique opportunity to launch such an initiative.

2. We should seek to defuse the present state of the relationship between the EU and the US and not follow the ideological controversies between the 'Atlanticists' and the 'Europeanists' or between Europe and the US. We should consider the thesis of Joseph Nye in which he states that the sole world superpower, the United States, needs partners like the EU states, rather than Robert Kagan's thesis pronouncing the decline of Europe (and the juxtaposition of a United States from Mars and a Europe from Venus). In the same thread of logic, we should not refer to Emmanuel Todd's thesis on the decline of the US, but try to find a common understanding with other actors regarding the opportunities as well as the threats coming from US power. Between the United States and the EU there are differences regarding their views and approaches, but it cannot be said that they prove any cultural or fundamental divergences between the US and Europe. Europe's awareness of its identity must derive from positive and affirmative discourse and not from the negation of America.

3. Analysts of international relations observe that this is the first time that US policy does not demonstrate any interest towards the European Union and to the unification or integration of Europe (i.e. to

the expansion to the east of the EU), but seems to seek the division of Europeans. We should create conditions to convince Americans that a strong and coherent European Union constitutes a guarantee of peace and European stability and will be a worthy partner in world policy.

4. The 'pre-emptive self-defence' doctrine and the strategic orientation of George W. Bush's administration to follow a unilateral approach in his foreign policy without the minimal consent of the EU states has to be one of the central issues of the debate between the EU and the US. Persuading the United States to be less unilateral could be better achieved by the initiative of internal reforms in the United Nations system, which could be launched together by the US and the EU. It seems difficult to presently obtain a consensus on changes in the composition and powers of the Security Council, but we could be thinking of suggesting a plan of successive reforms, to be announced within a short time and realized on a schedule. The promotion of human rights and democracy in international law and in the workings of the United Nations could be thought as an initial contribution of the EU, which will enhance the UN with the necessary powers and authority. Within this framework of facing international problems we should also consider the problem of international terrorism and weapons of mass destruction.

5. The problems of CFSP and of the formation of armed forces for the EU's rapid reaction force could be the subject of discussions with the United States. That could advance the CFSP at a time when the Intergovernmental Conference (IGC) and the Convention will be making important decisions. *At the same time we should seek a way to leave NATO out of the current crisis without debating on whom weighs responsibility for this situation.* The EU should take some lessons from recent experience to establish effective mechanisms for creating consensus in the domain of foreign policy. I dare to assert that if the 'French–German motor' seems to be of the biggest importance for the forward movement of European integration, I do not think that the CFSP could be reduced to a French–German axis: the attitudes regarding the war in Iraq have proven this.

6. Think tanks can do a useful preparation work – in a more effective way than parliamentary structures – but in the present situation it is up to the men and women in politics to play the active intellectual role and come together in think tanks *which could* join action to imagination and reflection. It seems to me also that during the necessary reconciliation between the US and the EU, countries such as the United Kingdom, Spain and Poland could and should use every aspect of their influence in the name and in aid of Europe.

Part III
Differences and Mutual Completion

6
Europe and the Transatlantic Relationship after the Iraq Crisis

Gilles Andréani

European integration and the transatlantic relationship have both suffered from the Iraq crisis.

Opposition to the war was dominant in Europe, whereas public opinion accepted an Iraqi policy presented as an integral part of the war on terror. The attitudes of governments did nothing to mitigate this polarization of opinions on the two sides of the Atlantic. The United States government, in particular, chose to isolate, then harshly criticize the European countries opposed to the war. The controversy was more serious than differences that usually occur in relations between allies, and memories of the clash will be slow to fade.

From the outset, European governments were divided as to the conduct to adopt in this affair, where the issue appeared to be less Iraq than the transatlantic relationship. The United States was part of the European debate throughout. The tone and terms of the debate within Europe increasingly mirrored those of the transatlantic debate.

The Common Foreign and Security Policy (CFSP) emerged from this episode unfairly criticized. It was not asked to play a role in Iraq. The CFSP was subject to the centrifugal forces at work in Europe and pressure from the US administration. US opponents of political union in Europe have expressed themselves without restraint and have attempted to divide the continent into 'two Europes'.

We must rebuild European unity, however, for two reasons. Firstly, a divided Europe would remain weak and without impact on US policy, leaving the transatlantic relationship in its current state. Secondly, a weak transatlantic relationship is far less of a problem for the Americans than a divided Europe for the Europeans.

49

1. The CFSP must overcome the divides created by the Iraq crisis

The Iraq crisis caused a split in European positions, highlighting not only profound substantive divisions, but, more importantly, divergences regarding the independence of EU policy from the United States (the Letter of the Eight and the Declaration of Ten have placed this theme at the centre of the debate).

CFSP cannot be based on a negative project, focused on the past (perpetuating European public opinion's opposition to war), rather than on an independent, forward-looking analysis of European interests.

On this issue, neither pole of the European debate can win. A reaffirmation of the Franco-German partnership as a driving force at the centre of the European system remains essential to the UE dynamic. It is particularly important to reassert Franco- German capacity as it has come under excessive criticism during the Iraq crisis. However, Iraq is a divisive memory for Europe. While France and Germany must take responsibility for their position on Iraq, they cannot present it as a unifying project for the future.

Conversely, it would be illusory for the European countries most engaged alongside the United States in Iraq to attempt to form an 'alliance within the alliance', a special relationship elevating them by marginalizing the opponents of the war. The fact is that the Americans do not really need them, as they said on the eve of the war. A 'hard core' of countries is conceivable within the European Union, but not the North Atlantic Alliance, where only the United States is in a position of natural leadership (the impulse for intervention in Iraq could not have come from Europe).

Europeans have become divided. But the idea that there are two Europes does not come from them. Such a conclusion would be contrary to their interests as Europeans and allies. They will move beyond the Iraq crisis, and already have.

2. However, it is important not to overlook the differences between Europe and America, which the Iraq crisis revealed more than it created

Differences in perception: the difference lay less in the technical analysis of Iraq's nuclear, biological and chemical capability than in the perception of the overall situation and the urgency of the threat represented by Iraq. For most Europeans (and quite a few Americans), Iraq did not represent a direct military threat to them or the region. They therefore believed that by applying dual pressure – the threat of military action and inspectors – the country could be disarmed peacefully. By contrast, the United States placed the war in a logic of self-defence, if not legally, at least politically and psychologically (a constant theme in the arguments of the president and vice-president).

Differences in diplomatic style: European countries have a more pluralistic concept of the international system. Aside from national sensibilities that are closer to multilateralism, the day-to-day operation of the European Union has made them more accustomed to a process of negotiation, influence and compromise leading to consensus as a precondition for action, at least in foreign policy. These working habits are deeply rooted in European diplomatic culture. The United States has always been more wary of this type of process. As the shift in US diplomacy after September 11 has shown (see Operation Enduring Freedom and the role of the Alliance), consultation and – even more – consensus are not perceived as necessary; at best they are an option, and often a hindrance, whose short-term usefulness is not obvious to the United States. In contrast, Europeans could not say 'with us or against us'.

These differences were caricatured by those in the United States who consider that the transatlantic relationship is a thing of the past and that permanent alliances should now give way to temporary coalitions. European's legalism and multilateralism are presented as signs of weakness; and their more global, political view of the threat as evidence of complacency or hypocrisy. One of our objectives must be to refute these stereotypes, which are unfair to Europe and dangerous for the transatlantic relationship.

3. On which bases should the transatlantic relationship be rebuilt?

European policy must not be too eager to repair the transatlantic relationship quickly by denying differences over the war and over the conditions for Iraq's reconstruction (if it were up to Europeans to define these conditions, they would spontaneously find an easy agreement). It would be as wrong to claim that no differences persist on Iraq as it would to build a European policy based on opposition to the United States and anticipation of its failure. We must develop a policy that is as pragmatic and positive as possible, given the legitimate divergences of analysis regarding the military intervention and its consequences.

If Europeans are seeking new ground on which to demonstrate their renewed unity and continued transatlantic solidarity, they must focus on the security issues central to their own interests and their alliance with the United States. They must combat unconstructive stereotypes of Europe as pacifist, versus America as belligerent. They must rise to the challenges that face them by applying their own European analysis, approach and style. The following are examples of areas on which to build a new transatlantic relationship:

- *Proliferation of weapons of mass destruction.* The next few months and years will be crucial. The Iranian and North Korean military nuclear programmes are not only security issues, but also a frontal challenge to the nuclear non-proliferation regime. On nuclear, as well as biological and chemical weapons, we must use all the instruments at our disposal: use and reinforce multilateral instruments without discrediting them through indulgence towards countries that violate them; use and reinforce the suppliers' regime; and integrate non-proliferation into our overall relationship with a country or a region. Reflection has been initiated by the Secretary-General of the Council. It must be pursued and expanded.
- *Fight against terrorism.* Most efforts are taking place within a national framework. Consequently, cooperation with the United States is mainly bilateral. However, there are a growing number of instruments at European Union level, relating to both prevention (police and judicial cooperation) and management of consequences of terrorist attacks. Cooperation between the EU and the US will be a natural complement to bilateral cooperation.
- *Human rights.* Europeans have an interest in rethinking existing multilateral mechanisms, primarily the Commission on Human Rights. To restore the Commission to its initial function and to remedy an undesirable situation in which the whole United Nations system is losing credibility, particularly, but not only, in the United States, because of its limitations. This is in line with both our values and our interests.
- *The Balkans.* The European Union allocates considerable resources to the region. It is important to further develop a comprehensive EU policy that is more structured and more integrated, covering political, military and trade issues. This is one of the essential prerequisites to the pursuit of the Euro-American partnership in the region, particularly since the European Union is set to take over from NATO in the Balkans, and soon in Bosnia, where the military dimension is only one aspect and not the most important.

First and foremost, Europeans must come together around a view of the world in which security problems are serious and from which threats have not disappeared. Europe has specific advantages to contribute to the analysis of international security and the assessment of threats: geographical and cultural proximity to the societies concerned; apprehension that those societies will become polarized in an anti-Western identity; sensitivity to the political and economic aspects of security; a preference for incorporating security arrangements into formal institutional mechanisms. This European approach to security issues is not a sign of weakness. It is legitimate and complementary to the United States' approach.

In the area of defence, also, Europeans must desist from constant emulation of the United States and instead increase their resources and develop their own military know-how and culture, compatible with their diplomatic style and concept of security. This can also be complementary to the United States' efforts.

In both the analysis of threats and the development of military capabilities, Europe must show that it is serious when it comes to security, without renouncing its own qualities and political personality. It is a narrow path to tread, but the only practicable one if Europe is to convince the United States of the mutual benefits of the Atlantic alliance and European unity, two historically mutually reinforcing projects, which ideology and divergences over the Iraq crisis dangerously threaten to tear apart.

7

Improving Transatlantic Relations in the Aftermath of the Iraq War

Joseph Stiglitz

The Iraq war has strained the multilateral system, a system which was already being sorely tested. Globalization, the closer integration of the countries of the world, requires with it closer cooperation among the countries of the world. There are more interdependencies, and more need for collective action. A commitment to democracy means that decisions must be made in a multilateral way. Multilateralism, in turn, means that there has to be both a process of consensus building, and a willingness to accept decisions that differ from those one would have wanted. Europe, in trying to develop a polity involving many countries, has long come to terms with this reality. The United States has not, and with its overwhelming economic and political power, it has not even felt the need to do so. Yet many Americans are uncomfortable with this state of affairs. Ideals of democracy, social justice, and liberalism more generally (though not universally) are woven into the fabric of America's own self-image and identity – a country which is a melting pot, which has welcomed others of all races and creeds to its shores, which fought, and continues to fight, the scourge of racial bigotry.

One needs, moreover, to see the current problems within this broader context. Even before the Iraq War, America repeatedly demonstrated a lack of commitment to multilateralism, as it repeatedly looked askance at the creation of an international rule of law, evidenced in its approaches to global warming, the International Criminal Court, secrecy in offshore banking (before 11 September), and so forth.

With these ideas as background, here are four aspects of a strategy to strengthen transatlantic relations:

1. *Strengthening non-governmental transatlantic relationships.* The starting point here is to deepen the ties between America and Europe at all

levels, including, and perhaps particularly, at the level of civil society and education. Governments see conflict, and they seek to bargain for themselves the best deal. Individuals working together look for areas of mutual cooperation, commonality of interests. Interests in creating a world with a better environment, more social justice, better health care and improved education, cut across national boundaries. But organizationally, efforts to accomplish this remain focused at the national level. Europe, perhaps working with American and European foundations, could help foster this kind of activity. Programmes like the Marshall Scholarships could be massively scaled up.

2. *Institutional development focused around common problems.* Efforts, including those of think tanks, to develop solutions to common problems remain remarkably nation-bound. The OECD (Organization for Economic Cooperation and Development) is an important exception, but it is too closely linked to governments. Transatlantic (and global) institutions are needed which would *challenge* the presumptions that often develop within a country and come simply to be taken for granted. While the Washington consensus strategy for development may illustrate an extreme case – the assumptions underlying that strategy are markedly different from economic philosophies prevalent in many market economies – there are numerous other instances. What is needed are both strengthened networks and new institutions, helping to foster transatlantic dialogue (and global dialogue) on key issues, such as global warming, intellectual property rights, and the rules for a global market economy (including corporate governance, accounting and bankruptcy).

3. *Hard bargaining (or tough love).* Unfortunately, I believe in order to strengthen transatlantic relationships it may be necessary for the United States to perceive that such improved relationships are in its *self-interest.* This is a delicate matter. If the United States believes, in the end, that it will get its way, then it has no incentive to develop better relationships. It is costly, and it requires compromise. Europe needs to make it clear that it perceives itself as a coalition of democracies, with obligations to its citizens, and that its citizens have perceptions of their interests which may be at variance with those of the US. Europe must stress that without more *meaningful* dialogue and cooperation, there are likely to be tensions, which *even within the existing limited multilateral framework* may not work to America's interest. The recent shrimp-turtle case which recognized the right of nations to use trade policy to advance global environmental concerns provides a case in point. There is a growing recognition that the WTO ruling on this case (brought by

the US against Thailand) provides the basis for Europe to impose restrictions on American products produced in ways which produce excessive greenhouse gases. Europe should begin strong actions, making clear that in doing so, it is not acting against the United States but is simply responding to global concerns and the concerns of its citizens. This may provide an incentive for the US to engage in more meaningful dialogue across a wide range of issues.

4. *Embedding the transatlantic relationships in a broader global context.* Many of the sources of friction between the United States and Europe are really not a division between Europe and the United States, but between the United States and much of the rest of the world. Relationships between Europe and the developing countries on the one hand, and America and the developing world on the other hand, are evolving rapidly. Europe's 'Everything but Arms' initiative may be limited, but is far broader and involves fewer conditions, than America's more limited efforts in Africa and elsewhere. The rest of the world is becoming increasingly committed to multilateralism, as America is seemingly moving in the direction of unilateralism. Embedding the dialogue in a global context will serve to diffuse any hostility aimed towards Europe, or any particular European country; Americans, hopefully, will see that if they hope to exercise global leadership, they will have to engage in meaningful dialogue both with Europe and with the rest of the world. The kinds of initiatives to enhance the transatlantic relationship called for in points 1 and 2 need to be done on a global scale. The costs will not be trivial, but neither will they be large, relative to the costs of continuing global tensions.

8
EU–US Relations in a Multipolar System

Dimitri Constas

The premise

Any discussion on the future of transatlantic relations has to address a fundamental question: Is US foreign policy unilateralism – with the latest case the war in Iraq – random and reversible or a trend which will continue in the future? To answer this question one should acknowledge some important facts. First, at the level of economic interaction, the transatlantic community manifests a highly inter-dependent relationship characteristic of the age of globalization. Interactions are affected only partially by state policies and, by and large, respond automatically to changing market conditions. However, at the political-security level, the picture changes. The relationship between a federal state and a collectivity of 15, now 25 states, becomes asymmetrical. The effects of this asymmetry are less evident in dis-agreements over trade where the EU is unified enough to respond effec-tively, but they are particularly striking whenever a conflict arises over issues directly or indirectly linked to security.

For some political elites in the US, the end of bipolarity presented the remaining superpower with a unique opportunity to prevent chal-lenges to its hegemony by a single or combination of opponents. With the advent to power of a Republican administration in November 2000, US unilateralism was clearly demonstrated in several instances: the International Criminal Court; the anti-ballistic missile treaty; the Kyoto Protocol, biological weapons conventions, landmines, etc. The 11 September terrorist attacks further aggravated the situation since US governing elites regarded the institutional framework of inter-national relations, as it stood since the end of the Second World War, as a hindrance to the effective exercise of American power. Because international terrorism respects no frontiers, American military might should ignore concepts of sovereignty and territorial integrity or other rules that restrict the use of force. Regimes that could offer haven to terrorists and supply them with weapons of mass destruction could become targets even if international law does not permit it.

Demonstrations of solidarity with the US after 11 September were widespread in Europe. NATO invoked Article Five for the first time in the history of the alliance. The EU adopted European arrest warrants, coordinated police action and established joint air safety measures. It gave substantial financial assistance to Afghanistan. Individual European countries were also helpful. The German Bundestag gave permission to use armed forces outside German territory for the first time since the Second World War. But none of this seemed to impress governing American elites. The war in Afghanistan was fought and won by a 'coalition of the willing' in accordance with the first application of the new dogma: 'The mission defines the coalition, not the reverse'. The second application of this dogma came in Iraq at the expense of United Nations Security Council rules.

Therefore, it seems that the answer to the question posed at the beginning of this essay is that US foreign policy unilateralism is likely to persist. The structural changes that the end of bipolarity introduced in the international system, the threat of international terrorism, even American military success in crises where multilateralism was disregarded, not to mention internal European divisions, make the perpetuation of unilateralism a strong possibility. But it is not inevitable. Domestic developments in the US or an early demonstration of the EU's ability to act effectively, at least as a regional actor, could eventually modify current American grand strategy.

Steps and initiatives

Regarding the EU, a first significant step would be to prevent further undermining of UN authority. The principles of the rule of law and multilateralism that the EU collectively endorses have little to gain from an *ex post facto* legitimization of the military operations in Iraq or by the UN performing a 'cleaning up' role. It is better to let the victors of the war in Iraq take full responsibility for their acts and limit the UN's involvement to urgent humanitarian operations.

The unprecedented mobilization of European public opinion could benefit CFSP and strengthen other collective EU initiatives. Europe needs to regain Washington's respect as a collective international actor. Priority issues in the internal debate are: the final formulation of CFSP clauses in the draft European Constitution and the use of qualified majority voting; the better coordination of financial aid, external trade, environment, justice and home affairs policies with EU's foreign policy objectives; the creation of a European diplomatic service and possibly the merger of the posts and functions of the high representative and the commissioner for external relations; and a substantial increase in national defence spending, along with common policies strengthening the European defence industry and improving research and development.

In addition, the EU should show America and the world that it is able to take care of its own backyard. It is in the Western Balkans (the former Yugoslavia), more than any other part of the world, that Europeans, but also Americans critical of the hegemonic tendencies of their own government, expect the EU to lead a troubled region of the world to a better future and turn a joint US–EU venture into a European undertaking. In the aftermath of the painful Iraq experience, an enlarged Europe should address the most urgent aspects of a potentially dangerous situation: the final status of Kosovo; internal security in Serbia after Zoran Dindjic's assassination; and peace and stability in FYROM. Current plans calling for a steady decline in assistance to the Western Balkans through 2006, to half the level provided in 2000, should be reversed. At the same time, structural assistance should be directly linked to the establishment of political conditions conducive to domestic and regional stability.

The Israeli-Palestinian conflict represents an even more vigorous test for European policy makers and transatlantic cooperation. There have been assurances before, during and after the war in Iraq, that coalition partners would consider as top priority a roadmap setting the stages for Palestinian statehood. After the war many have claimed that even democratic reform in the broader Middle East is linked to the outcome of such efforts. Certainly, students of this most protracted of conflicts, understand all too well the difficulties that lie ahead. But for the European side a consensus-building exercise on the conditions of a settlement along with the commitment of resources to facilitate the process, could at the very least have an intra-European healing effect. In turn, the formulation of concrete common policies toward that conflict could have some positive long-term spillover effects on other CFSP issues and benefit transatlantic cooperation.

European attention should also focus on America and its foreign-policy elites with the aim to deepen and expand the New Transatlantic

Agenda (NTA, 1995) as supplemented in 1998. The time seems ripe for an assessment and evaluation of these arrangements and their adjustment to rapidly changing needs, like the exchange of ideas on the current, post-Iraq war state of world affairs and the future of international norms and institutions. Mainstream American foreign policy analysts remain critical of US unilateralism and apprehensive of deepening divisions within the transatlantic community. At the same time confusion prevails as to what exactly the EU represents in foreign and security policy as contrasted to the individual policies of its members. An intensified intra-European debate on CFSP should lead think tanks and non-governmental organizations to engage in an extensive dialogue with their American counterparts on the current state of transatlantic relations and their future. This could happen either under the auspices of international academic societies, NGO networks, professional associations or, finally, within EU designed and financed networks.

9
Reshaping US–EU Relations: Toward a Broader Strategic Agenda

F. Stephen Larrabee[1]

US–European relations today are in one of their worst crises in decades. The Iraq crisis has led to a deep rift between the US and its European allies. However, the winding down of the combat phase of operations in Iraq provides an opportunity to begin to rebuild transatlantic relations and put them on a firmer footing. The foreign ministers meeting in Greece, May 2–3 2003 is a good starting point for initiating this process.

Getting on the US radar screen

The EU faces a fundamental challenge. Despite the fact that it is becoming an increasingly important international actor, it does not command high-level US attention – except in the State Department. In short, it's not on the US radar screen.

Institutional tinkering such as the creation of another EU president will not resolve this problem. *The basic problem is that the EU does not address the key security challenges that are on the minds of most high-level US policy-makers.* Most of these challenges lie outside Europe. Thus, if the EU wants to get on the US radar screen, it needs to address the broader strategic issues that concern US policy-makers.

What is needed is a *broader strategic dialogue* that goes beyond trade issues. The New Transatlantic Agenda, signed in Madrid in 1995, provides a framework for doing this. But it remains heavily focused on trade and other institutional issues. It needs to be broadened to address critical strategic issues of common interest.

Toward a broader strategic dialogue

Several issues could form the building blocks for this broader strategic dialogue:

Iraq

The reconstruction and democratization of Iraq will pose major challenges for the US and the international community. This is not a task that the US can accomplish alone. Washington will need help – for both economic as well as political reasons (to defuse the perceptions of a US 'occupation' and to give the reconstruction process broader legitimacy). The EU could play an important role in the reconstruction process. The quartet (the United States, European Union, Russia and the United Nations) could serve as a useful umbrella for a multilateral approach to the reconstruction and rehabilitation of Iraq.

The Middle East

A common US–European strategy toward the Middle East is a prerequisite for long-term stability in the region. The key to stability is a solution to the Palestinian problem. To date, the Bush administration has been reluctant to actively push for an Arab-Israeli settlement. But with the winding down of the combat phase of the Iraq war, it may be more willing to relaunch the Arab-Israeli peace process – something long advocated by EU members. Thus now more than ever there is a need for dialogue on how to move forward.

Iran

Iran's evolution will have a major impact on stability in the Gulf and the Great Middle East. The most pressing issue is to ensure that Iran abides by international law in developing its civilian nuclear programme. This will require close US and European cooperation. This cooperation should be easier to develop than in the past. In the last couple of years, US and European differences over Iran have narrowed. As a result, today there is a much firmer basis for a coordinated approach to Iran than in the past. The task now is to build on this greater consensus and develop a more coordinated policy. In particular, the US and the EU should press Iran to comply with international procedures in developing its nuclear programme and encourage a gradual democratization of Iranian society.

The war on terrorism

A successful war on terrorism requires broad multilateral cooperation, especially in areas such as banking, border control and intelligence. While cooperation has been quite good in some fields, obstacles remain in some areas such as protecting data, border security, and the development of a common arrest warrant.

Weapons of mass destruction

The danger of WMD proliferation is growing. However, US and European perspectives on WMD continue to differ. If the WMD problem is going to be effectively managed, the EU and the US need to develop a common policy, especially toward export controls.

North Korea

North Korea is the next looming crisis. The EU could play a useful role in helping to defuse tensions on the Korean peninsula. But any initiatives by the EU in this area need to be closely coordinated with Washington. An independent initiative by a self-appointed 'peace axis' would cause irritation in Washington and only serve to deepen the current transatlantic rift.

Turkey

Turkey's strategic importance is likely to grow in the next decade. It provides an important model of a democratic, secular Muslim regime in the Middle East. In the aftermath of the Iraq crisis, both the EU and the US need to begin to rebuild bridges to Ankara and develop a coordinated policy which helps to stabilize Turkey and keep Ankara firmly tied to the West. Without such a coordinated policy there is a danger that US and EU policy may work at cross purposes. A Cyprus settlement should be high on the agenda.

Of course, other issues – harmonization of NATO and EU enlargement, Russia, Ukraine and trade policy – should remain important elements of the US–EU dialogue. But the agenda needs to be broadened to include less 'Euro-centric' issues where common approaches are necessary.

Reaching out to Congress and think tanks

While working to get on the Bush administration's radar screen, the EU also needs to increase interaction and cooperation with Congress. The level of knowledge about and understanding of the EU in Congress is low. Many congressmen are simply not aware how much the EU is doing in places like the Balkans and Afghanistan. They also tend to be sceptical about the motivations behind the European Security and Defence Policy (see below). The EU needs to do more to educate Congress about its policies and their goals. Intensified exchanges between the European Parliament and Congress would be a good start.

The intensification of contacts, however, should not be limited to Congress. Party-to-party contacts also should be stepped up, as should contacts with think tanks. Informal contacts are often as important as formal contacts. By the time people get into office their perceptions are already formed and it is hard to change them. Unfortunately, these informal contacts have atrophied in recent years.

Speaking with one voice

The lack of a coherent Common Foreign and Security Policy (CFSP) also inhibits the ability of the EU to get high-level policy attention in Washington. While there are no easy quick fixes to this problem, merging the positions currently held by Javier Solana and Chris Patten and putting foreign policy in the hands of one official would help give EU foreign policy greater coherence. The elimination of the rotating Presidency would also be helpful. It is difficult for a US president to take the EU seriously when he has to deal with a different set of EU representatives every six months.

However, institutional tinkering is no panacea. It will not resolve the basic problem: the need for the EU to broaden its strategic focus and address the strategic issues that preoccupy high-level US policy-makers. The EU president or foreign minister will not receive high-level attention in Washington unless he has something of consequence to say to US policy-makers on critical international issues that concern them. This highlights the need to broaden the US–EU dialogue and make it more strategic.

The European security and defence identity

The EU also needs to clarify the goals of its European Security and Defence Policy (ESDP) more precisely. While ESDP does not engender the same scepticism or antagonism in Washington that it did several years ago, doubts about its motivations and goals continue to exist, especially in the Congress. Many congressmen fear that ESDP is designed, either consciously or unconsciously, to weaken NATO.

These fears have been strengthened by recent transatlantic differences over Iraq. There is a growing concern in Washington – and not just in the Bush administration – that some EU members, especially France, are trying to develop the EU as a 'counterweight' to the United States. EU members need to make clear that this is not the EU's goal and reject attempts by members to push the EU in this direction. If the perception continues to grow in Washington that the EU is bent on defining itself in opposition to the United States, or as a counterweight to it, then the US will have little interest in developing close ties to the EU, and the recent transatlantic rift will deepen.

Unfortunately some recent moves by EU members, particularly the call for the creation of a 'core Europe' in the defence field, are likely to exacerbate tensions, not heal wounds. A new push for autonomy in the defence field looks too much like an anti-US, anti-NATO move. While the US is likely to welcome proposals to increase defence spending, calls for the creation of a European military headquarters are likely to antagonize Washington and play into the hands of administration hardliners. The US wants contingency planning done at Supreme Allied Headquarters Europe (SHAPE) and opposes the establishment of a separate EU planning cell, which it fears could be decoupling. Adding a collective defence clause to the Constitutional Treaty, as some EU members have proposed, is also likely to deepen US suspicions about the long-term goals of ESDP. It would compete with Article 5 of the Washington Treaty on collective defence and create a direct conflict with NATO.

Toward a new partnership

Some observers have suggested a new division of labour in which Europe would concentrate on managing security problems in Europe while the US would have responsibility for managing security in the rest of the world. Such a division of labour is wrong-headed and ill-advised. First, it would erode the core of the US–European partnership, which is based on the 'indivisibility of security'. Second, it would produce an inward-looking Europe with little incentive to broaden its security horizons. Finally, it would be politically unsustainable in the United States. Most Americans would instinctively reject a partnership in which the US concentrated on the dangerous high-end of the military spectrum while the Europeans had responsibility for the more benign, low-end of the spectrum – i.e. peacekeeping in an increasingly stable Europe.

Instead, what is needed is a genuine partnership, one in which Europe and the EU increasingly share the responsibility for managing global security threats. But this presupposes that the EU broadens its strategic horizons and transforms itself into a more global actor. In return, the US needs to show greater willingness to address the non-military dimensions of security and engage in real consultation with its allies, not just inform them of decisions already taken.

Mars vs. Venus?

Some observers, such as Robert Kagan, have suggested that there is a growing philosophical and cultural gap between the US and Europe, especially in regard to the use of force. In his terms, Americans are from Mars and Europeans are from Venus. This gap does exist. But it is not as wide as many believe.

The German Marshall Fund poll in September 2002 – the most comprehensive poll on US and European attitudes ever taken – showed more similarities than differences in how people in the US and Europe view the larger world. Americans and Europeans identified very similar issues (including terrorism, weapons of mass destruction in Iraq and global warming) as their primary foreign policy concerns. Americans expressed discomfort with unilateralism, with 62 per cent in favour of a multilateral approach to foreign policy problems and 65 per cent saying that the United States should invade Iraq only with UN approval and the support of its allies. Even on the issue of the use of force, Europeans were at least in principle as ready as were Americans to use force to uphold international law (80 per cent of Americans vs. 76 per cent of Europeans).

In short, while differences between the US and Europe exist, they should not be exaggerated. Public attitudes on many issues on both sides of the Atlantic are broadly similar. Hence, there is a solid basis for enhancing cooperation in many areas. What is needed is to broaden the transatlantic dialogue to include the critical security challenges both sides face. At the same time, a new mechanism should be developed that allows more frequent and direct contact between the EU and the United States. The current US–EU summit format does not really satisfy that need.

Note

1. F. Stephen Larrabee holds the Corporate Chair in European Security at RAND. The views expressed in this paper are his own and do not represent those of RAND or any of its sponsors.

10

The United States and the European Union: is a Partnership still Possible?

Dick Benschop

Five suggestions for Europe, fully realizing how easy it is to give advice, but how difficult it is to take it:

1. Get off the moral high ground
A shouting match in self-righteousness between Europe and the US serves no sensible purpose. The problem of the past six months is that almost nobody could find or was willing to use the brakes. We have witnessed the dynamics of escalation between an 'activist' United States and 'legalist' Europe. The arrogance of power on the American side was countered by the arrogance of impotence on the European side. The political fallout was enormous, and it was especially harmful for the EU.

2. Get relevant
The problem that should concern Europe most is not whether America is the sole superpower in the world, but how Europe defines its relation with the US and what capabilities Europe organizes to match that relation.

For the US the relationship with the EU (or the intensity of its relationship) might be a relationship of choice. For the EU it is a relationship of necessity. Even when the US works on the basis of 'coalitions of the willing', we have to blame ourselves for our divisions and our lack of influence.

3. A partnership beyond Mars and Venus
The desired relationship between the EU and the US is one of partnership. Europe should avoid the temptation of defining itself as a counterweight to the US. We have too much in common for that.

The partnership is in danger of getting very typical. Dad (the US) is obsessed with security issues and Mum (the EU) is taking care of everybody. In modern partnerships the 'hard' and 'soft' parts are more evenly distributed.

Even if we use the less suitable Mars and Venus approach, it is good to keep in mind that they had an affair and gave birth to five children, including Phoebus (the God of Fear and Panic), but also Eros and Harmonia.

4. Make an agenda

Of course the rhetoric is improving across the Atlantic. But if we want to avoid the same rifts all over again, we have to agree on the agenda and the goals we are setting. What is our policy towards Iran? What methods are the US and the EU going to use to enforce the implementation of the roadmap in Israel and the Palestinian territories? How about the clear and present danger in Pyongyang? What about Pakistan and India?

The EU must try to get out of the position of always outlining the difficulties in doing something. The EU must recognize the value-driven aspect of American foreign policy.

5. Choose

Europeans very much want to see a more coherent and effective European foreign policy, including a policy on defence. They get frustrated by the gap between the solemn declarations and the failure over Iraq, which was a setback compared to what has been achieved in Kosovo and F.Y.R. of Macedonia. We have to choose. Either we get more realistic about the possibilities of a European foreign and defence policy, or we improve our performance, both political and in terms of capabilities. Saying one thing and doing the other, is the worst option.

PS:

Similar remarks, or even more nasty ones, could be made about the United States foreign policy. If asked, I am happy to provide the State Department with those remarks. In the meantime we have to focus on our responsibility: Europe.

11
The Choices in Euro-American Relations

Christopher Hill

The issue in Euro-American relations seems clear in the light of recent events (Iraq and the four-power defence initiative). Europe must decide whether to look towards a multipolar world with Europe as one of the major poles, or to accept the hegemonic position of the United States, with Europe working to ensure a benign hegemony through a partnership which implies not just support but also a voice which is listened to seriously in Washington. This is the new power politics, arrived on Europe's doorstep.

In practice the choice is not so simple, for several reasons:

- We cannot rival the US in military power in any manageable timescale and, indeed, have no wish to do so.
- The idea of a major stand-off between Europe and the US is unthinkable – indeed a nightmare scenario. Who wants to make an enemy of the hyperpower, even if its current policies are distasteful? The prospect is too unlikely to be worth worrying about unless we find that even moderate Republican or Democratic administrations are showing no interest in a rule-based international system. But it would be a serious mistake to risk creating a permanently alienated, aggressive American foreign policy.
- In terms of identity and interests, we have a great deal in common with the US. Whatever our differences, we also share some common threats, in terms of the fanatical enemies of the West for whom the differences between European and American capitalism or culture are a matter of mere pedantry.

The only real issue before European governments at present in this context is therefore the *terms* of a redefined relationship with the

United States, not whether or not to seek such a relationship. If we accept that full superpower status is unachievable and undesirable – what *did* Mr Blair mean when he said that the EU should become a superpower (but not a superstate) in his Warsaw speech of October 2000? – then we still have three broad options before us:

(i)   The Europeans can swallow their reservations and row along with Washington, calculating that the protection offered by Washington compensates for the extra enmity incurred on a wider front by association with 'the great Satan'. US leadership is then legitimate, NATO and bilateral relations remain more important than the European Security and Defence Policy, and the traditional attempts to prevent excessive linkages between economic competition and politico-military issues must continue.

(ii) They can continue along the current broadly 'civilian' path, towards the goal of Europe as a civilian superpower – if they can increase integration and make better use of their resources of soft power. This would involve putting a positive spin on Michael Mandelbaum's designation of 'foreign policy as social work', that is, trying to ameliorate the system within a structure determined essentially by US power. Enlargement might make the EU into a more impressive geopolitical presence in the world, at the same time as it makes more difficult the build-up of a European military-industrial complex (the precondition of achieving status as a true superpower). Yet Europe would still be an energetic global actor in this scenario.

(iii) Europe can pull up the drawbridge and behave like a large neutral, not agreeing with Washington, but not opposing it, except perhaps in its own 'Near Abroad'. In the post Cold War world, we need have no fear that great power conflicts in East Asia or elsewhere will lead to Europe being a battleground, and so the EU can safely sit on the sidelines over Korea, or Taiwan, or even Kashmir. We can try to avoid the worst of terrorism by behaving collectively, if not like Switzerland, then perhaps like Sweden or Germany, that is by displaying a reluctance to go to war and by avoiding excessive exposure in international politics. This behaviour carries the risk of all neutralism, namely that the bluff may be called and pressure exerted by aggressive outsiders. The EU is big enough to defend itself if roused, and if given sufficient warning, but it would have to gamble that it did not attract the attentions of a powerful and hostile state – including the United States.

The second of these options appears the most plausible path for the EU to follow, although the great challenges of enlargement, constitutional upheaval and an uncertain international environment make it difficult to make a confident judgement. It is more possible than at any point in recent years that the European project might seriously stumble and fall back to be what Michael Stürmer has called 'a customs union de luxe', which would force us into the first or the third options. What is clear is that Europeans themselves need to do more serious thinking about the future international role of the Union, and its relationship to American power. A 'new transatlantic bargain' may be too specific and grandiloquent to achieve, but there are at least four sets of issues which the EU ignores at its peril, even discounting the perennial problems of trade and agriculture:

Firstly, some ground-rules need to be established within the Common Foreign and Security Policy (CFSP) about who speaks to the US *on behalf of Europe*. Looking back it was understandable that the UK should have occupied the vacuum left by the EU's failure to have a proper debate over policy towards Iraq, but it had disastrous consequences in terms of intra-EU relations. The US itself would benefit if we could clarify what is a legitimate matter of bilateral discussion and what should be left – in the first instance, at least – to the Presidency, the High Representative, or whoever might succeed them. It might also be useful to look at the demarcations between EU–US relations and the roles of those other useful organizations, the Organization for Security and Cooperation in Europe (OSCE) and the Council of Europe.

Second, we have to reduce the incentives for the US to divide and rule Europeans – an irresistible temptation, but one where the damage can be limited. Yet this has to be done without merely appeasing Washington. Avoiding provocative gestures, calming gratuitous anti-Americanism, and stressing – not least to the Americans themselves – the positive elements in the relationship, such as the quiet work being done together in the war against terrorism, should gradually undermine the position of those in the US administration such as Donald Rumsfeld who have shown signs of actively wanting to derail European foreign policy.

Third, the issue of security cooperation evidently needs hard thought if we are not to descend into farce over multiple Rapid Reaction Forces and constantly changing inner groups. Given Europe's resource problems and the public antipathy to war, it would seem vital that we stress a division of labour with the US rather than competition, and that we gradually build on what we can honourably and practically achieve –

along the lines of what is being done in the Balkans. Competition is inevitable in the area of arms procurement and aerospace technology, but here change can be managed over a long period, as has been done with the slow but successful emergence of Airbus in the face of persistent hostility from Boeing.

Last is the problem of relations with third parties. The EU needs to address the issue of geopolitics more directly. That is, where should Europe be active, and where should it leave matters more to the United States, or indeed other powers? The US is already content in some respects to have the EU taking more of a lead in the Balkans, as it does in Africa, within certain agreed parameters. Conversely, with the exception of Cuba (and Central America in the 1980s), the EU has not engaged in turf disputes with Washington over Latin America. Asia is a more mixed picture and represents some important dilemmas for the EU. It should nonetheless be possible here as elsewhere for some agreement to be reached. This would be on the basis of neither side being necessarily committed to full-hearted support of the other in an area where it does not itself 'lead'. At the same time each side would undertakes not to oppose the other unless: (a) the rules (of the bilateral bargain, or of international society) are being flagrantly ignored; (b) a new vital interest has emerged – in which case the Euro-American channels of communication should have improved to the point where they can prevent open conflict, of the kind we have just witnessed, from flaring up. The EU should not forget that 'conflict prevention' applies just as much to its own relations with the US as it does to third states.

Transatlantic relations are vital to both Europe and the United States, whatever the ebb and flow of rhetoric. Yet we should not, in our eagerness to address the problem, give the impression to the rest of the world of a cynical Western deal to impose a particular order on the highly variegated international system, regardless of the opinions of the other 164 or so members of the UN. There is also the small matter of 'milieu' problems, which cannot be settled even by the most powerful single actors, such as the environment, economic stability and standards of international civility. On these both Europeans and Americans would do well to listen as well as to advise or instruct. Hubris, of beliefs as of power, is the great risk.

12
Europe and the US: Five Frank Thoughts and One Proposal for the Foreign Ministers of Europe

Timothy Garton Ash

1. There is no 'clash of civilizations' between Europe and America. We belong to the same historical civilization, and share most of the same values. There are important areas where our models of democratic capitalism differ (e.g. the role of the welfare state), but these are differences within the family. European identity should be defined positively, by what it is for, not negatively, against the United States. As we have seen over the last six months, any attempt to unite Europe against the US is destined to divide Europe, not unite it.

2. Americans are not from Mars and Europeans are not from Venus, *pace* Robert Kagan. The Kantian, internationalist, law-based approach to foreign policy that Kagan identifies with Europe has been repeatedly advocated and embraced by the US since 1945. For Europeans to accept American neo-conservatives' identification of their own views with those of 'America' is to fall into a trap. In calling for a return to multilateralism based on international law, we are not calling for a conversion to Europeanism but for a return to the United States' own best traditions.

3. A strong, united Europe is in the United States' own interest. The US itself understood this throughout the Cold War. Now it is much less sure. There is a tendency inside the Bush administration to believe that American interests are better served by *à la carte* alliances with individual European powers (e.g. Britain, Spain, Italy, Poland), rather than with Europe as such. *Divide et impera.* This is bad for everyone concerned. It must be resisted.

4. The only way to resist it is for Europe to pull together again. The key to this lies in a compromise between the British and French positions. Britain and France currently represent two fundamentally different strategic views of the right European approach to transatlantic

relations: the neo-Atlanticist and the neo-Gaullist. Each stymies the other. No good purpose is served by not acknowledging this deep difference. If the foreign ministers of Europe could have a frank discussion about this, it would be a useful start to seeking what will inevitably be a compromise that satisfies neither the Cartesian nor the Lockean spirit.

5. Where the old, threatening Soviet 'East' united the West, the Middle East divides it. This is the most urgent current policy issue between the US and Europe, and the one where there is most difference across the Atlantic. Our response to American proposals for a democratization of the wider Middle East, starting from Iraq, should not be a mere 'no' or 'what about Israel-Palestine?'

We know that a peace settlement producing a viable Palestinian state and a more secure state of Israel is an indispensable condition for progress in the wider Middle East. But this well-established European position should be embedded in a readiness to talk about a whole range of issues in relation to the whole Arab and Islamic world, whose stabilization, modernization and eventual democratization is even more directly in Europe's interest than it is in that of the US. These issues include immigration, trade, anti-terrorism, aid, cultural diplomacy and the EU's ever closer relationship with Turkey, as well as policy towards the Maghreb, Iran and, of course, post-conflict Iraq. If one looks at this whole range of policy instruments and relationships, the European role is different from, but not less important than, that of the US.

My proposal is that Europe (acting as 15 nations, but with substantial input from the accession countries and accepted candidate states) should attempt to work out a number of common elements of a broad 'détente' approach of constructive engagement in the wider Middle East, as a coherent response to the often one-dimensional American plans. (European involvement in the reconstruction of Iraq would also be placed in this context.) This European position should be worked out privately, rather than being hastily expressed in a public EU declaration which would inevitably have a fudged, 'lowest common denominator' quality. It should form the basis of discussions between European leaders and President Bush during his visit to Europe at the end of May/beginning of June 2003. It should then be discussed at the Thessaloniki European Council in June. Thereafter, it should be presented publicly in a form that emphasizes transatlantic cooperation in this larger endeavour.

13
Redefining the Transatlantic Partnership

Tom Bentley

The second half of the twentieth century was dominated by a competition between two forms of the modern state as well as between two ideologies: it was won by liberal-capitalist parliamentary democracies, acting together through the NATO alliance against the Communist Soviet bloc.

Ironically, the underlying logic of openness, pluralism and individual freedom, which helped win the Cold War by making command economies unsustainable, has now created a crisis of legitimacy for the forms of strategy needed to make peaceful, twenty-first-century societies safe.

Meanwhile, globalization has created new forms of interdependence and vulnerability so that even the most powerful nations cannot escape economic recessions, environmental damage or networked violence originating elsewhere. We are locked together in a century when the globe's own sustainability as a human habitat will be fully tested.

International legitimacy is a defining problem for the twenty-first century. Europe can make common cause with the US, and achieve positive strategic influence, by embodying and projecting new forms of democratic legitimacy rather than preaching about them.

Why have Europe and America diverged?

One reason for the insecurity is that the US is applying the rational, self-interested logic of a single modern nation onto an unstable world. Because a balance of power is not possible, the doctrine has become one of aggressive pre-emption. This will not change until Americans can see respect for others' perspectives and rights, even beyond US borders, as part of what it means to be American. In turn, this will not happen while the US sees itself as shouldering the burden of policing the world.

The fuzzy threat of rogue states and terrorism is being used to reinforce domestic American identity; the Republicans currently have little else in the way of a domestic agenda that could unite a critical majority.

American sovereignty is manifested by proclamations that American interests must not be encumbered by the claims of others: 'We really don't need anyone's permission'. Therefore, simply appealing to them to respect international rules will achieve little; it actually provides an opportunity for the US to show that it is different.

And some aspects of the threat are real and serious; the influence of domestic politics does not discount the need for a strategic response to weapons of mass destruction, failed states, or new forms of terror.

Is there an alternative? Should Europeans cluster under the wing of this strategy?

Ironically, America's Cold War strategy of 'extended deterrence' and containment created the conditions under which Western Europe could develop a unique innovation in governance – the EU – which goes beyond the security provided by the nation-state, however dominant. This now represents an irreversible form of positive interdependence between nations. European powers have made themselves safe from each other by allowing far higher levels of transparency and mutual domestic interference than classical military strategy would ever allow.

Many European citizens, cushioned by the modern welfare state and rising living standards, have developed new priorities, such as their quality of life, diverse ethical commitments, and social pluralism, as long as their basic security and living standards are maintained. This makes them increasingly sensitive to issues of international legitimacy.

But this historical achievement rests on two compromises: an EU of 'hybrid' status whose legitimacy rests on the sovereignty and democratic mandate of member states; and dependence via NATO on American military force to counter any direct threat. The result is that on issues of international strategy, collective action is incredibly difficult. Both need reshaping.

Enlargement should provide a new sense of regional identity and make all Europeans more conscious of their place in a wider world. The question is whether that place can be developed into a role which projects positive influence in legitimate ways. Unless Europe makes a concerted effort to do this, it has little chance of influencing US worldview or behaviour.

What should be done?

In the end, strategic influence reflects the distribution of power. But power is more multifaceted than the US doctrine implies.

Europe cannot realistically compete with US military dominance. It must find ways to project 'soft' power; making its wealth, population and norms count strategically by aligning its political positions with other forms of leverage.

The most effective way to do this is to put a finger on issues that Americans cannot ignore but do not know how to solve unilaterally.

There is a Western community of interest; the way to rebuild it is to engage Americans in ways which encourage a more nuanced understanding of their place in the world. Engagement with civil society and citizens as well as governments, could reinforce the pluralist and outward looking strands of American identity. But this will not happen if Europeans are making their own sense of identity by opposing American force.

The overarching question which a European strategy addresses should be:

How can we create security through interdependence?

The challenge is to show how security could be strengthened by a strategy of prevention, not pre-emption. Europe must lead the development of a position based on responsiveness, mutual respect and the evolution of democratic legitimacy, rather than hegemonic domination and thin, monocultural politics.

But to make this credible, Europeans must avoid being dewy-eyed about the legitimate use of violence. Europe's vast economic power does not count as it should because it is not properly backed with the capacity for military intervention. The EU's current commitments in Macedonia and the Balkans, while they arguably came too late, point to the kind of role that Europe will need to sustain more widely.

This means a hard-nosed commitment to ending, limiting and preventing conflicts, and to international economic development. It means connecting areas of European domestic concern far more strongly with transnational solutions in areas like crime and people movement.

Probably most importantly, Europe needs a 'near abroad' policy, which commits wholeheartedly to extending the zone of peace, prosperity and interdependence, if Europe wants to extend its strategic influence beyond Europe.

This could mean:

- Founding a *'European Commonwealth'*, a new intergovernmental network with members invited from the far North of Europe to North Africa, from Ireland to Russia and Ukraine. Encompassing and transcending the activities of the OSCE (Organization for Security and Cooperation in Europe) and Council of Europe, a European commonwealth could focus on projects strengthening democracy, trade and intercultural understanding, whether through infrastructure investment, education networks or grassroots civic development. Strengthening a much older sense of broad European identity would help, not hinder, the enlargement process.
- Making new shared investments in extending *cross-border collaboration* on policing, transnational crime, counter-terrorism, and preventive security
- Making the non-proliferation of *weapons of mass destruction* a fresh, EU-wide priority, but linking it to a broader agenda for conflict prevention and resolution, rather than just states arguing over treaties.
- Creating a *'European Volunteer Reconstruction Corps'* to assist in humanitarian relief efforts and strengthen civilian and civic roles in peacekeeping efforts.
- Using the accession of new member states to create a European *'democracy process'*, committed to understanding and investing in civic and institutional innovation across the European region, encouraging citizen engagement and creating a non-governmental transatlantic dialogue on routes to democratic renewal.
- Promoting transatlantic exchange on *how to govern cities* and regions well, exploiting America's federal system to build new networks of mutual understanding and knowledge exchange.

What role for international institutions?

This note has deliberately avoided discussing the UN. While it matters hugely, focusing too much effort on validation via highly imperfect institutional processes is a recipe for paralysis. The behaviour which creates norms of interdependence and cooperation should run ahead of incremental institutional reform and formal rules. European partners should be pursuing informal, network-based collaboration to forge a new agenda. If they establish enough momentum, the institutional map will follow.

14
Repairing the Transatlantic Rift

Joseph Nye

The war in Iraq not only split both Europe and the Atlantic alliance. It also gave rise to dangerous myths about an 'old Europe from Venus' locked in struggle against a unilateralist 'America from Mars'. The first task of repair is to strip away such myths. After all, as recently as 1999, the European and American democracies agreed to fight together in Kosovo in the absence of a Security Council resolution. And what is attractive about today's 'old Europe' is that it is so new! The EU countries are not all in the same sovereign boat, but their national boats are lashed together into an island of stability that is unique and powerfully attractive to its neighbours. Witness the desire of Central Europeans and Turkey to join. And those American who say that Europeans are from Venus while Americans are from Mars ignore recent polls by the Pew Research Center that show many Europeans with 'American' views on policy and many Americans with 'European' views. In fact, the polls show that nearly two-thirds of the American public prefer multilateral rather than unilateral approaches to diplomacy. Despite the frictions, no two parts of the world are more similar in their commitment to democracy and human rights than Europe and its cultural offspring in America.

Equally important, the sceptics have a myopic view of power that focuses too heavily on the military dimension, where the United States excels. They pay insufficient attention to Europe's hard and soft power. In the twenty-first century, power is distributed differently on different issues, and resembles a three-dimensional chess game. On the top board of military issues, where American military expenditure is equal to the next two dozen countries combined, the world is unipolar. There is only one superpower. It is likely to remain that way unless Europeans want to double the proportion of GNP spent on defence to

79

equal American levels. Even then, it is not clear how a military balance might work. But investment in more modest European capabilities should not be discounted. There are more European than American troops helping to keep the peace today in the Balkans and Afghanistan, and NATO remains an important institution which gives Europe influence in many such settings

The middle board of economic issues is a sharp contrast from the military board. Here the world has a multipolar balance of power. The United States cannot achieve a global trade agreement without the agreement of Europe and others. In the area of anti-trust, General Electric was unable to merge with Honeywell because the Commission of the European Community opposed. And recently, Microsoft had to make significant changes to its new passport system in order to meet European privacy regulations. This is hardly the 'American hegemony' that some proclaim. Moreover, despite the political popularity of the United States in Donald Rumsfeld's 'new Europe,' America is becoming less prominent in business and investment there. EU countries account for three-quarters of the 'new Europe's' trade. And two-way direct foreign investment knits America more closely to Europe than to Asia.

The bottom board of the three-dimensional chess game consists of transnational issues that cross borders outside the control of governments. Examples include illegal migration, drugs, crime, the spread of infectious diseases, global climate change, and of course, transnational terrorist networks. On this board, power is chaotically organized and it makes no sense to speak of 'unipolarity', 'hegemony', or 'American empire'. While these issues are having an increasing effect on the lives of ordinary Americans, they cannot be solved by military power or by the United States acting alone. Cooperation with other countries, particularly the capable Europeans, is essential to America's ability to solve such problems and protect its people.

Europe is not likely to become the military equal of the United States anytime soon, but it has enough sticks and carrots to produce significant hard power – the ability to get others to do what they would not otherwise do. In addition, despite internal divisions, Europe's culture, values and the success of the EU have produced a good deal of soft power – the ability to attract rather than merely coerce others. The EU is not as weak is it sometimes thinks. Rather than pursuing an ultimately futile strategy to create a classical balance of power against the US, it should use its considerable strengths to influence the US. Since values overlap, there is much to build upon, and the new transnational terrorism provides a very real common threat.

It is said that the UN Security Council failed over Iraq. That was true in the spring of 2003, but the failure goes back to the 1990s when members were unwilling to confront Saddam Hussein's clear defiance of both human rights and disarmament resolutions. The failure was not just of the institution but of the diplomacy among the major powers. There is enough blame to go around for both sides, but dwelling on the past will not be productive. We are at a point in history in which the law of the Charter descended from both Westphalian sovereignty and international humanitarian law sometimes come into conflict. Yet recent history shows that opinion in our democracies is sometimes willing to support the use of force for humanitarian as well as classic reasons. We need more discussion of how to identify and limit such cases where egregious human rights violators seek weapons of mass destruction and pose threats to their neighbours. Moreover, we need more discussion of how to work together to prevent and respond to the transnational terrorism that is a common threat to our modern urban civilization. Unless we do a better job of identifying the new principles that justify multilateral interventions in response to such threats, we will remain mired in the recent disarray. What a pity that would be, since there is so much more that unites us than divides us.

15
Note to the EU Presidency and EU Foreign Ministers

Sherle R. Schwenninger

In this short note I would like to offer for your consideration three observations and suggestions relating to US–European relations.

1. In the United States, the question of US–European relations has emerged as a key political battleground issue over which the future direction of American foreign policy will be fought. The alienation of our friends in Europe is cited by critics of the Bush administration as the principal failure of a unilateralist foreign policy that emphasizes *ad hoc* coalitions over established alliances, that seeks to marginalize the United Nations and opportunistically use NATO, and that seeks absolute security through American dominance and preventive wars Any dialogue the European Union undertakes with the United States must therefore not just be with official Washington but with the larger American polity.

The domestic political base for the current administration's foreign policy has not yet solidified into an enduring coalition of values and interests, and could erode further in response to new perceived domestic and international challenges. Indeed, there are a number of factors, from America's worsening fiscal position to the fact that the American public has little appetite for empire building to the possibility that the occupation of Iraq may be more difficult and costly than originally portrayed, that may constrain American policy and move it in a more internationalist direction in the coming years.

In light of these facts, it would be a mistake for European leaders to try to paper over current differences with Washington or to try to appease the Bush administration by raising no objections to its world-view. The United States is a diverse and multifaceted society, and the positions EU leaders espouse on many issues represent not just legitimate European interests, but uphold important world order values that are shared by many Americans, particularly by many influential Americans. The majority of Americans want an America that abides by international law, that is a constructive partner in international institutions, and that can work cooperatively to solve world social and economic problems.

This part of America sees Europe as its political partner in an effort to bring a degree of genuine internationalism and common sense to American foreign policy thinking. Europe is important because it offers an alternative multilateralist policy approach that reflects both European and American interests. If Europe fails to actively promote such an alternative or seems to be accepting the fallacies of current US policy, it weakens those in the United States who are pushing for a more enlightened policy and reduces the prospects for a new transatlantic partnership.

2. The first priority of EU diplomacy with regard to transatlantic relations must be to more accurately reflect the true relative power positions of the United States and the European Union upon which a transatlantic relationship must rest. Supporters of the Bush administration like to focus attention on Europe's military weaknesses and the lack of a unified European foreign policy. But the emphasis on the ability to project military power misrepresents not just the nature of power and influence in today's world but also exaggerates American dominance, particularly in relation to the European Union, and understates the European Union's many contributions to world order.

In fact, contrary to conventional wisdom, Europe enjoys an attractive position in relation to the United States, because Washington needs the help and support of Europe much more than Europe needs the United States. If looked at objectively, Europe no longer needs the United States for any real security or defence needs. Indeed, the European nations of NATO and the European Union now have primacy over their own security and over the security of the immediate European Rim region, stretching from the Ukraine in the north to the Balkans in the south. As much as certain Europeans might like the United States to do more in helping create stability in the Ukraine or maintain peace in Kosovo and Macedonia, the United States has essentially removed itself from these security-related concerns. Indeed, Europe's main security worry about the United States today is of entirely different nature – not that Washington will abandon Europe, but that it will use its power in the Middle East in a way that will destabilize the region and create greater Western–Islamic tensions.

But even in this case, Europe may have more influence and leverage than has been commonly recognized. Even though Washington is trying to build a flexible military structure that is less dependent on its allies, the United States still needs and relies on European bases and infrastructure for non-NATO missions, and it still needs a measure of European support and participation to gain domestic support for those missions. Beyond this, Washington depends upon European Union members for peacekeeping and nation-building, not just in the Balkans but in Afghanistan and most likely soon in Iraq, and it benefits from European assistance for other US security-related concerns, such as support for the Palestinian Authority. It needs Europe's active co-operation in tracking international terrorists and disrupting their networks and in dealing with countries suspected of having nuclear ambitions. It is dependent upon European as well as East Asian capital to fuel US growth which pays for its international policies. In addition, the European Union now has as much or more influence with other key members of the international community – such as Brazil, Russia and Turkey – and often better reflects their interests in world policy issues.

The occupation of Iraq may very well expose the limits of American power and show that the United States cannot successfully establish a stable, pro-American government in that part of the Arab world. It has greatly underestimated the costs and difficulties of establishing a democratic government in Iraq, and will probably increasingly welcome European and United Nations help and expertise in state-building. Indeed, the American weakness is that it has had very little successful experience in helping create stable democracies in any part of the world over the last two decades, including in its own neighbourhood. By contrast, the European Union has an impressive track record when it comes to democracy-building, particularly as it relates to the candidate countries of Central and Eastern Europe. For much of the last decade, the world has heard repeatedly about the superiority of the American model. But it has been the European Union that has had the most success in exporting democracy and economic reform. To create a true transatlantic partnership, Americans need to hear much more about these successes of European Union policy and about the many contributions to world order the Europeans make.

3. The true test of transatlantic relations in the coming months will be whether Europe and the United States can develop a common policy toward peace in the Middle East and toward the modernization of the Arab world. This will not be an easy task, especially given Washington's decidedly pro-Israeli leanings and the desire of some

leading foreign US policy figures to limit European influence in this part of the world. Yet EU members have no choice in my view but to come to grips with the fact that the centre of American foreign policy has moved from Europe (and East Asia) to the Middle East and that this represents both a danger and an opportunity for them. The danger stems from the fact that the United States is determined to redraw the political map of the Middle East and that its policies could easily destabilize the current order in a way that harms European economic and security interests. Indeed, if the current position in Washington continues to prevail, there are likely to be bitter differences between Europe and the United States over policy toward Iran, Syria, and the Israeli-Palestinian conflict.

On the other hand, the opportunity for Europe lies in the fact that the United States will soon recognize that it has taken on more than it can handle in the Middle East and that it lacks the legitimacy to promote democratic change in this part of the world. The Bush administration is correct that the current order in the Middle East is neither acceptable nor viable, but it is wrong to think that it alone can steer a process of reform in the region or that its Likud-like policies will succeed. Certain US groups may not welcome Europe's participation, but if the United States wants peace in the region and democratic modernization, it will need Europe's critical help and more balanced perspective.

To this end, European leaders must be willing to speak candidly about the Middle East to both the American leadership and the American people. They should make the following points. First, Europe has as much or more at stake in the settlement of the Israeli-Palestinian conflict as does the United States. After all, the region is Europe's neighbour, and any conflict or chaos there directly affects European interests and security. Second, American policy in the region has been most successful when it has been internationalized, when it has actively involved European powers, Russia, and the United Nations. Such was the case with the progress on the Israeli-Palestinian conflict from the Madrid conference in 1991 to the signing of the Oslo Accords in 1993. Third, Europeans need to point out to the American public what the rest of the world knows but what American leaders won't tell them: namely, as long as there are Israeli tanks in Hebron and Ramallah and as long as Israeli settlements occupy Palestinian territory, no American will be safe from Arab anger. Finally, European leaders need to make clear that there can be no double standards for Israel. If Israel chooses to ignore UN Security Council resolutions, it too must be subject to international pressures.

Engaging the United States in this way will require some courageous and determined leadership on the part of European Union leaders. It could very well lead to a more permanent rift in US–European relations, but given the importance of this issue to both the United States and Europe, I do not think Europe has a choice but to take a more active leadership role in the Middle East as a balance and complement to the United States. Helping the United States succeed in this part of the world would be the ultimate act of transatlantic partnership.

16
Transatlantic Security Cooperation
Jan Dirk Blaauw

The military campaign in Iraq served to highlight the different philosophies that already separated Europe from the United States in a number of areas:

- Europe does not share the US approach of linking the task of eliminating international terrorism with other problems such as that of dealing with 'rogue states' – which are seen as posing a threat to international peace – or with broader issues such as the question of restructuring the political landscape in the Middle East and in countries around the world.
- The war in Iraq would appear to have been the first time the new US national security strategy was implemented, suggesting that from now on pre-emptive military action can be a legitimate option even without a mandate or authorization from the United Nations. For a large majority of European countries, the UN Security Council must have the final word when it comes to authorizing any use of military force.
- As a result of what happened in the UN Security Council over the Iraq question, the US administration will now be reluctant to allow any multinational body to influence the use of its military forces.
- The US administration is likely to bypass multilateral institutions such as the United Nations or NATO and seek a coalition of nations willing to support its *de facto* unilateralist policy.
- The ambiguous US position regarding European efforts to develop a more independent security and defence policy might turn into open hostility.
- Europe has so far been unable to provide the United States with a credible alternative response to global threats to international peace.

Implications of the above for action by EU member states:

- The EU should draw up a 'European Security and Strategy Concept' in response to the US National Security Strategy, and identify common security threats and joint responses. What do we want our military capabilities for?
- There is no viable alternative to transatlantic cooperation. Initiatives designed to strengthen European cooperation are to be welcomed provided their object is not to seek any such alternative.
- The modified Brussels Treaty (mBT) gives the EU member states all the elements necessary to increase European security and defence cooperation without upsetting our transatlantic partners. Why not look at it again when you examine the latest proposals by the Convention Praesidium for Article 21 of the Constitutional Treaty? I attach Articles IV, V and VIII of the mBT to this contribution for information.
- The European Union member states should:
  o Continue to show understanding and active support for the United States' specific security needs in the wake of the 11 September 2001 attacks.
  o Explain to the US that the place for it to address its future security concerns is in international institutions, particularly the United Nations. Europeans should streamline their representation in these bodies. They should also signal their readiness to be at the disposal of the United Nations for the purposes of coercive action and to deliver the necessary forces.
  o Initiate a discussion in NATO on the consequences of the US National Security Strategy for transatlantic security and defence cooperation and in particular for NATO's strategic concept.
  o Engage in a robust policy to counter the proliferation of weapons of mass destruction (WMD). The control and prevention of WMD proliferation should become part of ESDP. The creation of a Euro-Atlantic centre to counter such proliferation should be considered.
  o Restructure their armed forces within the context of existing financial constraints and show a willingness to improve military capabilities. From a transatlantic perspective, only if there are European capabilities to count on will it be possible to share responsibilities and decision-making. Among other things, this implies reducing force numbers and transforming units into well-trained, high-tech forces.
  o Be prepared to take over military stabilizing missions in order to relieve the US and to show that the EU is a viable entity well able

to take on a fair share of the burden. This requires the creation of headquarters capable of leading a proper peace-enforcement mission.

o Rethink its stance on transatlantic cooperation in the field of missile defence with a view to finding common solutions to perceived security threats. This issue also holds great appeal for Russia.

o Contribute to the US administration's efforts aimed at creating a Palestinian state and ensuring the security of the state of Israel.

As far as the US is concerned, we must persuade our transatlantic partners to:

- Recognize the importance of maintaining a long-term partnership with the EU instead of trying to reap the short-term benefits of ever-changing coalitions of nations. A united, militarily capable Europe will serve US security and defence interests.
- Give more credit to Europe's involvement in international crisis management and the fight against terrorism, for example in Afghanistan and the Balkans, and lessen their resolve to withdraw from existing missions.
- Become much less reluctant to share their technological know-how with European partners so as to help close the existing capability gap.
- Work with Europeans on a binding and enforceable non-proliferation and anti-WMD policy

Further proposals

The EU should task the Institute for Security Studies, which was set up by the Western European Union (WEU) and which is trying to establish a follow-up to the WEU Transatlantic Forum, to seek a wider audience than its mainly academic partners as at present. It should increasingly seek to involve parliamentarians in its transatlantic dialogue.

It is national parliamentarians on both sides of the Atlantic who play a vital role in voting defence budgets, taking crucial decisions on armaments acquisitions, approving the deployment of troops or authorizing foreign armed forces to use national airspace and territory.

We need some way to amplify and coordinate interparliamentary efforts and dovetail our activities with what we are trying to do in intergovernmental terms.

The creation of a joint interparliamentary working group on global security policy should be envisaged, making provision for the participation of delegations from the

- US Congress
- European Parliament
- Assembly of the WEU – the interparliamentary European Security and Defence Assembly.

I would be happy to help develop this idea with all interested parties under the auspices of the Presidency, if you wish.

Appendix: Articles IV, V and VIII of the modified Brussels Treaty

(The Brussels Treaty signed on 17 March 1948 was amended by the Paris Agreements signed on 23 October 1954)

Article iv

In the execution of the Treaty, the High Contracting Parties and any Organs established by Them under the Treaty shall work in close co-operation with the North Atlantic Treaty Organization.

Recognizing the undesirability of duplicating the military staffs of NATO, the Council and its Agency will rely on the appropriate military authorities of NATO for information and advice on military matters.

Article v

If any of the High Contracting Parties should be the object of an armed attack in Europe, the other High Contracting Parties will, in accordance with the provisions of Article 51 of the Charter of the United Nations, afford the Party so attacked all the military and other aid and assistance in their power.

Article viii (paragraph 3)

At the request of any of the High Contracting Parties the Council shall be immediately convened in order to permit Them to consult with regard to any situation which may constitute a threat to peace, in whatever area this threat should arise, or a danger to economic stability.

17
Living with our Differences

Kalypso Nicolaidis[1]

It is telling that the war in Iraq has changed the very way the transatlantic question is habitually posed in Europe from 'how to resolve US–EU conflicts' to 'how should we deal with American power'? Differences that were simply taken as factors in the global and regional orders are now exposed as our central concern: the overwhelming asymmetry of military power between the United States and the European Union (and indeed the rest of the world); and the divisions within the EU as to what to do about it. There is of course a need to patch things up both on the transatlantic and intra-european front – the two are interconnected – and to devise a European global strategy for the new era of American Empire. This is the agenda of the Kastellorizo meeting of EU foreign ministers.

My purpose here is to make a simple point: a prerequisite for doing things together is to *learn to live with our differences*. This is true *between the EU and the US* where we need to define a constructive and conscious division of labour in tackling some of the most pressing problems before us and creating a more secure and just world. This is also true *within the EU* where we need to learn to disagree better, and moreover to draw strength from our diversity. Intra-EU diversity in turn can be better exploited to foster transatlantic cooperation. In short, we need to move beyond the universal assumption that pervades for instance our EU Constitutional debates that the one and only secret of success and effectiveness on the international scene is to acquire a more unified voice and a more 'common' foreign policy.

EU vs. US: avoiding the dual pitfalls of rivalry and Western hegemony

The discourse in Europe on how to deal with the United States has been ripe with traditional balance of power thinking. The French have brought back to the fore the old Gaullist theme of counterweight or counterbalance to the US. The Belgian and Germans follow suit *sotto voce*. On the other side, the British and the 'other Europe' proclaim their continued loyalty to the alliance and argue that being 'inside the tent' is the most effective way to constrain or tame the US: balancing vs. bandwagoning as the two traditional responses to hegemony. It is important to note what the two sides have in common: in both cases, the strategy is about influencing the US, from without or from within, harnessing its unilateralism, making the case for multilateralism. In the context of the Iraq crisis, some have argued that France and the UK only disagreed on means not on ends. If this is true, it certainly has not pervaded public discourse and perception.

Perhaps member states in the EU do not need to agree on a general concept or a label for their strategy towards the US. Each member state will continue to have its diplomatic culture and slogans, notions which chime with its public opinion. Nevertheless, ministers may ask, what ideas may help both side moves towards each other?

To start with, Europeans could agree on one thing, that is to *move beyond such a balance of power thinking*. What is the point! Unipolarity in the security realm is a fact. So is multipolarity in diplomatic terms. The EU approach to US power should not be defined in structural terms – unipolar vs. multipolar world, friends vs. rivals. If clash there is between the current US administration and some governments in Europe this is a *clash in civilization*. It is the very sense that we share basic political values (rule of law, democratic self determination, human rights as individual rather than collective rights), but that we disagree on how to promote them consistently, that has made the recent dispute so acrimonious. The US does not qualify as the EU's 'other' – if the EU needed one at all it has its own past. Nor can the EU's values-based foreign policy be captured by another power's reading of these values, even if it claims to share them.

Moreover, the EU's position vis-à-vis the US can only be *contingent* on the policies and attitudes of the US itself. It is bound to vary over time, across issues, administration in power and global developments. Therefore, Europeans should define the relationship in terms of ad-hoc *Madisonian checks and balances*, whereby respective roles oscillate on a case by case basis. Under a Madisonian logic, parties form a single cooperative system, and adjust their strategies according to changed circumstances.

Under this logic, cooperation need not be among equals – concerts of nations, alliances or international regimes are all about how to manage peaceful relations given asymmetric power. The call for an 'equal partnership' between the US and the EU is premature and wishful thinking or at best irrelevant. It does not help make sense of the mix of centrifugal and centripetal forces that characterize the relationship.

Instead, strategic thinking in the EU must undergo its *Copernician revolution*. To the extent that the EU is a Union of post-colonial nation-states, its guiding principle in defining its role in international affairs must be to reverse the logic of traditional colonialism: giving a voice to the rest of the world inside its own polity. To start with, why not ask today: what kind of EU strategy with regard to the world superpower would the rest of the world like to see? Indeed, seen from the rest of the world, transatlantic rows must appear very parochial.

There is no single 'rest of the world' of course. But it is fair to say that most countries know what they do *not* want the US–EU relation to be: *all-out rivalry or Western hegemony*. Heightened and continued rivalry between the US would be bound to spell global instability. It would weaken the reach and effectiveness of international organizations – above all the UN – which would most probably be increasingly deemed irrelevant by the US. And on an issue-by-issue basis, most countries usually resent being asked to take sides as we have seen with the dispute over the International Criminal Court.

At the same time, there is little appetite in the developing world for the kind of 'Western hegemony' that characterized the heydays of neoliberalism. The combined economic power of the two sides already overwhelms the rest of the world. And while the US does not need the EU on the military front, the latter's growing military capacity is not irrelevant to NATO. Prospects of the US and the EU 'making up' through exclusive transatlantic economic deals, or that of NATO supplanting the UN (or filling the vacuum) as global police conjures up a world entirely shaped by 'Western' interests.

A European strategy must be inspired by the imperative of avoiding these two pitfalls, destructive rivalry and hegemonic arrogance. But the diversity of issues and actors involved make it impossible to prescribe a magic formula to encapsulate such a middle strategy. Instead, and most likely, the European strategy that is likely to develop in the near future will oscillate between two poles – call this schizophrenia, ambivalence or simply differentiation. On one hand, well-intentioned liberals on both sides of the Atlantic are right to insist on the shared values and interests that must continue to guide transatlantic cooperation on all fronts. Our longstanding transatlantic partnership will need to be revisited based on a multi-faceted division of labour between the two sides and drawing on our complementary strengths and inclinations.

On the other hand, and to satisfy the yearning for a new kind of international relations of many of its members, the EU should not hesitate to take stands on a case by case basis as *an alternative power* to the United States, with its different methods, policy concerns and priorities and its own ways of making friends and indeed enemies. In parallel, rather than with or against. At its best, this alternative power would lend its know-how and resources to the advocacy and implementation of alternative approaches to social, economic and political management, as is currently the case for instance in the GMO affair under WTO. It may even come to refer to itself not in terms of 'power' at all, but as an intervenor, a global partner, a 'vanishing mediator' in the words of Etienne Balibar. The test here for Europeans lies not with US appreciation but with their ability to do their own thing in a world dominated by US hegemony.

There is little doubt that these two poles for middle strategy will continue to coexist in Europe, along with the more extreme temptations of rivalry and western hegemony. Not only because some member states are more inclined towards one or the other; or because, in fact, the choice of emphasis between them needs to be issue-specific. But because the emphasis will depend, to no small extent, on the attitude of the US itself. In any event, actors who shape the EU's role in the world are far from having articulated the meaning of this 'European alternative' – a global role for the EU which does not aim to replicate traditional parameters of powerhood.

The EU as a civilian power with military assets

In the wake of the Iraq war and at this crucial constitutional moment, can European diplomats agree anew on some of the relevant parameters for this global role? On both sides of the Atlantic, Robert Kagan has come to provide the intellectual benchmark – reflecting the view of the current US administration and a great part of the US foreign policy establishment and scholarship. Accordingly, Europeans, rather than humbly and gratefully accepting that their Kantian paradise can only survive in a Hobbesian world thanks to American military strength, are trying to make a virtue out of necessity by propounding their own, alternative and allegedly naive view of international affairs.

Of course, Europeans must acknowledge that Kagan's view is right on many counts: that having successfully built a zone of peace on their continent colours the way most of them see the world. That they have achieved this peace under the umbrella of the US security guarantee in the last half century. That the end of the Cold War was cashed in by Europe as a peace dividend in contrast to continued military build-up for the US. That there are places and instances in the rest of the world where the occasional use of military force by outside actors may be legitimate. And that they, the Europeans, have been unable as of yet to forge a meaningful post Cold-War strategy because of their disagreement over what such use of force means for them in practice. Beyond these important truths, *EU politicians must articulate a collective response to Robert Kagan so as to be better understood in Washington through the EU lens. For a start can they agree on the following propositions?*

1) *As it stands today, the EU is not Kantian because it is (militarily) weak, it is (militarily) weak because it is Kantian.* If valuing the sources of power other than military force underpins the EU internally then it must also do so externally. This is the EU's great lesson, the result of a painstaking collective learning process, not a second best. Europeans do not defend the rule of law, the pre-eminence of the UN and multilateral institutions or question the role of military force as a means of resolving conflict because they are weak (although of course, there is no denying that the law serves the interest of the weak). Rather, Europeans have *chosen* not to go down the military route on a scale comparable to the US, preferring instead to allocate significant resources to ambitious social programmes. This philosophy is increasingly being translated into an EU foreign policy approach, where nation-building and a more generous – if still insufficient – laid budget are seen as the external corollary of states that are active in the domestic arena.

2) *The EU is not wielded to pacifism but to peacemaking.* The historical experience of European states has promoted an explicit recognition of the fact not only that fighting wars is of little use if the subsequent peace is not won, but also that war itself is a recognition of failure. For Europeans, conflict avoidance and prevention is the name of the game. Yet, this does not preclude the development and deployment of military force, and therefore the expansion of intervention capacity (Petersberg task) and even defence commitments as the new EU Constitution makes clear. But it implies that the use of force should be

seen only as a necessary prerequisite to the deployment of *civilian* tools and at the service of *civilian* goals. Civilian powerhood refers not only to the civilian *means* of foreign policy – as the favourite but not the only instruments of influence – but also to the civilian *ends* of inter-vention, notably reconstruction. As the joint declaration of the Member States in February 2003, at the eve of the Iraq war testifies, Europeans can agree on the threat of force at least if the emphasis is on its use as last resort. *In this sense, civilian powerhood is compatible with increased military strength, for member states in the EU who may decide to choose such a route together. But there will always be divergence among as well as within states as to what the use of force as 'last resort' actually implies.*

3) *The world beyond is EU-compatible.* Ours is a world that is far from being a desolate 'Hobbesian' landscape beyond the Kantian European island. It is closer to a pre-Kantian world with a great number of Hobbesian islands, in the form of rogue states, failed states or local zones of conflicts. The progressive socialization of governing elites as well as the growing interconnections between civil societies around the world has meant that zones of peace and democracy by contagion coexist with zones of chronic instability. This does not make the terror-ist threat less real. Clearly, rogue states and other Hobbesian realities need to be dealt with. But we must consider that our very actions in these cases will themselves contribute to the Hobbesian vs. Kantian character of the international system. The great majority of countries that have affirmed their commitment to or at least their reliance on international organizations must be taken at their word. This is at least what the EU has tried to do, from Iran to Central America.

A US–EU division of labour? Along which lines and to what extent? And how explicit should it be?

Even in its latest version incorporating military capacity, this European story of civilian powerhood suggests that differences between Europe and the United States must be valued, and reinforced, if we are to counter the challenges facing us in the decades ahead. Irrespective of the policies of its individual member states, the EU as a whole will not change the essential parameters of the US superpowerhood; but it can aim at a more optimal division of labour, by striking implicit or expli-cit bargains with the US or by doing its own thing. A division of labour drawing on our respective strengths and inclinations as well as simply acknowledging our divergent policy concerns. Differences and comple-mentarities exists along various dimensions:

1) *Geographical:* Both the US and the EU are global actors with regional strategies. The EU must reassure Washington of its commitment to global order. At the same time, for the EU to recognize and proclaim that its next strategic priority will be to export justice and stability to its own 'zone of peace' would not mean retreating in a regional role while leaving the global stage to the US. The global impact of progressively expanding the EU's zone of peace and prosperity cannot be under-estimated. First through enlargement, the EU's most powerful foreign policy tools: the prospect of membership for Turkey would constitute the most powerful signal that the EU is indeed a 'world partner' who will not banish the Muslim world as Europe's 'other'. And clearly, an EU bordering Iraq and Russia is not irrelevant to the supply of global order. Beyond enlargement, the construction of a Euromed region constitutes the best hope for the peoples bordering the *Mare Nostrum* – notwith-standing the crucial role of US arbitration in the Middle East in the immediate future. Beyond, the EU's wider neighbourhood should be its grand project of the next decade and the next frontier of its constitu-tional ambitions.

2) *Functional:* Cartoons, pride and prejudice have obscured a crucial point. When it comes to global intervention, the different policy agendas of the US and EU have led, through painful trial and error in the last few years, to a rather productive division of labour between the front-end and the back-end of missions. There is nothing wrong with Europeans continuing to invest in reconstruction and stabilization, anticipating the requirements of nation-building in conflict-prone regions – from policing to support in developing a legal infrastructure. Good-cop – bad-cop routines can be effective, as competition in winning 'hearts and minds'. But the EU must stubbornly keep on the table the core bargain eschewed by the US in the case of Iraq: the US must recognize limitations of its own power and the need for pluralism in world governance *in exchange for* the EU helping to legitimize this power and mobilizing its own civilian capacities. Why shouldn't Europeans accept to do the dishes if Americans consult on the menu? At its best, the US can create worthy recipients for Europe's construct-ive engagement. At its worse it will alienate more renegades whose impulses the EU can seek to moderate as the 'alternative power'.

3) *Temporal:* Crucial to their respective roles, the US and the EU also have different temporal horizons. Europeans are turtles, Americans are hares. Where Americans like to drop by, Europeans have staying power (there is widespread acknowledgement in the Middle East that it is the Europeans' long term presence on the ground which prepared these grounds for the Quartet and American public diplomacy). The long

term is the EU's comparative advantage and prevention should be its response to the US's preemptive strike. Since 9/11 US policy makers have made much of dealing with root-causes. But this requires engagement, cooperation and assistance, rather than containment and coercion. Since the measure of success in the prevention field is that there is nothing to report, this strategy is not likely to win many votes. Similarly, micro involvement and assistance, requiring the acquisition of detailed local knowledge is unglamorous and painstaking. But the less democratic EU can afford slow and discrete results. Its machinery is not subject to short term Union-wide electoral cycles but to the long term constraint of its own civilian logic. The EU needs to spend more on these cost-effective approaches and explain their logic to its publics. And even as it becomes more accountable with time, European public opinions might stay more patient.

Along each of these dimensions, the EU can and should be the United States' partner at times, while simply following its own logic.

The EU mosaic: can weakness be turned into strength?

The standard assumption these days is that Europeans agree on most things – including the above description of EU comparative advantage and most topics on the global governance agenda – except how to deal with American power in times of crisis. It is unsurprising that the Iraq war found EU member states hopelessly divided. As witnessed at the European Convention, the standard response is, unsurprisingly to tinker with institutions and processes in order to mould a single purpose out of the EU mosaic: institutions and mechanisms that can enhance the likelihood of a 'European reflex' (consult first, early and intensively); institutional machinery to foster a more unified voice in foreign policy, emulating to the extent possible the relative success of the trade area. The arguments have been well rehearsed and are now translated into constitutional reform – including a foreign affairs minister with double accountability and joint European civil service.

Yet neither a treaty article nor even in the short term institutional habits are likely to change deeply entrenched national diplomatic cultures. The obligation of loyalty has been in the treaties since Maastricht. Is loyalty not more likely to become the rule if the Union focuses on the causes and occurrences of 'dis-loyalty' and adopts practices which seek to turn diversity into strength? Can the leveraging of complementarities *within* the EU replace confrontation or false harmony? I believe so, along the following five principles:

1) *Member States must learn how to agree to disagree.* Heads of States have little incentive to consult with their European colleagues if they fear that they will be precluded from acting on their own in case of disagreement, or perhaps worse, that if there is agreement, this will only be on bland minimal positions or actions – a favourite of EU bashers and satirists. This was the dilemma on both side during the Iraq saga. If EU consultation as a first resort is to have any meaning, there must be an understanding that member states can agree to disagree without mutual accusations of letting the Union down or 'caring only about one's national interest'. For what is wrong with national interest! Isn't an enterprise like the EU premised on the understanding that national interests are often best served by acting together? Those who bemoan the fact that *national* interests too often trump the so-called *common* interest fail to understand the logic of positive sum games. This first principle still leaves many questions open: does this mean deciding that the Union will only act in relatively consensual areas (e.g. Bosnia etc.)? Or does it mean a generalization of coalitions of the willing, constructive abstention and enhanced cooperation in foreign and security policy? Does it mean a carving out of areas of foreign policy between member states? Or simply a new approach to 'multi-voice' declaratory diplomacy?

2) *The EU itself must remain mulitpolar.* At the institutional level, turning diversity into strength implies a definite commitment to a multipolar EU with strong coordinating mechanisms – as with a new foreign minister. The EU was invented to forestall age-old temptations of hegemony within Europe as reflected in the original bargain of the Treaty of Rome, balancing weights according to size with equality within states. Small and medium states will not indefinitely acquiesce to an EU where the population principle increasingly prevails. Equal access to leadership by less powerful states *within* constitutes a powerful signal to the rest of the world that the EU does not only follow the logic of power politics. In this light, the suggestion of the Convention to almost abandon rotation among member states in the Council can only be detrimental. For the sake of a multipolar Europe, the IGC must re-establish the best elements of the old system of rotation *alongside* the new European Council chair.

3) *Special bilateral relationships must be made to work for the Union.* Special relationships between individual or groups of member states and outside actors may rest on history or geography; they may be conjunctural or structural; rely on personal, cultural or bureaucratic ties. They may reflect different allegiances linked to different views as to how to deal with the rest of the world. They can also reflect world

politics of the moment (e.g. Chirac's popularity in the Arab world). The question here is whether and how a set of special relationships at a given moment in time can be made to work for the Union as a whole to address a particular problem. Here we must ask together: how can individual member states put their credibility at the service of the Union, without necessarily acting and speaking in its name?

4 *Diplomatic and popular mutuality need to be pursued alongside consensus.* Part of the answer lies in greater mutual trust and mutual knowledge between national diplomacies in the EU, a deeper respect for each others' positions – even obsessions. Paradoxically, the problem lies in the fact that meetings at all levels in the EU, from diplomats to political directors, ministers and heads of states concentrate on basic commonalities and the crafting of infamously innocuous communiqués (e.g. 'the EU will never use force ... except when absolutely necessary'). Instead, more of these meetings could be devoted to the plain-speaking exposition of different national priorities and the concerns that lie behind them (this might have avoided Jacques Chirac's ill-advised outburst against new member-states in February 2003). Beyond the world of diplomats and bureaucrats, one of the lessons from the Iraq crisis is that European public opinions may not lag behind but lead in this spirit of mutuality. When the history of Europe is written 20 years from now, we may well see a fundamental divergence between diplomatic history and social history. There seems to have been more (or at least better) dialogue across borders between the peoples than the elites of Europe. This crisis should motivate EU leaders to explore new avenues of communication with EU citizens on foreign policy but also in engaging more forcefully in trans-European debate over Europe's role in the world.

5) *It is as a microcosmos that the EU can influence the rest of the world.* The EU's global influence lies in its power of attraction more than its projection of power. And this power of attraction in turn lies in its diversity. Ultimately, the EU's claim to fame is that it is one of the most formidable machines for peacefully managing differences ever invented. The formula of the EU as a model for both regional and global governance is certainly too crude. The EU cannot be a model to be promoted or emulated wholesale, but it can serve as an inspiration for other instances of cooperation or at least an interlocutor. It may be more appropriate to speak of the EU as a pioneer in long term inter-state peace building, a pioneer acting through trial and error and thus designing options for peaceful governance. The EU and its experience can serve as a well of precedents, good or bad, exportable or not, for

the rest of the world. The success of its attempts at conflict resolution in the rest of the world is predicated on its practice of the politics of recognition and the politics of empathy inside its borders – a practice too often found wanting. The characteristic of the EU as a micro-cosmos, managing within itself many of the tensions present in the rest of the world constitutes its greatest source of legitimacy. In some ways, such legitimacy from diversity is the twenty-first-century equi-valent to what the American melting pot may have represented a century ago.

Finally then, how can such a European 'constructive diversity' contribute to fostering progress in specific areas of transatlantic relations?

1) *Devising a transatlantic strategy for the Middle East.* According to Tony Blair, his hand would have been strengthened if the EU could have pressed Washington to recognize that 'dealing with Iraq has to fit into a broader vision of the Middle East that also encompasses a resolution of the Israeli-Palestinian conflict.' What he should have added is that this is an area where differences must be exploited to their fullest. First because, in a final settlement process, the division of labour between the EU and the US is clear but requires intense coordination: the former must deliver the Palestinians, the latter deliver Israel. It is only as part of a broader strategy that the efforts of the EU keep the Palestinian authority afloat; but as importantly, because different EU member states can, if not deliver, at least use their clout respectively with different Arab states, ruling families, non-state actors and sub-regions.

2) *Revisiting the United Nations*: The time has come to revisit the premises of the UN Charter regarding the link between enforcement of its fundamental norms (human rights, non proliferation) and the use of force – or coercive diplomacy. Europeans should not be associated with the status quo and the upholding of traditional sovereignty norms, while the US would stand for freedom and the 'aggressive' pro-motion of human rights. Indeed this has not been the case in the 1990s from Kosovo to Sierra Leone. But to be consistent in its loyalty to the UN and multilateralism, should the EU not campaign for the institutionalization within multilateral institutions of a generalized strategy of human rights-based intervention? In doing so, the fact that different attitudes to the use of force – from neutral states to nuclear powers – coexist within the EU itself will be a key asset.

3) *Linking the Doha Round and transatlantic economic cooperation.* Global economic governance is clearly an area where the US and the EU must rekindle their cooperation. But they must resist the sirens of introverted transatlantic initiatives, free trade areas and the likes. Instead they must focus on a joint commitment to the Doha round as genuinely a 'development round'. A good place to start would be the promotion of *regulatory development*, where the US and the EU have different and complementary experiences and resources to offer: the US standards of regulatory consultation; the EU experience in mutual recognition, e.g. the management of continued regulatory diversity. For instance, the managed liberation of the movement of people as professionals (temporary) through the mutual recognition of qualification, licensing and certification requirements is high on the list of many third world countries. The US and the EU could commit to the negotiation of 'open' MRAs in this field and devise procedures for their multilateralization, not only as a means of reinforcing transatlantic ties but as the basis for addressing the needs of developing countries for greater access to the benefits of globalization.

4) *Reinvigorating transatlantic networks.* Finally, for differences between Europe and the United States to be constructively exploited rather than denied requires much deeper and sustained dialogue between all levels of our societies and political classes. European leaders must combat anti-Americanism in Europe and the rest of the world for fear that it might become a self fulfilling prophecy and drive the US out of multilateral forums. Clearly however, the different nations of Europe would do so in different voices.

Note

1. Kalypso Nicolaidis is University Lecturer at Oxford University and advisor to the then Minister for Foreign Affairs, George Papandreou. This contribution was written in preparation for the EU Foreign Ministers informal meeting on Transatlantic Relations. For their feedback I would like to thank Peter Dunn, Thierry Fabre, Andrew Hurrell, Robert Howse, Anand Menon, Dimitri Nicolaidis, Michael Petrou, Simon Saunders and Jennifer Wesh. This article is based in part on Nicolaidis and Howse, 'This is my EU-topia: Narrative as Power,' *Journal of Common Market Studies*, October 2002; and Menon, Nicolaidis and Welsh, 'In Defense of Europe,' *Working Paper*, ESC, Oxford University, 2003.

Part IV
Short-Term Causes

18
On EU/US Relations

Stanley Hoffmann

The present crisis in EU/US relations cannot be ended by EU measures aimed at appeasing the Bush administration. This crisis results from a major shift in American foreign policy and strategy. The postwar policy of leadership (or primacy, after the fall of the Soviet Union) through multilateral cooperation has been replaced by a quasi-imperial policy, justified by the notion that the US is at war since 11 September 2001, that deterrence must be replaced by preventive action, that the constraints exerted by alliances, international organizations and international law are no longer acceptable, and that the concept of terrorism must be extended to states that support terrorism and to states that want to obtain or build weapons of mass destruction. A potent symbol of this momentous shift is the predominance of the Department of Defense over the State Department.

In the crisis over Iraq, the US has 'succeeded' in provoking a division of NATO and of the EU, and in devaluing the UN, which it deemed insufficiently supportive. In the case of the EU, Washington was unfortunately helped by Tony Blair, eager to isolate France and Germany.

The lessons seem to me extremely clear. If the EU wants to be taken seriously by the Bush administration, there is only one way: the reinforcement of the EU as an organization capable of playing an important role in world affairs (and thereby capable of serving, in fact, as a counterweight to a US whose understanding of other countries' outlooks and concerns remains often cloudy or limited). This means:

A. That Britain, whose participation in the 'coalition' has not brought to Tony Blair all the benefits he had expected (and certainly not a genuinely 'central' role for the UN in postwar Iraq), must now emphasize again the role of the EU instead of undermining it, and be able to present itself in friendly Washington as a powerful advocate of the EU.

B.   That France must draw the consequences of the fact that its opposition to the US has put it in a very delicate situation versus Washington and that the ideas that it has tried to promote (including that of preventing a confrontation between the Muslim and the Western 'civilizations') have a chance of being heard only if France also gives priority to the reinforcement of the EU, in cooperation especially with London and Berlin.

C.   That the EU, in order to be taken seriously in Washington, must give priority to:

(1) The streamlining and strengthening of its institutions, which have, alas, often proved their insufficient efficiency. A good first step would be the quick conclusion of the Convention, and a project of institutional reform whose two main features would be the priority of effectiveness over perfect representation, and a greater association of delegations of the national parliaments with those of the European Parliament, so as to close the all too frequent gap between national politics and the EU.

(2) A major effort to develop:
   (a) The common security policy that was promised in St Malo in 1998, but derailed by the combination of German budgetary policy, often shrill US opposition, and the crisis over Iraq. Only serious progress here could persuade the pragmatists who still exist in Washington that the EU could actually be useful in Iraq as it is beginning to be in Afghanistan or in the Balkans.
   (b) Common foreign policy positions on key issues in world politics, such as the Palestinian problem, an issue pressed by Blair, to which the US has paid little attention, relations with Muslim countries, many of which may feel threatened by the US war on terrorism, North Korea (which is not just, as the Americans say, a regional issue, but a global one), the development of weapons of mass destruction – a central problem of world politics for the near future – and finally the issue of 'regime change' when a regime violates human rights on a massive scale at home. (This is an issue that should not be handled by unilateral intervention, for obvious reasons, and it is not likely to be handled by the UN Security Council, as we saw in the case of Kosovo.)

One of the links between institutional reform and the urgent development of a common foreign and security policy is the importance for the EU having a strong and experienced Minister of Foreign and Security Affairs. Mr Solana, who was Secretary General of NATO before becoming the key figure of the EU in these areas, would be the ideal person. Given the Bush administration's lesser emphasis on NATO than any previous administration, I believe that those new members of the EU that appeared, during the Iraq war, to be 'Atlanticists' first, and 'Europeans' only for economic and social questions will, if treated with genuine respect by the other members of the EU, rapidly become convinced that the EU is not only an enhanced free trade area.

19
Healing the West's Wounds

Theodore A. Couloumbis

Through the din of countless reports, analyses, commentaries and critiques surrounding the recent war against Saddam Hussein in Iraq, a proposition – shared by a number of pessimistic thinkers – is emerging as follows: The world, after regime change in Iraq, is crossing the threshold to a radically changed era. In this allegedly emerging 'new global order', the USA is expected to continue playing the role of a lone superpower that acts unilaterally, seeks *ex post facto* legitimization, and is highly impatient with the gridlocks of international institutions (such as the UN, NATO, EU, *et al.*). Neoconservative thinking in the Bush administration is said to view the world in Hobbesian terms as grey, miserable, unpredictable and dangerous, with Islamist international terrorist networks heading the agenda of global threats. In such a 'new system', traditional concepts – such as sovereignty and territorial integrity of states – are being replaced by newly-minted doctrines of 'preemptive war' and 'humanitarian intervention'. The proponents of 'grand systemic change' refer to the 'death' of the United Nations, to a 'permanent' rift in the Euro-Atlantic community, and to the impending dissolution of an enlarging 'Old Europe' that will not be able to withstand the tremors caused by the absorption of a post-communist 'New Europe'. For the rest of the world, the pessimistic prognosis involves increasing marginalization of Russia, China and Japan, while the Arab world is expected to be facing mounting challenges that will place traditional monarchies and other authoritarian regimes high on the risk list. A new 'domino theory', made this time in the USA, is expected to result in a chain of pre-emptive invasions against 'rogue states and governments' in the name of democratization, anti-terrorism and the neutralization of weapons of mass destruction.

In my view, the changes that have taken place after 11 September 2001 cannot be compared to the grand systemic change that followed the dissolution of the Soviet Union, the fall of the Berlin Wall and the end of the Cold War. In the crucial years 1989–1991, we were escaping from a system of bipolarity and the balance of nuclear terror, as well as from a cosmic confrontation of two incompatible ideologies: communism and capitalism. Even then, for a short while, some Cassandra-minded scholars predicted the birth of a neo-Westphalian 'order' based on multipolarity, with tendencies toward the atrophy or fragmentation of post Second World War institutions such as the United Nations, the European Union and NATO. These dire predictions were soon challenged by the flow of events: after the wars of Yugoslav succession and the rise of new risks (later to be upgraded to threats), such as international terrorism, the proliferation of weapons of mass destruction and transnational criminal cartels, NATO reshaped itself into an alliance that, beyond collective defence and deterrence, would assume important functions of collective security (peacekeeping and peacemaking), while acting beyond its traditional area of operations. The USA was universally accepted as the uncontested global superpower, and multilateral structures (UN Security Council, NATO, Group 7/8, the Bretton Woods institutions, the EU, etc.) markedly increased their regulatory responsibilities.

The post Cold War system (let us call it uni-multipolar) reached the apex of its functionality after the 11 September attacks against the United States. The US, for the first time since the Second World War, fell victim to the 'bombardment' of its own territory and instantly secured the sympathy and solidarity of humankind. The French newspaper, *Le Monde*, did not accidentally use the front page headline 'We are all Americans'. The quick, efficient and relatively low cost (in blood and treasure) operation against the Taliban regime in Afghanistan secured also the support – or at least the acquiescence – of the majority of the planet's governments. Unfortunately, however, the unquestionable success in effecting regime change in Afghanistan strengthened the hand of neoconservatives in the Bush administration, such as Dick Cheney, Donald Rumsfeld, Paul Wolfowitz and Richard Perle. Following its decision to attack Saddam Hussein without the authorization of a second UN Security Council resolution, the Bush administration has managed to squander the unconditional goodwill that the US had enjoyed after the 11 September terrorist attacks.

The fighting phase of Gulf-War II appears to be over. Indeed it almost caused a major rupture in Euro-Atlantic and intra-European relations. But a great challenge lies ahead. It involves damage control, humanitarian assistance, post-war administration and state building in war-ravaged Iraq. In a paradoxical sense, winning the peace may give the West a grand opportunity to return to a status of interdependence, complementarity, cooperation and unity. In other words, it is high time to return to what was needed after the end of the Cold War: a global concert of powers.

Looking to the future, we need to draw conclusions from the time-less lessons of history. Simply, the planet's great powers (one could think in terms of the G-7/8/9 or the Quartet plus) have every interest to conserve a state of affairs that perpetuates their position of pro-minence. Together they can act as the guarantors and legitimizers of the earth's regulatory mechanisms. Needless to say, 'fire fighting' is necessary but not sufficient. It needs to be supplemented by a global strategy of 'fire prevention' that will address the key structural chal-lenge of the twenty-first century: the growing gap separating the rich in the global north from the poor, and therefore conflict-prone, in the global south. For the EU, involved simultaneously in a deepening and widening process, rebuilding a system of global order with equity and economic sufficiency is both a challenge and an opportunity. We should all remember that, in years past, whenever great powers resorted to force in order to exert their influence, it was a sign of impending decline, if not their fall.

20
EU–US Relations in Worldwide Context

A. A. Fatouros

1. Relations between the European Union and the United States are going today through a difficult period, one might even say a crisis. While in international affairs policy differences between states (or groups of states) are commonplace, this particular crisis exhibits several special features that give to it added importance and meaning. To understand this crisis and be thereby able better to cope with it, it is necessary to place it in its proper context.

2. To begin with, three particular elements of special character and importance colour and exacerbate the present situation. *First, the current policy conflicts* with the United States have arisen at a time when the European Union has not yet fully developed its foreign policy apparatus (rules, procedures and approaches). In the process of completing its political and economic integration, however, it has reached the stage where such a development is among its top immediate priorities. A this point, the European foreign and defence policy area is therefore particularly sensitive, if not vulnerable, and the current crisis with the United States raises difficult institutional problems for the European Union and involves fundamental structural questions. *A second element of the situation* is the particular policy style of the current US administration, that is to say, the manner and rhetoric in which policies and positions are advanced and implemented. Partly as a consequence of the 11 September events, which have promoted a public sense of insecurity, the US government tends to stress differences and conflicts in approaches and policies in order unequivocally to reaffirm the country's strength and ability to deal with external threats. *Finally, it is significant that a war is involved.* The use of armed force remains the most sensitive of issues among nations, even where

force is not directed at the countries immediately concerned. In combination with the two factors just mentioned, this tends to bring to a head the policy differences and the reactions to them.

3. It is, however, significant that the differences in question involve, not so much, or at least not primarily, policies towards one another (i.e., US policies concerning the EU and EU policies concerning the US), but policies towards other countries or towards the international community at large. Because the US and the EU are important global actors, each of them is affected by policies directed at and primarily concerned with other countries and regions. While there is no lack of bilateral policy conflicts between them, especially in economic matters (e.g., US steel tariffs or EU import polices), these conflicts are not the ones that have led to the current 'crisis'.

4. A first question that arises is whether and how far the current 'crisis' reflects a fundamental change in the international situation, which may lead to long-term conflicts between the basic interests – and thereby the policies – of the United States and the European Union, or is it merely a temporary problem reflecting the particular attitudes and policies of specific governments at the present time. The elements identified above suggest that, while significant world changes may have occurred, the intensity of the present crisis between the US and the EU may largely be due to the coincidence of factors which are not long-term or permanent, especially the current stage of European integration and the particular style of the current US administration. More fundamental factors are likely at play as well, pointing to possible longer-term conflict potential, but the role of the 'accidental' elements mentioned cannot be denied.

5. In view of the above, one might start by suggesting that, in the case at hand, patience and a willingness to wait out the policies of particular governments may be appropriate. The European Union and its member states should adopt a firm position on the questions at issue between them and the United States, keeping in mind that, as the recent past has shown, long-term interests and policies of the two parties are more likely to be in harmony than to conflict and that a deadlock between the US and the EU is in nobody's interest. The EU should also try to ensure at the very least that the decisions and actions to be reached should not foreclose future movement in desired directions.

6. Such prescriptions, however, while valid as far as they go, disregard the actual character of the problem at hand and do not take adequately into account the US positions that have led to the current crisis, nor in fact the responses of the states that have opposed them. It should be recalled that the argument over Iraq has to do primarily with the role of international, multilateral institutions and procedures, mainly those of the United Nations. The US position has been that the current world situation and the problems that must be confronted today (post 9/11) cannot be adequately addressed by the existing UN structures and procedures. Opposing states have essentially argued, not so much that UN procedures are the most appropriate for current conditions, but that they are all we have and must be made to serve.

7. It would seem to follow that the real challenge for the EU (and its members) is to address the actual problem, to direct its institutional imagination, the imagination it has successfully used in the past and is now using to devise its own institutions and their evolution, to formulate proposals for the creation of international structures more appropriate for the times than those constructed after the Second World War – or to the improvement of the existing structures. Up to now, the EU as such (regardless of legal niceties) has not been an important participant in multilateral (universal) international processes. This is due to a number of reasons, some of them legal or institutional, some political. It would seem that it is high time for the EU and its member states to disregard formal considerations (e.g., the fact that the EU is not a member of the UN) and seek to address the real problems of their international position (and thereby those of their relations with the United States) directly. The likely diversity of views within the European Union itself is in this context an advantage, because it allows for a first debate and makes extreme or dogmatic positions rather unlikely. Such a task would moreover give the EU an opportunity to recruit other states and groups of states (including, why not, the United States itself) to help in the invention of new multilateral structures and procedures.

21
The Future of the Relationship between the EU and the US: Managing Interdependence and Global Responsibility

Georgios Papastamkos

The transatlantic relationship: a legacy of mutual benefit and a challenging future

The transatlantic relationship, the centre point of Western Europe's security and defence architecture, as well as of its political and economic agenda for at least five decades, is characterized by symmetry in the economic power of the US and the EU and asymmetry in their international presence.

The starting premise of this statement is that the recent crisis in Euro-Atlantic relations is the by-product of the unresolved question of how to manage interdependence. As such it has unquestionably prejudiced the continuity of the transatlantic security balance and has created new political and security challenges for the EU. Arguably, the EU may effectively meet these challenges only by devoting considerable energy and resources in the reform of its security and defence structures.

This statement offers some scenarios and policy proposals on the future orientation of the EU security and defence policy focusing on the transatlantic relationship.

The Transatlantic Declaration of 1995, adopted by the EU and the US, stipulates that NATO would remain the indispensable link between North America and Europe around which the transatlantic relationship would continue to revolve. As a result, the new European Security and Defence Identity was viewed as reinforcing the European pillar of NATO. This approach was reaffirmed as the cornerstone of the transatlantic relationship in NATO's New Strategic Concept, enunciated in the 1999 Washington Communiqué. The European Security and Defence Policy (ESDP), as conceived in the Treaty of Nice as well as in the post-Nice process, has arguably overreached the boundaries of the

1990s Transatlantic Consensus. Thereby, for the first time, the EU asserted itself as a security and defence entity that may act unilaterally and that has recourse to NATO's assets.

Three scenarios for the ESDP and the transatlantic relationship

In this section, I provide three scenarios regarding the orientation of the ESDP, indicating the projected US reaction.

(a) The static scenario: responding to new global challenges with shared responsibilities

The EU and the US reach a new understanding in a number of global challenges, including all forms of security (e.g., terrorism, humanitarian intervention), trade relations, and 'millennium goals'. This understanding may be achieved through the reaffirmation of shared principles and aims that have underpinned the model of collective action in the post-Cold War era.

This scenario necessitates the reinforcement of the role of the UN and NATO as main forums used for the formulation of a common strategy, in the context of the EU–US partnership. This will enable the two sides to preserve without substantial changes the strategic balance that has prevailed during the past decade. In accordance with this scenario, the EU and the US should reach a new understanding in responding to pressing global security challenges, such as the combating of transnational terrorism and the crystallization of the doctrine of 'humanitarian intervention', through a process of transparent dialogue and constructive consultation. These two components could contribute to the prevention of further divergence of the EU and US interests in the field of international policy, on the one hand, and the deepening of the current feeling of alienation between the two sides, on the other hand.

(b) The dynamic scenario: an autonomous ESDP

This scenario may only occur if EU member states, after enlargement, consent to participate in a 'strong ESDP', which may act autonomously from NATO's defence capability. This will result either in considerable change to the foundations of the transatlantic relationship (whereby the two sides will act as co-operating, but autonomous partners, thus, leading to a new division of global responsibilities and capabilities), or to the formation of two systems of action, which will alternate between co-operation and competition.

(c) The fragmented ESDP scenario: enhanced co-operation of some EU member states

The occurrence of this scenario, although provided by the EU Treaty, will mean the fragmentation of the EU's common external action. A fragmented ESDP will weaken the EU's position and its role in the framework of the transatlantic partnership. This will release the forces of disengagement, reinforcing US unilateralism both within and outside the boundaries of the transatlantic relationship. In addition, closer security and defence cooperation between a few member states ('a minor ESDP') should further EU political integration and be guided by the principle of 'an ever closer union', and it should not be the result of temporary overreaction to the international political meteorology.

Policy proposals

(a) Global governance: transition from declarations to regulation and implementation

The common desire for shared action in response to global challenges may be fostered and materialized only if it is transposed from the declaratory stage to a comprehensive, transparent and stable institutional framework. Any increase in the number of fields of common action will have positive spillover effects in the enhancement and deepening as well as the widening of political co-operation.

(b) Merging the EU foreign action into a single constitutional framework

The EU at first should reach a political consensus enabling it to form and follow a consistent and uniform position in the management of major global challenges and international crises. Merging all forms of EU foreign action (e.g., external economic relations, security policy and cooperation for development) within a single institutional setting should be viewed as the preferred option. This emerges as one of the major tasks and visions of the current European Convention and the upcoming Intergovernmental Conference

(c) Reforming the UN

It is suggested that the EU and the US work together to reform the UN, including its organizational structure and the composition of the Security Council; its principles concerning international crises, humanitarian relief, combating international terrorism, international crime and drug trafficking, prevention of communicable diseases; and its policy responses toward debt relief for developing countries, environmental protection, and the support of sustainable development.

(d) Building bridges across the Atlantic and beyond

Major changes should be implemented in the framework of preventive diplomacy in order to facilitate the adoption of positive and effective policy initiatives in this area. In this manner, the US and the EU will discharge properly their responsibility to be active partners in effective distribution, globally, of the product of their partnership at the level of security and economic and social welfare.

22
Pursuing Common Security Goals

Misha Glenny

The crisis over Iraq in the run up to war demonstrated beyond doubt that where the US has an ability to formulate and execute decisive policy initiatives, the European Union does not.

Over issues such as Iraq in which the US bids to define an entire foreign policy strategy, EU member states (critically the three most influential) revert to foreign policies framed by national interests. This neutralizes the ability of the EU's institutions to modify US strategy.

The present US administration works actively to undermine a European coherence by playing on our insecurities, e.g. by proclaiming Europe's division into two irreconcilable and hostile blocs, one old and one new. The division is fatuous and inaccurate (the 'new' bloc is led by Europe's most enduring state while public opinion in New Europe is decisively hostile to American policy in the Middle East). But such is Europe's self-doubt that we begin to believe it.

All this flows from the ability of the US, the world's most powerful economy, to project its political energy into military force through a single agency, a presidential administration, bolstered by a sympathetic Congress. The diverse interests of America's 50 states are rarely if ever reflected in foreign policy. The diverse interests of the EU's members are always reflected in foreign policy.

It does not follow, however, that EU member states share no concrete interests which could and should act as a powerful adhesive. If applied correctly, this could transform Europe's enormous economic power into much greater global influence. On many of the most contentious issues such as the Israeli/Palestine question, Britain, Spain, Italy, France and Germany are much closer to one another than to the US.

I cannot paper over the difficulties which the British relationship with the United States poses for the EU. I do not believe that Blair acts as a bridge, and London's primary commitment to Washington makes the development of any common European strategy extremely difficult.

Similarly, however, French particularism is immensely problematic, especially its support for the common agricultural policy (CAP). The abolition of the CAP would be the single most beneficial policy that the EU could undertake – it would put the US on the back foot regarding its farm subsidy policy, but it would also show a tremendous commitment to an equitable global market. Until we do this, the outside world will look at us with considerable contempt as merely a slightly more palatable version of the US.

I have not addressed the CAP issue below because the responses would be entirely predictable.

But on issues closer to home where the unique values of the EU can be readily appreciated, the long-term strategic interests of the member states are almost identical. By attending to these interests, Europe will maintain good relations with the US while becoming an alternative pole of attraction for the rest of the world.

On the surface, Europe's position in the world at the end of the Iraq war looks weak and tattered. In fact, the European Union still has a great opportunity in the next decade to offer an alternative foreign policy strategy to the US.

This strategy does not imply a confrontational relationship with the US (which would be most unwise). We cannot and should not compete militarily with the United States. But we can develop a very different vision of global development that other states and areas will find considerably more attractive than US policy.

The European strategy must use those tools dismissed as ineffective by America's neo-conservative thinkers, such as negotiations, multilateral institutions and engagement through economic development. US military intervention underscores its global might but it does not provide the long-term answers to Western security concerns. Bosnia, Kosovo, Afghanistan, and almost certainly Iraq demonstrate that America does not have the capacity to follow through.

The EU is sometimes rather modest about its most remarkable achievements. But it has an enviable track record of providing answers to questions raised by dysfunctional, underdeveloped societies.

Greece, Ireland, Portugal and Spain have witnessed the most spectacular social, economic and political changes in the last twenty years thanks to the mighty engine of EU accession. The EU has absorbed four states that:

a) emerged from different forms of fascist or clerical rule;
b) were overwhelmingly rural with high rates of unemployment; and
c) whose administrations were regarded as incorrigibly corrupt.

All four are now modern, secular states with an ever-improving economic and political performance. If ever there was ever an advertisement for the advantages of the European model, these four states are it. We can ascribe their success to many things, but chief amongst them is the uniquely innovative policy of cohesion and infrastructural funds.

Notwithstanding a couple of loose ends, the latest round of enlargement is now complete. Europe should take pride in a process that has lain to rest some of the bitterest causes of European conflict in the nineteenth and twentieth centuries.

Now the challenge is absorption or digestion. Europe's next goal is to show that it can eradicate the totalitarian legacy for eight of the new ten states. The discrepancies between Western and Eastern Europe remain considerable. But the mere prospect of EU accession has triggered profound changes in the incoming member states that no other process could provoke.

Romania's fortunes act as a simple measure of the extraordinary impact that the concrete prospect of EU membership can have on the perception of apparently weak societies and economies. Five years ago, foreign direct investment (FDI) in Romania stood at $1 billion per year. Once accepted as a candidate country, FDI began to rise exponentially, reaching $9 billion last year, and it is estimated to reach $18 in five year's time.[1] Despite the pain involved, the Romanians have worked hard at ensuring the passage and implementation of legislation to meet the Copenhagen criteria. All the signs are that Romania will be ready for membership in 2007.

But there is one region where the EU's progress is too slow: the Western Balkans. This is the greatest challenge for the EU, because it must apply its stabilizing tools in an area of highly dysfunctional states where potential for major armed conflict and social unrest remain.

The stabilization of the Western Balkans is in the vital interests of the EU. Failure to succeed here has two implications:

a) Organized crime will consolidate the area as its base for operations inside the European Union.
b) Europe's failure to deal with its own backyard will expose it as an ineffective player on the global stage.

Success, on the other hand, will demonstrate the superiority of European tactics in the arena of conflict resolution and nation building. But this matter needs to be addressed with the greatest urgency.

The states and territories of the Western Balkans need a date for accession (even if it is 2015). Reformist governments in the region must be able to show their electorates that the road map is real and not just theoretical.

In its present constitutional makeup, much of the Western Balkans cannot meet the criteria for entry. In order for the EU to assert itself as the primary international actor in the region, it must take the lead in finding a solution for the dangerous constitutional uncertainty in the Western Balkans, above all the anomaly of Kosovo. If the EU does not seize the initiative on Kosovo's final status soon, it will have to suffer some serious consequences.

The centrality of regional cooperation in this strategy, and the critical role that economic underdevelopment plays in fostering conflict, will have significant implications for the Middle East and the Maghreb.

The EU must concentrate on these areas because it is a magnet for migrant labour from all conflict areas in Europe, Africa and Asia (only a very small percentage of migrant labourers travel to the United States).

This makes the question of immigration policies central to any EU strategy. The long-term reduction of illegal immigration into the EU can only be achieved by assisting the economic development of those regions producing migrant labour. But EU member states must urgently fulfil the commitments made at Tampere in 1999 to develop a coherent, EU-wide immigration policy. Because of our ageing population, we need a healthy infusion of labour to guarantee economic growth. The United States has been cherry-picking the global labour force for many decades. Unless the EU adopts similar policies, it is bound to decline as a global economic power. The cultural fears of Europe's indigenous populations arising from immigration issues need answers that also satisfy our long-term economic requirements.

Note

1. The Economist Corporate Network, London Meeting, February 2003.

Part V
The Recommendations

23
TPN Outreach Project: Interim Report from the Co-Chairs (April 2003)

Transatlantic Policy Network (TPN)[1]

Executive summary

Since its founding in 1992, TPN has helped shape a broader and deeper transatlantic partnership, responsive to the new global realities of the post Cold War world. Since May 2002, in response to growing tensions, TPN is now developing a long-term strategy for building such a partnership, to be completed – following further discussions – by a high-level meeting before the end of the year to mobilize broad support. US Senator Robert Bennett, Congressman Cal Dooley, and Members of European Parliament James Elles and Erika Mann serve as co-chairs for this project.

Set out in the attached interim report are emerging points of consensus from a series of meetings in Europe and the US, based on TPN's consistent call for strategic 'linkage' between transatlantic political, economic and security interests.

Political

Strong transatlantic partnership can only be built on common global interests and agreed purposes, as well as willingness to build on the lessons of past experience (particularly Iraq). Full partnership requires a strong and effective EU, but the EU must not attempt to pursue a strategy of geopolitical opposition to the US which can only fail. We must improve political dialogue and understanding.

Economic

Transatlantic economic relations are embedded in the broader political relationship. The world's two largest economic players can deal with each other as equals. Our growing bilateral economic interpenetration must be further developed through approximation of market conditions where possible. Our broader purpose must be to spur global economic growth and development as part of our long-term strategy for a secure and democratic world.

Defence and security

Asymmetry in political and operational capacity remains acute. The potential for future security partnership will depend on Europe's willingness to invest in relevant military capability progressively over an extended period of time. The European political will to do this remains unclear. In the meantime, we must continue to reshape NATO, driven by practical responses to real world conditions, further clarify the NATO/EU relationship, and pursue integration of transatlantic defence industries and markets.

Institutions

Americans may be seen to value institutions for what they can do, Europeans for their durability and continuity. We will need to adapt the existing institutional framework to take account of the rapid evolution of common purposes and priorities. Where the EU has developed its competence and ability to act, it offers the US a more efficient partner interface for effective cooperation. International institutions also need to be reviewed.

1. Political

Emerging points of consensus

A strong transatlantic partnership can only be built in the context of:

- Common global interests and agreed purposes in a longer-term framework.
- Close linkage between political, economic and defence and security collaboration.
- A strong and effective EU. But the EU must not attempt to pursue its own further political development in a strategy of geopolitical opposition to the US, which can only fail.
- Partnership strategy must therefore reflect the present and foreseeable degree of symmetry or asymmetry in US/EU competences and capabilities. Viewed in this light:

o The economic foundations for EU/US partnership are strong.
o The defence and security foundations for partnership are weak and depend on developments on the EU side.
o Potential for extended political partnership now exists in areas of vital common interest. These need to be pursued with enhanced political dialogue at all levels.
• Willingness on both sides to build on the lessons of past experience (particularly Iraq).

Possible actions

• Identify bold, practical steps for rebuilding collaborative trust and momentum, inscribed in the pursuit of longer-term common purposes. More specifically, create a long-term collaborative framework and action plan for the war on terrorism, based on broad coalitions of linked interest.
• Shift the emphasis from a transatlantic 'community of values' to a transatlantic 'community of action'. Develop collaborative strategy and action for:
    o post-conflict cooperation in Afghanistan and Iraq
    o relations with the Arab world
    o a renewed Middle East peace process
    o North Korea
    o infectious diseases
    o nuclear proliferation
    o integration of Russia into the family of democracies.
• Measure/articulate the real *value* of the transatlantic relationship to each partner, and highlight/build on common interests and purposes. Open our domestic political processes to each other, listen to each other, and do not reflexively criticize or ignore each other's views.

2. Economic

Emerging points of consensus

Transatlantic economic relations are clearly embedded in, and sensitive to, the broader political relationship. Moreover, the US and EU are and will remain the world's two largest economic players, able to deal with each other as equals – a necessary condition for effective partnership. Beyond that, joint economic action must in future serve – and be seen to serve – the most central political priorities of both partners. Therefore:

- *Our vast and growing bilateral economic interpenetration* must be further developed and linked to the effort to help stabilize and strengthen our broader relationship;
- *Common global economic interests and joint action* must provide the broader strategic framework, focus and motor for the economic dimension of future transatlantic partnership. The driver must be a joint leadership commitment to spur sustainable worldwide economic growth and development, as part of a broader common long-term strategy for a secure and democratic world.

Possible actions – bilateral

- Give much greater prominence to the breadth and depth of trans-atlantic economic interpenetration, particularly its spectacular growth over the past decade.
- To facilitate the next phase of development (and counter possible conflict from 'extraterritorial' effects), pursue the approximation of Atlantic zone business and market conditions with an agenda and timetable for step-by-step EU/US joint policy development and action in the following areas:
  o financial services and capital markets
  o aviation
  o the digital economy
  o competition policy
  o the ethical dimension of trade
  o performance of regulatory systems.
- Reinvent the Transatlantic Business Dialogue (TABD) to better serve its multiple constituencies and purposes, as a key instrument for economic partnership.

Possible actions – global

- To stimulate global growth and integration of the developing world into the global system, and to provide stronger joint leadership for:
  o the Doha Development Round
  o the OECD (Organization for Economic Cooperation and Development) Policy Agenda for Growth.
- Jointly reassess EU and US development aid (and humanitarian assistance) strategy and instrumentality (including Bretton Woods institutions), with particular focus on performance and complementarity.
- Intensify efforts to enhance regulatory cooperation, and the stability of global financial markets.

3. Defence and security

Emerging points of consensus

Transatlantic asymmetry in military capacity remains acute, and will limit for the foreseeable future politically viable options for linking this dimension into a strategy for full EU/US partnership. There is also asymmetry at the level of strategic planning capability, concept and geopolitical focus.

With a reconfiguration of US forces in Europe under review, the goals of European security policy need to be more clearly defined. The potential for future security partnership with the US in given areas will depend on Europe's willingness to invest in relevant military capability progressively over an extended period of time. The European political will to do this remains unclear.

Possible actions

- Continue to redefine and reshape NATO, based on the Prague Summit agenda but primarily driven by practical responses to real world conditions (currently centred on a NATO role in Afghanistan, and possibly Iraq).
- Further develop the NATO/EU interface, while continuing to clarify respective future roles and capabilities in the military sphere.
- Pursue integration of transatlantic defence industries and markets, including a policy and regulatory framework allowing for the transatlantic flow of defence technologies.

4. Institutions

Emerging points of consensus

Americans may be seen to value institutions for what they can do, Europeans for their durability and continuity. We will need to adapt the existing institutional framework to take account of the rapid evolution of common purposes and priorities. Where the EU has developed its competence and ability to act, it offers the US a more efficient partner interface for effective cooperation.

Institutions will need to provide an adequate but flexible framework for managing this evolution. It will be particularly important to create ways to link the various processes and dialogues, which is the only practical way to achieve the 'linkage' necessary to drive the development of full transatlantic partnership.

Possible actions

- Restructure the annual TA summit (and process) to provide strategic direction and impetus to the TA partnership agenda; it must not focus on minutiae.
- Create an institutional structure for ongoing transatlantic strategic discussion, including for example a prototype annual 'Transatlantic Assembly' to initiate a genuine 'Legislators' Dialogue'.
- Review international institutions, including the UN Security Council, G-8 and OECD.

Note

1. www.tpnonline.org

24
Agenda for a New Transatlantic Relationship: the EU's To-Do List

Elmar Brok

Introduction

The inability of the Europeans to define a common position with regard to the Iraq conflict has ruthlessly exposed the EU's shortcomings:

- In the EU, recourse to intergovernmental action still gains the upper hand.
- It would be possible to continue to develop joint structures and institutions in Brussels dedicated to greater coordination; however, these will merely perform a decorative function unless the member states demonstrate the political will to pursue joint action.
- It is clear that common values that could serve to underpin a common foreign policy are missing in the case of both current and future EU member states.

As a result, EU behaviour in the context of international alliances, especially in the United Nations and NATO, is decidedly erratic.

The EU is facing its most serious crisis of the last decade. Now the all-important questions are: Will the EU be able to return to the integration track and develop a new dynamism, and will it also be able to fine back to a constructive partnership with the US?

In spite of the damage that has been done, there is still both potential and necessity for developing a renewed transatlantic partnership for the third millennium.

A stronger Europe as a condition for the survival of NATO

As recently reaffirmed by the European Parliament, NATO remains not only a fundamental guarantee for Euro-Atlantic stability and security, but also the essential framework for coalition operations. Cooperation within the Atlantic Alliance continues to be of decisive importance for security and stability in the Euro-Atlantic region, and it is in the interest of the transatlantic partnership to strengthen NATO's capabilities and European defence. Therefore, in the aftermath of the Iraq war NATO must once again become the main framework for addressing security questions that affect all Alliance members. A strategy aimed at forming 'coalitions of the willing', mainly with countries outside the Alliance, must be forestalled.

The following questions must now be addressed among the partners:

- What purpose does the Atlantic Alliance serve?
- How should it be structured, and what means should be placed at its disposal?

NATO reform initiatives must include:

- Military restructuring: This must take into account not so much new technologies but the way in which force can be exercised in a much more efficient and much less costly way.
- Institutional reform: Efforts in this regard should comprise the 400 committees as well as structures in Brussels more generally.

Enhancing CFSP (Common Foreign and Security Policy) and ESDP (European Security and Defence Policy) as the best way of reinforcing NATO

The US will only accept the EU as a partner in international affairs if the Europeans will be able to develop their capabilities in the field of foreign and security policy. The EU therefore faces a threefold challenge:

(1) Coherent performance at home and abroad

The EU must not only meet political and economic expectations within the Union vis-à-vis intergovernmental decisions, it must also project an image of unity to the outside world, and especially to the only remaining superpower, the US. This is particularly important in areas in which different approaches to the issue of collective security seem to exist on both sides of the Atlantic, such as the non-proliferation of weapons of mass destruction, missile defence systems and the role of the United Nations and the Security Council. Balanced cooperation between the

EU and the USA in the field of external relations is vital to solve the major conflicts in the world and to develop conflict prevention strategies, such as the positive results achieved in joint post-war actions in the Balkans.

(2) Strategic thought and action

The EU must overcome the present crisis concerning the formulation of a CFSP and begin to make a contribution to the development of strategic answers to global questions of international and security policy. A necessary precondition would be to define the vital political and security interests of the Union. These should be mapped out in a *European Security Doctrine*, which would take into account the National Security Doctrine of the US. This would also include the Union's position on issues which the US seems to interpret differently. The two major ones are the legitimacy of the use of military force in the absence of a UN mandate and the concept of pre-emptive strikes.

(3) A decisive step forward towards a genuine and autonomous CFSP

A constitution cannot compensate the lack of political will on the part of member states, but it can create a framework in which a common will can be more efficiently created. Therefore, it should be a constitutional duty of all members of the EU to define and observe the common interest in all foreign and security policy matters, and to subject all such matters to a common institutional process at the level of the Union, allowing for joint decisions and permanent consultations in the overall interest of the Union. The EU needs to recognize the indivisibility of its security. It needs to tackle the enormous duplication that exists in territorial defence. It needs to reform its institutions (Council and Commission), establish the position of a EU minister for foreign affairs, come to majority voting on non-military matters, pool its defence resources and reinvest the resources freed up thereby in those areas where a more urgent need exists. Therefore the EU also needs its own budget for security and defence policy.

Political issues first in the aftermath of 11 September 2001

Making pursuit of *common global interests* (spread of democracy, modern governance, open societies and markets, sustainable economies, freedom of expression, fundamental human rights and respect for the rule of law around the world) should be the central defining political purpose of the renewed transatlantic partnership. Furthermore, the concept of close *linkage,* whereby aspects of political, economic, and defence and security collaboration are closely tied together, remains a cornerstone of any future relationship.

Two possible initiatives seem of the utmost importance and are therefore strongly recommended:

(a) We should create a long-term collaborative framework and 'action plan for the war on terrorism'. International terrorism must be combated firmly, not only by military means, but above all by addressing the roots of the tremendous political, social, economic and ecological problems of today's world.

(b) We should also promote a 'transatlantic community of action' by developing collaborative strategy and action for, at least, the following cases: post-conflict cooperation in Afghanistan and Iraq; relations with the Arab world; the Middle East peace process; North Korea; infectious diseases; nuclear proliferation; and the integration of Russia into the family of democracies.

Overcoming the threat by economic strength and joint action in the framework of a transatlantic marketplace

The degree of transatlantic interdependence and the potential of future cooperation are nowhere more visible than in economic relations. Economically, Europe and the USA are the two most closely bound regions in the world.

Already, a large proportion of bilateral trade takes place free of any restrictions, but major exceptions remain, such as non-tariff trade barriers. This is why Americans and Europeans should agree on a continuous liberalization initiative designed to accelerate the implementation of World Trade Organization rulings which, in the context of a renewed partnership and as a long term objective, could even lead to the establishment of a 'transatlantic marketplace' guaranteeing the free movement of goods, capital, services and persons. However, it seems more urgent now to pursue the development of business and market conditions in the Atlantic zone by developing joint actions at least in the following areas: financial services and capital markets; aviation; the digital economy; competition policy; the ethical dimension of trade; and the performance of regulatory systems.

Acting together on other important global challenges

Developing solutions to global challenges – such as the environment, migration or social and ethnic conflicts – is not about preserving the power of security policy. Anyone who wants to make a real contribution requires partners and coalitions. Together, Europe and the United States represent the right critical mass. Therefore, responding in the same direction to important global challenges such as the issue of global warming (i.e. ratifying and implementing the minimum standards of the Kyoto Protocol) and the issue of global justice (i.e. the functioning of the International Criminal Court) are issues which certainly deserve preferential treatment in the reinforcement of transatlantic relations.

Finally, it seems particularly important to jointly reassess EU and US development aid and humanitarian assistance strategies and instruments (including Bretton Woods institutions), focusing in particular on performance and complementarity.

Expanding the existing dialogue in the renewed transatlantic partnership

First of all, the annual EU–US Summit should be restructured (as well as the process itself) to provide strategic direction and impetus to the transatlantic agenda. In addition, the political dialogue within the partnership should be enhanced at all levels. As far as the strengthening of the parliamentary involvement in the process is concerned, the following improvements should be introduced:

- given their respective competencies, especially in the field of trade and foreign relations, the president of the European Parliament and the speaker of the US Congress should be involved in EU–US Summits, when they are organized at presidential level;
- in addition, the political association with legislators (TLD) should consist in a formal session with the senior level group prior to each summit; this has only happened once under the NTA (New Transatlantic Agenda) in Washington in May 1999;
- as a final step, the existing inter-parliamentary exchange should be gradually transformed into a de facto 'transatlantic assembly'.

Moreover:

- the Transatlantic Legislators' Dialogue (TLD) should be fully activated and an early warning system should immediately put in place between the two sides;
- the Transatlantic Business Dialogue (TABD), should reorganize its management structures, refocus its goals and streamline its activities, and the Transatlantic Economic Partnership (TEP) should be renewed;
- Other transatlantic dialogues such as the Transatlantic Consumer Dialogue (TACD), the Transatlantic Labour Dialogue (TALD) and the Transatlantic Environment Dialogue (TAED) should finally become effective and coherent.

Defining civil society as an anchor

Besides the importance of political and economic relations on the top level, the ties between the civil societies on both sides of the Atlantic will remain the basis for the transatlantic relationship. But the network that was built up after the Second World War has lost over the last years its spirit and speed. The old ties are getting more and more fragile. Clear indicators are for instance the lack of interest of American politicians in European affairs. In order to avoid the relationship becoming driven by a lack of understanding and knowledge on both sides, the EU must support – even financially – the exchange of young leaders from relevant parts of society (politics, economy, media, art) to guarantee that mutual understanding between partners can grow and can be developed from generation to generation.

The reconstruction of Iraq as a first case study of a renewed transatlantic partnership

As a matter of priority, the EU must develop an agenda for Iraq in order to demonstrate its ability to provide a comprehensive approach to the US plans for reconstruction of the country, based on the following guidelines:

- The transition process should be overseen by a multinational task force under the auspices of the UN and include domestic actors at the earliest possible stage.
- The establishment of an inclusive and accountable political system in Iraq requires first and foremost the distribution of the oil revenue among several centres of power.

- An effective approach to Iraq's problems requires a regional dimension. Iraq should be integrated gradually in a security system which includes Iran and other Gulf states and, at the same time, create a free trade zone with its Arab neighbours to the west with whom it shares important economic and cultural ties.
- Cohesive action by the EU and its member countries requires basic agreement on long-term goals in order to be effective. A common EU approach on Iraq may kick-start a more comprehensive approach for the Middle East. The impact of EU policies and institutions on long-term transformation and democratization processes, especially in Southern and Eastern Europe, is well documented and generally acknowledged. The Union's approach of fostering structural change through trade liberalization, transnational communication and regional integration, based on the success of its own model, is well established. Europe may not be a superpower, but it certainly is a project.

Conclusions: first of all, the Union must put its own house in order

1. The EU will only be recognized as a partner if it can accompany its economic strength with a strong position in external relations. This requires:

   - *extension of QMV* (qualified majority voting) in the Council to services in external trade;
   - QMV in foreign and security policy and enhanced cooperation in defence policy, as well as stronger military capabilities which would be complementary to NATO.

The goal must be to make the EU and its member states so interesting as partners that the United States needs to include the Europeans in strategic planning within and outside NATO. Europe will not be called upon to follow suit.

A project for a transatlantic marketplace is the best way of strengthening the political dialogue

2. The EU and the US have treaties and agreements with almost all states in the world, but not with each other. As NATO is no longer sufficient as the unique common institution, *a new common*

framework has to be created in economic and trade policy – without endangering the multilateral institutions – in order to solve questions of dispute but also to further common interests:

- EU/USA relations need a *project*, which will enhance the political discussion. The proposal for a transatlantic marketplace could be such a project, even if not immediately achieved,
- TABD has to be organized in such a way that enterprises may serve also as reinforced bridging elements.

A bigger implication of the Congress as a fundamental element to enhance the whole transatlantic process

- Only with a wider implication at all levels of the Congress, the EP and national parliaments will it be possible to really enhance the whole process. It has therefore become urgent now to seek and develop new formulae for doing so. For example, the Transatlantic Legislators' Dialogue (TLD) must be strengthened at an early stage of legislation.
- Commission and Council must start an information campaign in Congress. An EU/US treaty for a transatlantic marketplace should involve Congress.
- The issue-by-issue approach will only have success if an overall framework is an essential part of the strategy. Experiences of the last decade show that new questions arise faster than old ones are solved. The present mechanism does not have the right psychological effect to keep the peoples of both sides of the Atlantic Ocean together.

25

Europe and the United States face the Challenges of the New Century

Kemal Dervis

There have been moments of transatlantic tension before. But recent events reflect a deeper and more far-reaching challenge than has been previously experienced. The fundamental changes in the international system that the world has experienced since the fall of the Berlin Wall and the accelerating pace of globalization, with its threats and opportunities, require new thinking and decisive actions.

What are the basic 'stylized facts' that define the new reality?

- Europe is no longer divided by the Iron Curtain and is no longer threatened from the East. It no longer needs American protection the way it did until the 1990s.
- Nonetheless the world remains a dangerous place, as was driven home to all of us by the terrible tragedy of 11 September. Globalization increases the potentially catastrophic dangers from terror, organized crime, contagious diseases and environmental degradation. The world economy also remains fragile with a widening gap between the richest and the poorest and between expectations and actual achievements, even in the advanced countries. Global interdependence has increased the potential benefits from the coordination and joint management of global public goods and bads.
- The United States has, and for decades will continue to have, overwhelming military superiority compared to any potential competitor. Europe's gross domestic product (GDP) will be larger than that of the United States, but the United States *is* 'united' while Europe is *debating* the degree of cohesion it wants to develop in foreign and security policy. The United States will be in a position to project power worldwide and to block any development of which it does not approve in the domain of international security or economic architecture.

- Despite this strength, however, the world has become far too complex for the United States to be able to 'manage' globalization successfully on its own. To be effective, US leadership has to be able to count on the active cooperation of other major players, because US economic resources alone cannot suffice and in today's world, thankfully, there is need for a sense of moral and democratic legitimacy. Television, the Internet and the progress of democratic and value-based politics constrain the use of power.

If these are the 'stylized facts', some key reforms are needed in the international institutional architecture.

Greater European cohesion in terms of coordinated economic, foreign and security policies would contribute to greater overall stability in the international system, provided the aim of such cohesion is to improve the world and guard against dangers, rather than just counter the United States. The European Union would take major steps forward by adopting some of the key proposals backed by a large majority of the members of the European Convention, such as the election of the European Commission's President by the European Parliament, and establishing the office of a European foreign minister who is also a member of the European Commission. In my view there should also be a more direct form of European taxation to finance the budget of the Union.

Despite weaknesses and problems, the United Nations system, including the specialized agencies and the Bretton Woods institutions, is the only source of real legitimacy in the international sphere. But the system needs reform to reflect the realities of 2003 rather than those of the 1940s. The UN Security Council must be restructured if the UN is to remain relevant. The ideal would be for most decisions to be taken by a 'super-majority' of Security Council votes, with votes weighted by population, GDP, resources contributed to the UN system and military capability. The weighting would result in a union of the United States and the European Union, as a Union having veto power. The vote of the Union should be determined by a qualified majority of the European Council. Russia and China would retain their permanent seats but would lose their individual veto power, as would France and the United Kingdom, to allow the system to function. To make this happen, Europe and the United States together should be ready to press very hard for reform, and those unwilling to cooperate would face the possibility of being excluded altogether. The fact is that if Europe wants to make the UN more capable of handling crises, the UN must be reformed in the general direction indicated above, with the cooperation of the United States.

European common defence policy should be strengthened, but NATO should remain the basic joint defence framework for the US and the EU. NATO's mandate can change and expand to reflect the fundamental change in the nature of the threat faced by the countries in Europe and North America. It should include cooperation with all other nations who want to contribute to a more peaceful and safer world, and who want to help enforce decisions of the UN Security Council when needed. NATO taking over the command of the international forces in Afghanistan has been an appropriate step in the required direction.

A key task for both the UN and NATO will be to bring lasting peace and development to the Eastern Mediterranean and the Balkans, which remain a source of instability and vulnerability for the world as a whole and Europe in particular. The misunderstanding and tension that exists between large parts of the Moslem world and the American and European 'West' is a threat to all. A democratic, strong and prosperous Turkey, fully anchored and integrated into Europe, would make a crucial contribution to overcoming the potential cultural divide and securing peace in the region.

Europe should promote the creation of an 'Economic and Social Security Council' within the United Nations system to oversee the fight against poverty, to help coordinate economic and foreign aid policies, to fight and prevent the spread of disease and to preserve the environment. The Bretton Woods institutions and the UN's specialized agencies should remain the operational branch of the international economic system, but they should benefit from the legitimizing umbrella of a strengthened and restructured United Nations, with the US and Europe in full partnership, driving the reforms forward. The Bretton Woods institutions are valuable and quite effective instruments for the world community. But for the programmes they support to have more domestic support and more lasting impact, they must be perceived as being imbedded in a more legitimate worldwide structure which has greater support from the general public.

Europe and the United States should turn their joint attention and energies to such difficult but necessary reforms rather than undermining each other within the old institutional architecture which no longer reflects current realities, and within which it is impossible to create the sense of purpose and legitimacy that the world needs so much. The construction of Europe has already been, despite temporary setbacks, a wonderful example of how to overcome a history of conflict and build a future of cooperation and understanding. It is time for Europe to show that it can lead the whole world with ideas and that it has the courage to set examples. France and Germany gave up their currencies for the sake of a stronger and more prosperous Europe. France and the UK should be willing to give up their Security Council veto for the sake of a stronger and better United Nations. In the end, peace and prosperity can only be secured if the world functions as a system based on ethical values, participation and democratic legitimacy. Europe can lead if it lives by these values and supports them globally. At this time of crisis but also promise, it should invite the United States into a new partnership appropriate to the twenty-first century.

26
Transatlantic Relations: the EU Stance

John Bruton

We must get a firm grip on two fundamentals.

Firstly, the economic relationship between the European Union and the US is by far the most important in the entire world.

For example, European investment in Texas alone is responsible for 233,000 jobs and is greater than all US investment in Japan. And trade figures underestimate the importance of this relationship because they don't account for sales by European-owned affiliates in the United States and vice versa. This economic relationship is vital to jobs on both sides of the Atlantic, so we have no choice but to manage it politically. We should also keep these trade disputes in perspective. The areas of trade in which there are currently EU/US disputes amount to less than 1 per cent of the total.

Secondly, the United States will not take Europe seriously unless Europe gets its own act together on all relevant issues, including defence. Europe needs to speak with one voice. It is in the interest of the United States that Europe does this, because the United States needs to manage its trading and security relationship with Europe in a coherent and predictable way. It is easier to do this with one interlocutor than with several.

What must we do now?

Security questions

We must recognize that the new United States doctrine of preventive or pre-emptive wars is a big and potentially dangerous departure from existing norms of inter-state behaviour. But the concerns the United States has about the proliferation of weapons of mass destruction and the threat of global terrorism are genuine and predate the 11 September terrorist attacks. United States public opinion does not realize how much the European Union has already done in the battle against international terrorism, both by legal changes and by the sharing of intelligence. Nor does it fully understand the limitations of purely military power in the war against terrorism, even though this is the kind of power in which the United States is so pre-eminent.

The European Union should establish a comprehensive and formalized dialogue with the United States on the linked questions of pre-emptive wars, weapons of mass destruction and the battle against terrorism. A specific strand to the transatlantic dialogue should be established for these three issues. This strand should involve government-to-government contact, as well as contact between people in the academic and security communities. The aim should be to develop a new, predictable, well-understood and intellectually sustainable doctrine for managing the post-11 September world, with understood rules about when war is justified and when it is not. This should inform a joint EU/US approach to the United Nations.

Public opinion

Europe must recognize that it needs, after recent events, to mend its fences with large segments of the US population. United States public opinion does not understand the nature of the European Union or its achievements. The EU, as such, has little contact with the West, the South and the Midwest of the United States. European studies departments are mainly to be found in East Coast Universities.

The Israel/Palestine dispute causes strain in EU–US relations. It is important for Europeans to recognize the influence of evangelical Christianity on United States public opinion and particularly on the Republican party. Evangelicals believe that the second coming of Jesus Christ can only occur once the Jewish people have been converted to Christianity. Therefore evangelicals have special religious interest in the preservation of the state of Israel. This is a reality which must be understood by European policymakers.

Divergent views on many issues arise from the fact that Europeans and Americans have different attitudes to science and to problem-solving capacities generally. Europeans are pessimistic about both. Americans are optimistic. This leads us to react differently to the same issue.

To promote better understanding, the European Union should intensify its visitor programmes for young Americans, selecting young

Americans, of all religious persuasions, who are likely to rise to leadership positions, with a particular emphasis on people from the West, the Midwest and the South.

European Union spokespeople should undertake a concerted programme of appearances in the media and at public events in the United States to explain what the Union is about and to explore the source of recent differences and misunderstandings. United States audiences are open-minded, and they are more willing to have their preconceptions challenged than are some on this side of the Atlantic.

27

After Iraq: Permanent Transatlantic Tensions

Ted Galen Carpenter

America's longtime European allies have become increasingly disturbed by aspects of the Bush administration's foreign policy. Criticisms of US actions are most pronounced in France and Germany, the core of what US Secretary of Defence Donald Rumsfeld derisively refers to as 'old Europe'. Disagreements about Washington's drive to war against Iraq have been the most acute sources of transatlantic tensions, but they are hardly the only ones. Indeed, early in President Bush's term, acrimonious disputes arose between the United States and the leading European Union countries over such issues as the Kyoto Protocol on the environment, the international criminal court, and ballistic missile defence. The gap between US and European policy preferences became even more pronounced following the issuance of the Bush administration's new national security strategy document in September 2002, with its emphasis on 'pre-emptive action'.

Those transatlantic tensions are not likely to go away merely because the guns in Iraq fall silent. One especially potent source of animosity will occur if the administration decides that pre-emptive action is justified in cases other than Iraq. There are worrisome signs. Not only did the new national security strategy document point to that course, but in the years before they joined the Bush administration, key officials were on record as arguing that Iran was as dangerous (if not more dangerous) to regional and global peace than was Iraq. This antipathy suggests that, with Saddam Hussein's regime ousted from power, the United States may turn its attentions toward the Islamic fundamentalist regime in Tehran.

Iranian leaders have ample reason to worry about US intentions. Not only did President Bush explicitly include Iran in the 'axis of evil' in his January 2002 State of the Union address, but US military deploy-

ments since the 11 September 2001 terrorist attacks must seem menac-
ing from an Iranian perspective. It would not require an abundance of
paranoia in Tehran to conclude that the United States is carrying out
an encirclement strategy and that Iran is next on Washington's list of
rogue state targets.

The logic of the 'Bush doctrine' outlined in the national security
strategy suggests that a war against Iran is a serious possibility in the
next few years. In addition, the doctrine increases the risk of tense,
highly confrontational relations with such countries as Syria and Saudi
Arabia. The former has long been regarded by many in the American
foreign policy community as a rogue state, and negative attitudes
toward the latter have soared in the months since 11 September as
evidence mounts about Saudi flirtation (financial and otherwise) with
Islamic extremist forces. Indeed, some members of the American foreign policy community now argue openly that Saudi Arabia is part of
the Islamic terrorist threat and that the desert kingdom should be targeted for military action. Although the Bush administration has not
embraced that view, relations between Washington and Riyadh have
grown noticeably cooler in recent months. A hostile relationship
between the United States and its nominal ally can no longer be ruled
out.

The application of the Bush doctrine in the Middle East has major
implications for the transatlantic relationship. It is increasingly evident
that the Bush administration wants – and expects – its European allies
to be junior partners in its interventionist ventures throughout that
region. Washington's strong lobbying effort to create a rapid response
force within NATO is clear evidence of that goal. Moreover, in the final
months of 2002 and the initial weeks of 2003, Washington pressed the
NATO allies to participate in the coming military campaign against
Iraq. True, the United States did not expect the Europeans to provide
large numbers of combat forces for the conquest of Iraq. Rather,
Washington's principal objective was to have a European military presence in the postwar phase of garrisoning and stabilizing the country.
US officials also hope that the NATO members will contribute financially and otherwise to the postwar nation-building task in Iraq.

Washington's enthusiasm for a rapid response force reflects the
expectation that it will be needed for other interventions in the Middle
East in the coming years. The concept of a NATO rapid response force
is not new, nor is the belief that the Alliance's primary focus in the
twenty-first century should be on 'out of area' security missions – that
is, missions outside Europe. In an important article in the *New York*

Times in 1997, former secretary of state Warren Christopher and former secretary of defence William Perry suggested that NATO be transformed into an instrument for the projection of force wherever in the world the West's 'collective interests' were imperiled. In a moment of exuberance, Secretary of State Madeleine Albright urged that NATO become a force for peace 'from the Middle East to Central Africa'. The Clinton administration presented a proposal in late 1998 to have NATO play an active role in countering the proliferation of weapons of mass destruction (WMD) – the principal rationale for the hardline US policy toward Iraq. It was as clear at the time as it is today that the probable arenas for WMD proliferation lie far beyond Europe.

Washington's policy is a snare for the Europeans. The successful effort to have NATO agree to create a rapid response force, the continuing US lobbying campaign to have the Alliance play a role in Iraq, and the desire of the Bush administration to make the war against terrorism the *raison d'être* for NATO in the twenty-first century are initiatives that point to the same policy goal. Washington is expecting the European allies to sign on as junior partners to implement *US* policies in the Muslim world.

Therein lies the major problem. The European members of NATO often disagree with the substance of US policy in that part of the world. It is not coincidental that, with the partial exception of Great Britain, the key EU governments expressed reservations about the policy the United States pursued toward Iraq. European publics seemed even more hostile than their governments toward that policy.

Iran threatens to become the next arena for transatlantic squabbling. Washington has long pursued a hardline policy toward Iran, seeking to isolate that country and subject it to economic sanctions. America's NATO allies have been monumentally unenthusiastic about that approach, believing it to be counterproductive. Such key European powers as France and Germany favour a strategy of engagement with Iran, and both countries have developed thriving economic relationships with the Islamic republic. Chris Patten, the EU's commissioner for external affairs, urged the United States to emulate the EU's policy of engagement with Iran. 'I hope both Tehran and Washington take into account the developing relations between Tehran and the EU and accept it as a pattern for developing relations with each other,' he said.

Given the differences between the United States and the EU on this issue, forming a common NATO strategy towards Iran would verge on being impossible. This is especially true if the United States, after finishing military operations against Iraq, targets Iran for military coercion as another member of the axis of evil. Many of the European allies have been reluctant to go along with Washington's policy toward Iraq; they might well join France and Germany and erupt in open rebellion if the United States sought to apply a similar policy against Iran.

If policy disagreements regarding Iraq and Iran were not enough to make transatlantic unity problematic concerning the Middle East, there are profound US–European differences about the Israeli-Palestinian dispute. European governments and publics view US policy as horridly one-sided in favour of Israel. In late 2002 EU foreign ministers issued a strong statement demanding a freeze on Israeli settlements on Palestinian land, while Washington's pronouncements on the settlements issue have been noticeably tepid. US policymakers and opinion leaders, for their part, regard the European countries as dangerously pro-Palestinian. Some members of the American opinion elite even believe they detect a whiff of European anti-Semitism regarding the Israeli-Palestinian conflict.

The divergence of US perspectives and interests should not come as a surprise. Indeed, it may be surprising that the trappings of policy unity lasted as long as they did once the Cold War came to an end. Nearly a decade ago, Owen Harries, the editor of one of America's leading foreign policy journals, wrote presciently that the concept of a unified West was dubious. Harries pointed out that despite the many common roots of their civilizations, there was little concept of political unity between the United States and Europe before the Second World War. Indeed, each side tended to view the other with contempt. Despite the rhetoric of solidarity by US and European officials and the continued expansion of that quintessential transatlantic institution, NATO, that is a fair description of US and European attitudes toward one another in recent years. It is therefore more than a little likely that relations between the United States and European countries are returning to their 'normal' (i.e., pre-Second World War) pattern.

It is not apparent that such a result can be averted. US policymakers hope that the terrorist threat can play the role of alliance unifier that the Soviet threat did during the Cold War. But there is reason to be pessimistic about this outcome. Although most European governments have cooperated enthusiastically with the United States in tracking down Al Qaeda cells and attempting to disrupt the financial resources of terrorist organizations, they resist Washington's attempt to broaden the definition of the terrorist threat. The divergence of US and European perspectives and interests is likely to intensify regardless of the intentions of statesmen on both sides of the Atlantic.

The European powers face a fundamental choice. One option is to accept the role of America's junior partner in various military and nation-building ventures in the Muslim world. But the Europeans are going to dislike many (perhaps most) of those ventures, and most of the interventions will not serve tangible European interests. In addition, the European powers will have to tolerate an increasingly arrogant 'take it or leave it' attitude on the part of US leaders. (That point became especially evident in January and February 2003 in the lead up to the military confrontation between the United States and Iraq.) Members of the American foreign policy community already speak contemptuously of European military capabilities, and they ask why the United States should take criticism from its allies seriously when those countries add so little to American power. Increasingly, the prevailing attitude will be that if the Europeans wish to support a specific US policy, fine. But if the Europeans choose not to support the policy, it is a matter of no great consequence. Most significantly, the United States will exhibit little willingness to alter any significant aspect of its policies to suit the Europeans. As America's junior partner, the European powers can expect to experience a growing amount of impotent rage as it becomes evident that Washington does not take their criticisms seriously.

European attitudes toward US power have a fatal flaw. Too often, Europeans want an activist United States that will be responsible for global security and take a leading role in resolving Europe's specific security problems, such as the Balkan crises of the 1990s. Yet many of those same Europeans want the United States to defer to the wishes of its allies on key policy issues. They seek a United States that is powerful enough to be hegemonic, but humble enough not to exercise that awesome power unilaterally. In essence, they want the United States to be a tethered superpower. That, however, is an inherently contradictory concept.

If Europe wishes to avoid the fate of being Washington's barely tolerated junior partner, it must choose an alternate course: to build a coherent, cohesive security identity of its own and back it up with serious resources. Both elements are crucial yet difficult to implement.

Developing the necessary cohesion on security issues within the EU would be a daunting task even under the best conditions. But the split that developed between France and Germany on the one side and Britain on the other over US policy toward Iraq has intensified the difficulty. Moreover, the role played by the so-called Vilnius Group – the eight European governments that signed a statement emphasizing solidarity with the United States – has added a new dimension to European disunity. There is little doubt that Washington encouraged (perhaps even suggested) the statement by the Vilnius Group. That is consistent with longstanding US attempts to scupper European efforts to build a coherent security and defence capability that could eventually balance American power. US officials see the new Central and East European members of NATO and the European Union as Washington's proxy votes in both institutions. Overcoming that self-serving meddling by the United States will be one of the great challenges facing the statesmen of 'old Europe' in the coming years.

Building credible military power to back up a common EU foreign and security policy is equally crucial. Unfortunately, the signs are not encouraging. Spending in Germany and other key EU countries is woefully inadequate and continues a downward spiral that began almost as soon as the Cold War came to an end. Those trends must be reversed if the EU hopes to be taken seriously in the realm of security affairs by the United States or anyone else.

Whatever the course the European countries choose, the Cold War era of transatlantic solidarity on security issues is over. The task facing statesmen on both sides of the Atlantic is to manage the ever more frequent disagreements and prevent them from poisoning the entire relationship.

28

Strengthening Transatlantic Relations: Statement for the Informal Meeting of EU Foreign Ministers on Strengthening Transatlantic Relations

Friedbert Pflüger

America remains our friend and partner. The transatlantic community is based on a unique foundation of shared values, similar civil societies and the will to ensure that democracy, human rights, individual freedom and the market economy prevail all over the world. The European Union and the USA are, globally, the economic areas most closely interconnected by trade and investments – and thus also the most highly interdependent.

The transatlantic community can, however, only fulfill its function if it constantly adapts to changing circumstances and challenges. In order to meet the new global challenges, Europe and America need a *common global agenda*. To achieve this, Europeans and Americans must, step by step, create a more efficient mechanism, allowing closer and more continuous consultation and cooperation. Issues on the *common global agenda* should include: the Middle East peace process, the stabilization of Southeast Europe, transformation in the successor states of the Soviet Union, the fight against international terrorism, drug trafficking and organized crime, environmental protection, the non-proliferation of weapons of mass destruction, as well as questions relating to economic growth, the creation of jobs through the dismantling of trade barriers, future provision in the energy sector, the battle against poverty and the reinforcement of the World Trade Organization. Where close cooperation already exists in these areas, it must be intensified.

The value of transatlantic cooperation becomes particularly clear when consultations lead to concrete actions. In addition to combating international terrorism and organized crime together, Europeans and Americans must develop a strategy which enables the more effective stabilization of states suffering from political disintegration and internal conflicts and the elimination of zones where order has broken down and terrorists find a safe haven and breeding ground for their ruthless fanaticism. Programmes designed to prevent children and young people being brought up to embrace hatred and fanaticism must also be a part of this. As in the late 1960s, America and Europe should agree on a common security concept, and again, a dual strategy like the one proposed in the Harmel report is required: in addition to military security, and solidarity in the struggle against terrorism and weapons of mass destruction, Europeans and Americans have a wider political task. They should demonstrate to the countries of the Middle East, the Persian Gulf and Central Asia their willingness to jointly contribute to the stabilization of the region through dialogue and cooperation.

Issues such as combating poverty (joint AIDS projects and technical aid), energy security (joint research projects) and the digital economy (joint measures against cyber crime) also belong on the *common global agenda*. With a view to closer trade and economic cooperation, a joint scientific commission should be set up, within the framework of the WTO or between the EU and USA, to reach binding conclusions on controversial questions of consumer protection; likewise, it is essential to press ahead with the harmonization of anti-trust proceedings.

The opportunities for dialogue must be expanded in order to identify potential transatlantic differences early on. A high degree of transparency in the decision-making processes of executive and legislative bodies allows many disagreements to be settled at an early stage. EU–US summits should once again be held every six months. The effects of legislative and administrative plans on the transatlantic relationship must be assessed at an early point, without in this way granting the other side veto powers. In order to ensure that differences are identified at an early stage, the transatlantic dialogue between our societies – between companies, consumer organizations, employee associations, churches, environmental organizations, universities and think tanks – must also be expanded.

One vital aim with regard to strengthening relations between the EU and the USA must be to revive NATO. Europe can only counter the new threats to its security effectively together with America. Thus,

NATO will have to be the decisive stabilizing force in the conflicts of today and tomorrow. So it is only logical that NATO takes on the leading role in Afghanistan. It was for the same reason that I called, even before the end of the Iraq war, for NATO to take on the leading role, under the auspices of the United Nations, in the tasks of military stabilization in Iraq.

Yet the revival of NATO will only be achieved if Europe increases its efforts to narrow the widening gap between American and European capabilities. The numerous declarations of intent must finally be followed by action. In other words, the EU must actually create the necessary capabilities. It will be crucial that the EU meets its commitment to ensure the planned rapid reaction force is ready for deployment on time. All attempts to establish Europe as a counterweight to the USA should be avoided, though. Europe needs America more than America needs Europe. For Europe will, in the foreseeable future, remain dependent on the USA for essential aspects of its security.

The grave deficits which exist in the area of strategic transport, together with those in the areas of reconnaissance, communication and armaments, must be eliminated. These gaps in capability cannot be bridged through additional financing alone. Defence measures must also be coordinated more closely and potential synergies fully exploited. The needs of the armed forces must be met by a European armaments base which allows efficient production of sufficient quantities, through consolidation of demand and capacities, and avoids the current squandering of resources as the result of products being developed or manufactured in two, or even several, places. Such a European armaments base would then be able to compete against and forge partnerships with the US industry in important fields.

The treaty signed on 27 July 2001 by six EU states, in which they agree to facilitate the work of the European armaments industry and to restructure it, is a step in the right direction. In the future, EU member states are not only to define the tasks of their armed forces jointly, but also to meet jointly the demand for equipment and materials to carry out these tasks. In the future, therefore, EU member states should also coordinate their defence budgets, examining the overall level of finances necessary to perform the joint tasks and create the necessary capabilities, and then the national contributions required for this.

Considerable potential still exists for the exploitation of synergies in the area of European security and defence policy. The 25 future EU member states do not *all* need to have their own fighter wing. It would be far more sensible for the European NATO states to set up three to four air wings, which would then protect all member states, with the big states always making a contribution. Major cost savings could also be achieved by the creation of a joint air transport wing. In addition, where the same armaments systems are in use, joint EU-wide training and maintenance units should be created.

Military deployments will, again and again, be a necessary aspect of the battle against terrorism. The majority of the EU member states, as well as several of the accession candidates, have their own special forces. For the foreseeable future, these forces will continue to be organized at national level. But, in view of the new type of threats which exist, these task forces should not only be strengthened, but prepared on a wide basis for possible joint operations on behalf of the European Union. This requires intensive and sustained joint training. The EU should, if required, have access to special forces with a strength of around three to five thousand men.

29
A Structural Approach to Transatlantic Unity

Alan K. Henrikson

Structures matter. Just as the United States was, to a great extent, 'built' with an eye toward Americans' relationship with Europe, so today is Europe, to a degree, being 'built' with an eye toward Europeans' relationship with the United States. Both have emphasized their 'independence', not just in an abstract sense, but also from each other.

President John F. Kennedy recognized the risk involved in American and European independentism when on July 4, 1962, in Philadelphia, he stated that the United States would be ready for a 'Declaration of Interdependence' with a united Europe, and would even welcome the formation of 'a concrete Atlantic partnership'. One of the strengths of America's political system, he then noted, was its 'checks and balances', by which individuality and plurality could be preserved within a larger unity, even with strong central leadership. This seems applicable to the present situation of the Atlantic partnership – which has not yet been 'concretely' formed.

A 'partnership', by definition, implies the existence of a whole. It is more than an 'alliance'. It is premised on the partners' awareness of belonging to the same community. A transatlantic community does exist, and this has been confirmed by the experience of two World Wars and the Cold War. Americans and Europeans believe in freedom, democracy and the rule of law. In recent decades the economies of North America and Europe have grown so close, in terms of investment as well as trade, that they are almost a single economy. This reality has not been matched in the political realm, however. There collaboration also is needed, especially now that common American and European action is vital for *global* purposes.

The historical successes of the 'constructions' of the United States of America and, during recent decades, the European Union, strongly recommend an effort to give more *form* to transatlantic cooperation. Both James Madison and Jean Monnet understood and themselves impressively demonstrated the power of institutions as factors in community-building.

Could something of a structural nature – following a constructivist approach – be done to 'build' Europe and America closer together? A number of suggestions here are offered.

Starting at the highest – the *ideological-conceptual* – structural level, the governments involved in transatlantic discussions would do well to recall, and perhaps again to articulate, the *purposes* of transatlantic unity in the context of a globalizing world. This is not necessarily to propose drafting an 'Atlantic Charter for the twenty-first Century', but it is to emphasize, by this historical reference, that 'Atlantic' ideals have not been narrow or exclusionary ones. They have been, in principle, universal. The original Atlantic Charter (August 14, 1941) was the basis of the 'Declaration of the United Nations' (January 1, 1942), to which much of the world could and did subscribe.

At the next level – the *organizational* level – there should be formed a transatlantic 'Leadership Group' to set policy priorities, to concert long-term plans and to manage crises as they occur. Henry Kissinger has proposed, along these very lines, an 'Atlantic Steering Group' that would be composed of the United States, the integrated European Union, nations not part of the politically integrated Europe, the Secretary-General of NATO and the EU's High Representative for the Common Foreign and Security Policy.[1] This idea could be further developed. In order to prevent the leadership group from becoming too large for serious discussion, a system of rotation could be built into it, thereby permitting smaller and medium-sized countries to have a real voice in Atlantic leadership, along with the institutional voices of NATO and the EU and, presumably, of all the larger European and North American countries.

The reasons for forming an Atlantic Leadership Group, whose meetings would be of the informal Camp David or Fontainebleau type, are many. Perhaps the most important one would be to *bring together* the NATO and US–EU relationships within the same framework. A second would be to rise above the current system of US–EU meetings, which tend to focus, somewhat bureaucratically, on the 'problem areas' in the relationship. A third would be to enable *all* of the Atlantic partners (if some of them only on a rotational basis) to think grand-strategically, and in so doing to help meet the complaint made by US officials that the United States *must* be prepared to 'go it alone' because it really doesn't know, in advance, whether it can count on European help, even outside the military sphere. A fourth would be to widen the circle of Atlantic decision-making intellectually, for no longer can *international* decisions be made, wisely, at the national level within the political structures of individual countries, even that of the United States. A fifth would be to increase transatlantic 'checks and balances', so that more objective interests are taken into account.

At the level of *economic* cooperation, nothing would be more important, or exemplary, than US–European cooperation in completing the Doha Round of the World Trade Organization. Beyond close cooperation in multilateral trade, serious consideration should be given by Europe to negotiating a comprehensive economic pact with the United States to include its NAFTA partners, Canada and Mexico (with which the EU already has concluded a free trade agreement).

At the *social-cultural* level, a major *global* educational project should be launched. This would involve not only increased educational exchanges directly across the Atlantic, but also European–American *cooperation* in educational exchange and distance learning with developing countries in the Middle East and in other parts of the world. The existing Fulbright and Erasmus programmes are partial models, but a 'whole' model is needed, such as expansion of the proposal for The International Open University under the auspices of the United Nations.

http://www.unicttaskforce.org/perl/matchmaking.pl?id=13

Note

1. (Henry Kissinger, *Does America Need a Foreign Policy?* Simon and Schuster, 2001)

30
Cooperative Ways to Bridge the Gap

George Soros

The rift between Europe and America is real. It is in the interests of both sides to heal it. To this end, it is necessary to find common ground. While it is difficult for some European governments to accept the Bush doctrine of pre-emptive American military action, it should be possible for both sides to agree on the need for pre-emptive action of a non-military kind.

It is not possible to change all the repressive regimes in the world by force. Military intervention must remain the last resort, and it ought to be preceded by pre-emptive action of a constructive nature: resolving conflicts by peaceful means, helping countries to move in the direction of democracy, and enabling democratic countries to flourish.

We must recognize that the greatest source of conflict, poverty and misery in the world is bad governments: repressive, corrupt regimes and failed states. Yet it is difficult to intervene in the internal affairs of other countries because the principle of sovereignty stands in the way. But constructive action that improves the rules that govern the international trading and financial system and which offers countries incentives to improve the governments of nations does not infringe on their sovereignty. They can take the assistance or leave it.

Constructive action is the missing element in the current world order. There are many penalties for bad behaviour – from trade sanctions to military intervention – but few incentives and reinforcements for good behaviour. We need a better balance between rewards and penalties. Developing countries ought to get better access to industrialized countries' markets; countries following sound policies, such as Brazil, ought to be assured of an adequate supply of credit; and there ought to be a genuine attempt to meet the United Nation's millennium goals for poverty reduction.

Europe and America could agree on some common objectives and cooperate in pursuing them. This would help to rebuild the unity of the West, and to reduce tensions between the West and the rest (and Islam in particular).

It may not be possible to agree on the principle of international cooperation in the abstract, because a dominant faction within the Bush administration follows a different ideology: it believes that international relations are relations of power and that legality and legitimacy are mere decorations. Because the US has the power, it can impose its will. It would be hopeless to try to find common ground by challenging this ideology directly. Moreover, there are ideological differences among European governments themselves.

What may be possible is to identify specific goals to which all sides can subscribe. One specific goal on which all parties could cooperate is greater transparency and accountability for revenues derived from natural resources. Many poor countries are rich in natural resources but the revenues are not used for the benefit of the people; they accrue to the benefit of corrupt and repressive regimes. This is a major source of instability in many parts of the world. The British government has sponsored an 'extractive industries transparency initiative' (EITI), which has considerable support from industry and civil society. Countries like Angola, Botswana and Azerbaijan seem prepared to participate at the governmental level. It ought to be possible to gain American support for this initiative. After its experience with Saudi Arabia, the US should be concerned with how Angola develops, given that it will be supplying the US with 3 million barrels of oil a day in a few years' time.

This is but one example where constructive cooperation could pay off. Others could be identified. The US is establishing the 'millennium challenge account'; it has also made a major commitment to fighting HIV-AIDS. These are both areas where Europe can offer to cooperate. Cooperation could help ensure free elections in countries like Kyrgyzstan and Georgia. Smart sanctions could be used against repressive regimes like Zimbabwe, Burma (Myanmar) and Belarus. The Doha round can be saved only by a determination to succeed on all sides. A whole menu of these and other such proposals for areas of cooperation could be prepared for the meeting between the presidents of the EU and of the US, for discussion in addition to the obvious subjects of Iraq, Palestine and North Korea.

31

The 'Washington Consensus' and the EU–US Relationship

Emilios Avgouleas

1. Introduction

The echo of the headline-grabbing news that emerges from the trials and tribulations of the Euro-Atlantic relationship over a number of issues, ranging from NATO's intervention in Kosovo to the recent Iraq crisis, often makes us forget that the US and the European nations were the founders of the International Monetary Fund (IMF) and of the World Bank (hereinafter the 'Bretton Woods twins'). Even when the headlines, and, as a result, the attention of politicians from both sides of the Atlantic turn to economic issues, the agenda tends to be dominated by the threatening noises surrounding the perennially 'imminent' trade war between Washington and Brussels, or the painful negotiations, in the context of the Doha round for the amendment of the WTO Agreements. It has widely escaped the agenda of the EU–US relationship that the Bretton Woods twins were intended to be at the heart of the UN system, and that the US and the EU (along with Japan) are not only their main providers of funds and loans, but also dominate their executive bodies. EU and US policymakers include them, particularly the IMF and its governance structures, in the agenda of their meetings, only in the wake or aftermath of an international economic crisis, in order to evaluate the means used by the IMF for the alleviation of a monetary crisis. Once the crisis has passed, and, along with it, the threat to the stability of the global and regional economic and financial systems, the issue of the reform of the Bretton Woods twins is soon forgotten, at least, up and until the emergence of the next international monetary crisis. In this essay, I shall argue that rethinking and reconceptualizing the economic policies that both institutions dictate to the developing world is a very important issue, and worth taking central stage in the economic agenda of US–EU relations.

2. The Bretton Woods twins and the 'Washington consensus'

As mentioned earlier, the types of economic policy that the IMF and the World Bank dictate and impose on borrower countries, which are often in desperate need of their loans or grants, and the means for the implementation of such policies, take very little space in the discussions developing in the context of the Euro-Atlantic relationship. In addition, academic and political debate surrounding the IMF has mostly focused on whether or not it should become a global lender of last resort, working towards the prevention of credit and financial sector crises in the context of a 'New Global Financial Architecture'.[1] At the same time, the Bretton Woods institutions' insistence on the rapid implementation by borrower countries of a set of economic policies, based on the so-called 'Washington consensus', has, arguably, had the same catastrophic effects on the economies of the countries concerned, and, as a consequence, on the global economy, as has any major monetary crisis experienced in the 1980s or 1990s.

The term 'Washington consensus' is used to signify the neo-liberal policies formulated by the Bretton Woods twins since the early 1980s. Such neo-liberal policies include the fast privatization of state dominated industries, and particularly those relating to the financial, natural resources, manufacturing and agricultural sectors. The shift in the policy direction of the Bretton Woods institutions towards an extreme version of free market economics is usually attributed to the arrival of William Clausen as president and Ann Krueger as chief economist at the World Bank in 1981.[2] In addition, the early 1980s signalled the beginning of a period during which the activities of the two institutions became increasingly 'intertwined', enabling me here to speak (somewhat licentiously) about the common policies pursued by the Bretton Woods twins, although the IMF and the World Bank remain separate, and often rival institutions, with distinct missions. Joseph Stiglitz attributes this increasing overlap in the activities of the two institutions to the IMF taking an imperialistic view of its mission.[3] A number of other factors, however, may have played a role, including the World Bank's loss of direction in the period between 1985 and 1996, and its involvement in infrastructure projects, which caused very strong and widespread criticism with regard to their environmental impact, thus weakening its political status. Whatever the political undercurrents that led to this development, the fact remains that, since the emergence of the Washington consensus, the Bretton Woods twins act as carriers of a certain economic model for developing countries, which is that of free market economy. In this context, they have also become the unchallengeable 'fountains of economic wisdom', using their influence (and money) to 'dictate' the fast implementation of privatization policies, regardless of local political, economic and social conditions.[4] The results of the rapid implementation of these policies, while ignoring the great number of structural and institutional weaknesses that made state intervention necessary in a number of sectors, have been disastrous. They have, *inter alia*, contributed to the genesis and exacerbation of the Russian, Latin American and Asian monetary crises, and have created much hardship for the people of the countries concerned.

Besides the non-favourable social and political conditions prevailing in these countries, which should have impelled the Bretton Woods twins to exercise some restraint in dictating the fast privatization of almost all kinds of economic activity in the countries concerned, at least economic conditions (which in the specific cases constituted clear market failures) should have prevented them from doing so. State subsidies and guarantees were withdrawn from poor farmers, even though it is a widely held economic truth that commercial (banking) credit may not be obtained without good collateral. Valuable state assets were auctioned off, in order to implement the dictated privatization policies, while competition on the demand side, a necessary ingredient of any successful (or even worthwhile) auction, was totally missing. To validate the aforementioned claim, I shall discuss, in the next section of this essay, the results of rapid privatization of priceless state assets in Russia, and some East Asian countries, and, secondly, the hardship experienced currently in Ethiopia, as a result of the IMF's intervention in the structure of its food markets.

3. The plight of Russia and Ethiopia

3.1. The privatization of Russian state assets

In the former communist countries, and, especially, in Russia, the rapid and unprofitable auction of state assets, ranging from media licenses to transfer of ownership rights over gas and oil fields, through legally and politically dubious procedures, led, in most of those countries not only to the creation of new, privately owned monopolies, but also to the creation of a new class of oligarchs or 'plutocrats'. The members of this class had, almost invariably, been party apparatchiks, who were subsequently clothed in the role of free market entrepreneurs and ensured privileged access to the privatization process.[5] Admittedly, the infamous US 'robber barons' of the nineteenth and early twentieth centuries, such as the Rockfellers, the Morgans and the Vanderbilts, must – wherever they are – feel very proud of their modern-day emulators in Russia.

On the other hand, all true believers in free market economics know very well that the most important element of a liberal economy is unfettered competition. Thus, they look with horror at the conglomerates that resulted from the Russian privatizations of state assets, and the enormous concentration of market power in very few hands, at the expense of every notion of economic efficiency. The consequences for the Russian economy have clearly been catastrophic in terms of loss of employment, reduction of the country's GDP and devastating effects on the welfare of Russian people.[6] In addition, the involvement of this new class into politics and the 'running' of the country has led to feuds with the political leadership, and arguably, to a sometimes serious adulteration of the democratic process.[7] Although the Bretton Woods twins were not the initiators of this process of state asset looting, they did not object to the processes that led to them.[8]

Furthermore, in some Asian countries such as Indonesia, the Philippines and Myanmar (Burma), rapid privatization has led to a serious reinforcement of the economic position of tiny market-dominant ethnic minorities, fostering, lamentably, racial hatred and tension among the majority of the population in these countries, who did not have the economic sophistication and the necessary education to benefit from the auctioning off of state assets, and the opening up of national markets.[9]

3.2. The privatization of Ethiopia's grain markets

Another case study that very clearly illustrates the failure of the rapid implementation of economic policies based on the 'Washington consensus' is the privatization of the grain market in Ethiopia. Under pressure from the Bretton Woods' twins, and, especially from the World Bank and some other international donors, the government, during the mid-1990s, withdrew from the grain market, in order to allow the private sector to take its place. According to this view, Ethiopia would be better able to fight famine through the complete withdrawal of the state from the market for agricultural products, including the withdrawal of state guarantees for the granting of private (bank) credit to farmers to buy seeds and modernize their farms.[10] The private sector remained, of course, under-funded, because farmers lacked collateral that would be acceptable to private lenders, and they did not have the organizational skills and experience to create storage, transport and distribution facilities. A good harvest in 2001 caused grain prices to collapse. No government action was undertaken to stabilize prices in the market. Farmers barely covered their costs through selling their harvest to the market. In addition, no provision for the creation of corn stocks was made, as the nascent market could not be expected to undertake food coordination projects on such a large scale. In 2002, because state support that would help farmers cover their losses had been withdrawn (including state guarantees of farmers' bank loans), farmers bought lower quality seeds and no fertilizer, and they worked in much smaller plots of land, as planting corn seeds in the largest part of their land seemed financially disastrous. So the drought that ensued turned the plants to dry dust and the spectacle of famine has re-appeared in this country, bringing to mind pictures of horror coming from Ethiopia in the mid-1980s.[11]

The contribution of the Bretton Woods twins' policies over Ethiopia's current food crisis is not an isolated incident. It comes in addition to the IMF's decision to discontinue grants and loans directed toward this country (devastated by both famine and civil war), because it did not strictly comply with the IMF's dicta in respect of its fiscal and welfare policies.[12]

4. The reform of the Bretton Woods twins and EU–US relations

The paradigms discussed above, clearly illustrate how the premature and enforced application of free market policies based on the 'Washington consensus' have failed, creating serious economic and social hardship. They also make a strong case for the reform both of the economic policies emanating from the Bretton Woods twins and of their role as supervisors, carriers and facilitators of such policies. IMF loans, and its 'conditionality', and World Bank funds should be based on much milder free market policies, which evaluate and consider local economic and social conditions, and the sensitivities of the people in borrower countries. The reform of economic policy suggested here would preserve the long-term beneficial effects to the wealth of nations and welfare of their peoples, that properly implemented free market policies usually achieve, without generating the same amount of hardship and bitterness as policies based on the 'Washington consensus'. Therefore, the reform of the economic policies emanating from the Bretton Woods twins must be regarded as an issue of equal, if not greater, importance with those other issues dominating the agenda of US–EU relations, such as access to capital markets, commercial distribution of genetically modified products and subsidies that farmers receive in the EU and the US, which keep the agricultural products of the developing world away from the table of consumers in the developed world.

5. Conclusion

Only the joint effort of the US and EU – probably over and above the objections that will be posed by the US Treasury, but possibly with the blessings of Congress – may bring about this urgent and sensible change of policy. A programmatic agreement between the EU and US to effect the discussed change in the quality, sensitivity and direction of economic policies emanating from the Bretton Woods twins will facilitate economic development, prevent starvation, and alleviate, to the extent possible, social hardship in the developing world. Consequently, it will assist in combating political instability in the interior of these countries, benefiting international security, and, to some degree, the war against terrorism, the highest item on the US domestic and foreign policy agenda.

Notes

1. S. Fisher, 'On the Need for an International Lender of Last Resort' (1999) 13 *Journal of Economic Perspectives* 85; R. Gilpin, *Global Political Economy: Understanding the International Economic Order* (Princeton: Princeton University Press, 2001), at p. 274. See also Michel Aglietta, 'The International Monetary Fund: Past and Future' & Andrew Gamble, 'Regulating Global Finance: Rival Conceptions of World Order' chapters in Meghnad Desai & Yahya Said (eds), *Global Governance and Financial Crises* (New York: Routledge, 2003).
2. A very authoritative account of this shift in policy is offered by Professor Stiglitz, who served as the chief economist of the World Bank between 1996 and 1999: 'The most dramatic change in these institutions occurred in the 1980s, the era when Ronald Reagan and Margaret Thatcher preached free market ideology ... The IMF and the World Bank became the new missionary institutions, through which these ideas were pushed on the reluctant poor countries that often badly needed their loans and grants.' Joseph E. Stiglitz, *Globalization and its Discontents* (New York: Norton & Co., 2002), at p. 13. [Hereinafter, Stiglitz, *Globalization*].
3. See Stiglitz, *Globalization*, at pp. 13–14.
4. See generally R. Gilpin, *The Challenge of Global Capitalism: the World Economy in the 21st Century* (Princeton, NJ: Princeton University Press, 2000).
5. R. Brady, *Kapitalizm: Russia's Struggle to Free its Economy* (New Haven: Yale University Press, 1999); Stiglitz, *Globalization*, Chapters 5 & 6. See also Amy

Chua, *The World on Fire* (New York: Doubleday, 2003), at pp. 76–9 & 82–94. [Hereinafter, Chua, *The World on Fire*].

6. Russia's GDP in 2000 was 'less than two-thirds of what it was in 1989 ... Ukraine's 2000 GDP is just a third of what it was a decade ago.' See Stiglitz, *Globalization*, at pp. 152–5; J.F. Hough & M.H. Armacost, *The Logic of Economic Reform in Russia* (Washington, DC: Brookings Institution, 2001). The best and most provocative journalistic account of Russian privatizations is offered by Chrystia Freeland in her book: *Sale of the Century: the Inside Story of the Second Russian Revolution* (London: Little, Brown, 2000), which became the subject of extensive discussion in the US and international journalistic and academic circles.

7. M. McFaul, *Russia's Unfinished Revolution: Political Change from Gorbatchev to Putin* (Ithaca, NY: Cornell University Press, 2001). See also Archie Brown & L. Fedorovna Shevstkova (eds), *Gorbachev, Yeltsin and Putin: Political Leadership in Russia's Transition* (Washington, DC: Carnegie Endowment of International Peace, 2001).

8. A. Cohen, 'Russia's Meltdown: Anatomy of the IMF Failure', Heritage Foundation Backgrounders No. 1228, 23. 10. 1998; Stiglitz, *Globalization*, at pp. 157–75.

9. Chua, *The World on Fire*, at pp. 23–47.

10. 'The [World] bank has long prodded poor African governments to privatize their agriculture sectors and abandon any type of farming subsidies.' R. Thurow, 'Ethiopia's Privatization of its Grain Markets Yielded a Bitter Harvest', *The Wall Street Journal*, 1.7.2003, A1, at p. A10. [Hereinafter 'Ethiopia's Bitter Harvest'].

11. Ethiopian farmers describe the causes of crisis in a most persuasive way: ' "First the market failed ... [a]nd then the weather." ... ' "I know that when I cut the size of my farm, I'm contributing to the food shortage ... [b]ut at least I'm not losing money." ' See 'Ethiopia's Bitter Harvest' at p. A10.

12. For the IMF's attitude towards Ethiopia and the policies that the Bretton Woods twins dictated to it see Stiglitz, *Globalization*, at pp. 25–32.

32
Mending the Transatlantic Partnership

David Andrews and Helen Wallace

The transatlantic relationship is at an impasse. The basic premises and reciprocity that once informed this political consensus no longer carry much weight on either side of the Atlantic. Yet the further deterioration of the Atlantic framework would only serve to reinforce American impulses towards unilateralism, to fuel existing European distrust of the US, and to weaken the multilateral framework for international relations that has served both Europe and America so well for the past half century.

The situation is precarious. The political crisis within Europe, and between Europe and the United States, regarding Iraq has not yet affected the economic relations that bind the Atlantic community. But there is no guarantee that this will remain so, and pressures to involve the economic dimension in the ongoing dispute will only grow – with potentially severe and long lasting results.

The immediate aim of European policy must be to keep the economic relationship insulated from the current political crisis. The longer-term aim must be to use the economic relationship as a lever to refashion a more positive political relationship with the United States. Some of the same political genius that facilitated intra-European reconciliation at the end of the Second World War will be needed to reconstruct Europe's relationship with America, including a willingness to think creatively and to harness economic tasks to political ends. Preliminary suggestions towards this end follow.

Analysis

- From its consolidation in the 1950s, the Atlantic partnership has always involved an implicit bargain: Europe extended legitimacy to

US foreign policy activism (or unilateralism) in exchange for US support of arrangements guaranteeing European regional security and prosperity.

- With the end of the Cold War, the circumstances that sustained this arrangement no longer apply, and more recent changes of government and generation in both Europe and the United States unmasked significant underlying strains in the Atlantic framework. The crisis over Iraq merely confirms how great these shifts have been.

- Current American priorities are focused on political, military and hard security issues. The US is preoccupied with terrorism and 'failed states'. Europe is no longer the focus of American geopolitical strategy. Accordingly, many within the Bush administration regard the existing Atlantic framework as an intrusive distraction.

- Conversely, the focus of Europeans is on political economy and soft security issues. As Europeans acutely recognize, economic instability and weakness fuel political instability; European policy priorities tend to reflect this realization. The enlargement of the European Union, a huge foreign and security policy achievement, is a prime example. Enlargement is aimed at overcoming the continent's dangerous and dysfunctional historic divisions. The 'new' Europe is a reworking of the 'old' Europe, not an alternative to it; the challenge for all Europeans is to ensure that this new Europe delivers on its potential.

- Because of these differing priorities and preferences, many Europeans regard the existing transatlantic bargain – trading the legitimization of US foreign policy for assurances of US military protection and limitations on US demands for access to European markets – as no longer suitable. Changed circumstances make acting on this judgement a tempting prospect. The absence of an immediate and credible military threat to Western European security has discounted the value of the American security guarantee, while the introduction of the euro has resulted for some Europeans in a new sense of economic insularity and autonomy.

- With important actors on both sides disenchanted by the Atlantic framework, and while the European and American economies remain bound together by deep ties, the partnership has reached a critical moment. Permitting the political bacillus to spread into economic relations would be disastrous for Europe's peoples, Europe's governments and European integration; preventing this should be a chief policy aim.

Prescription

- *The immediate aim of European policy must be to keep the economic relationship insulated from the current political crisis.*

  The extent to which the Atlantic economies are bound to one another is generally under-appreciated. The US is the EU's major trading partner, and vice versa, but 'trade' represents only about 20 per cent of Atlantic commerce, with far more economic activity passing through foreign affiliates based on opposite sides of the Atlantic. Were the overall Atlantic economic relationship to become endangered, the consequences would be severe. Despite the attention they generate, current US–EU trade disputes account for less than 1 per cent of transatlantic commerce; allowing that proportion to expand would threaten the livelihood of millions of Europeans (and Americans).

- *The longer-term aim must be to use the economic relationship as a lever to reconfigure a positive political relationship with the United States.*

  Upgrading the economic relationship will be the key to restoring the transatlantic relationship. The alternative – a major political initiative – is currently untenable. Any major political proposal floated by the EU at this juncture will undoubtedly be received in Washington with extreme scepticism. Nor is it clear that 'Europe' is in any position to mount a coherent diplomatic initiative in the near future. Nevertheless, creative efforts to develop a new framework for transatlantic relations could be developed within Europe and explored informally with US counterparts, especially if they promised to upgrade the underlying economic relationship. Two such proposals are examined below.

1. Trade and investment

There are a variety of policies that have divided the Atlantic community, and have assumed totem status in Europe (e.g., the Bush administration's rejection of the Kyoto Protocol and the ICC) and vice versa in the US (e.g., European attitudes towards GMOs). Throwing additional resources at these questions is likely only to add fuel to the flames. A preferable alternative is to upgrade the common interest in areas where there is already substantial agreement, or the basis for substantial agreement. One such area is trade and investment policy.

Despite the Bush administration's imposition of tariffs on steel, soft lumber, etc., the overall orientation of US trade policy remains substantially multilateral. Indeed, Washington's payouts to various special interests are consistent with past American trade policy in the run-up to a new multilateral agreement – offering short-term concessions to protectionist industries in order to buy their acceptance of longer-term liberalization. Thus trade policy offers a significant point of entry into American politics, including the politics of the Bush administration; and Commissioner Pascal Lamy's relationship with US Trade Representative Robert Zoellick is an under-exploited aspect of the transatlantic relationship.

This could change if European political authorities offered Lamy greater room to manoeuvre. Currently, leading trade officials on both sides of the Atlantic are intellectually respected but politically exposed actors; despite removing some irritants, neither Lamy nor Zoellick has been able to deliver trade agreement of genuine political consequence. But if European political authorities were to authorize a substantially wider brief for Lamy – easier within the context of the Doha Development Round or in a separate, transatlantic initiative – the transatlantic dynamic could be very positively influenced. An initiative that represented the creation of substantial new economic value might not only produce immediate and substantive effects in the domain of trade and investment, it could elevate the position of Atlanticists within both European and American politics.

Progress is needed on two fronts. First, the EU and the US administration need to give strategic attention to breaking the deadlock in Doha in order to give substance to the issues of global stability that must be at the core of a genuine development round. Second, momentum must be maintained in reinforcing the multilateral and bilateral mechanisms of the trade and investment relationship.

Two recent studies spell out the economic weight of the relationship: Mark Pollack et al., *The Political Economy of the Transatlantic Partnership* (European University Institute, Florence, 2003), and Joseph P. Quinlan, *Drifting Apart or Growing Together: the Primacy of the Transatlantic Economy* (Center for Transatlantic Relations, Washington DC, 2003). Both these reports make specific policy suggestions; the EUI study, for example, addresses ways in which a transatlantic trade dispute resolution mechanism might be framed.

2. Money and growth

The global economy is going through a rough period, with disappointing growth prospects and worrying signals on both sides of the Atlantic. The difficulty of identifying the critical ingredients of and remedies for this situation notwithstanding, some palliatives need to be found to prevent the situation from deteriorating further.

The creation of the euro provides Europe with a powerful tool but, as with trade policy, it is a tool better employed in co-operation with the US than in opposition to it. The single monetary policy, and the resources of the European System of Central Banks, should be deployed as a carrot rather than a stick in the transatlantic relationship, with the offer to respond jointly to problems that threaten the welfare of citizens of both Europe and America.

One such problem is likely to be an eventual correction of the dollar's value. The US current account deficit is large and growing, threatening a precipitous drop in the value of the dollar. While a slow and measured depreciation of the dollar is probably necessary to unwind the US deficit in an orderly fashion, a rapid and disorderly depreciation would be calamitous for both the US and the EU. On the European side, a rapid and substantial rise in the value of the euro against the dollar would snuff out the prospects for early economic recovery in a number of member states. On the US side, Washington has relied on foreign capital inflows to compensate for low domestic savings rates, and a crash in the dollar's value would bring that policy to a rapid end.

This mutual vulnerability creates a common interest in developing arrangements for co-operative exchange market intervention by US authorities and the ESCB (European System of Central Banks). Unfortunately, the positive institutional characteristics that mark the US–EU trade relationship are not replicated in the monetary realm. On the US side, the very existence of a common interest in market intervention arrangements is likely to be denied by political officials in the US Treasury. On the EU side, the relationship between EMU's (European Monetary Union) political authorities and the ESCB are poorly specified in the treaty, and no informal traditions have been developed to compensate for this formal weakness.

Nevertheless, the beginnings of a run on the dollar could provide a rapid education on the benefits of co-operation for both European and American monetary authorities. The content of such arrangements would have to be worked out discreetly by representatives of the ECB and American counterparts from the Fed and UST, but the EU's political authorities should be prepared to suggest (once again, discreetly) their willingness to support such arrangements. And in any event, Europe's national political authorities should resist the temptation to comment publicly on such arrangements except through prescribed EU channels.

Conclusion

There is no quick fix for the deep problems that bedevil the transatlantic partners. Nonetheless it is evident that further drift in the Atlantic relationship, with accumulating tensions and frictions, would be damaging to both sides and would further prejudice much needed efforts to improve global stability. Both the EU and the US need therefore to work urgently on those parts of this agenda where co-operation is possible and could yield practical dividends.

Part VI

The Studies and their Recommendations

33
Recommendations for a New Transatlantic Charta: A Strong Europe – A Partner, Not a Rival to the United States

The Potsdam Centre for Transatlantic Security and Military Affairs: Margarita Mathiopoulos

1. Introduction

The transatlantic relationship is in a serious crisis after the Iraq war. The mood prevailing in Washington these days was elegantly expressed by the US-National Security Advisor Condoleeza Rice: 'Punish the French, ignore the Germans, forgive the Russians.' That alone will not heal the wounds which we inflicted upon each other. From the European perspective two main aspects need to be addressed: First and foremost, Europe must match its own standards with the reality of the twenty-first century's strategic environment, and Europe must speak with one voice on the international stage. This one voice must be backed by credible capabilities. However, we need to recognize that a New World order in the twenty-first century can only be achieved if the nineteenth-century pattern of power politics – recently in fashion again – ceases to guide our thinking.

Accepting these premises, Europe can become both a global player and equal partner to the United States. Only then can an EU–US strategic dialogue take place across the Atlantic that enables both sides to heal the rift and jointly address the global security and non-security challenges of the twenty-first century.

If it is to 'make the world safe for democracy in the twenty-first century', the United States will – despite all its military might – need a strong democratic partner. The Bush administration, with its emphasis on global security, will recognize the attractions of a new contract with Europe if the European Union can live up to its own ambitions of becoming a full fledged international partner. Such partnership would amount to a 'New Transatlantic Charta' in which Americans renew their commitment to remain a European power and Europe pledges to assume its responsibilities in maintaining the European–Atlantic space as a sphere of stability, democracy and progress.

Clearly, we need each other. But forging a new bond will require political lucidity and willpower on both sides of the Atlantic, especially in Europe. At the same time, a crisis always opens windows of opportunity: An enlarged New Europe, with a new spirit, dynamism and good will, is evolving. Transatlantic values never disappeared, and we should not let a mass-murderer like Saddam Hussein bury in the Iraqi desert the values that have bound Europe and the United States together since the French and American Revolutions, and the American Constitution. It's time to stop contemplating a split between the United States and Europe. This is not an option.

Appreciating the 1990 'Transatlantic Declaration' and the 1995 'New Transatlantic Agenda', this paper proposes the following recommendations for a 'New Transatlantic Charta' that should be developed and lead to a report in perhaps six months under the auspices of a senior European and a senior American politician.

2. Recommendations for the future of the transatlantic relationship

An agenda for the New Europe as a global player and partner of the United States

Europe has a success story to tell. The launch of the European Monetary Union in 1999 and the introduction of the Euro laid the foundation for the future competitiveness of Europe's economy and prosperity for its citizens. Equally the introduction of the Euro laid the political and economic fundaments for the European Union to become a global player and an economic powerhouse.

The Euro, after a weak start against the dollar, is gradually evolving into a respected world currency. Internally, a strong Euro will put the necessary pressure on countries to follow through with overdue reforms. It is the Euro and the Stability Pact that impose fiscal discipline on member states. The Euro is much more than just a currency. It is a symbol of European integration, one of the most significant political and economic accomplishments of the twentieth century.

The new, enlarged Europe has the potential to become a major force in world affairs as a partner to the United States. To achieve this, all European states must pursue a common strategy. The prerequisite for this is the definition of our interests, answering the questions; 'What world do we want to see twenty-five or fifty years from now? What should be Europe's political, economic and military contributions to achieve such a world? And does it have the political will to invest in the necessary means and capabilities for that endeavour?'

With the enlarged New Europe bringing in new dynamism into the EU – with a fresh mind, fresh visions and new interests – it is now the time for the EU to become what is has failed to become after 1990: a global player and responsible strong partner. The following issues must be addressed in order for Europe to take up a responsible role in world affairs.

(1) Completion of EU enlargement

When ten countries – Cyprus, the Czech Republic, Malta, Poland, Hungary, Slovakia, Slovenia, Latvia, Lithuania and Estonia – signed the EU accession treaties on 16 April 2003, they decided to join what George Papandreou called the 'largest, most fascinating peace project in the world and possibly in mankind's history'.

The new EU members signed a contract to become part of the most innovative economic and political project of the last fifty years. Too often we tend to take what has been achieved in this regard for granted, discussing this process in terms of the problems ahead rather than in terms of the enormous achievements done.

The signing of the Treaty of Accession in Athens should be seen as a new beginning, a new chance for Europe to complete what the EU's founders had envisaged for the organization: to foster peace and stability in Europe and beyond.

The Challenges after EU enlargement 2004

The EU and the current candidate countries have been debating the future of Europe, concentrating on how the EU will operate after the inclusion of ten new members. But with few exceptions, such as the UK government as well as Chris Patten and Javier Solana, there has been little discussion of EU policy towards the *new* neighbours of the EU. These, of course, will be the Eastern Europe/post communist countries that will *not* become members of the EU after the grand enlargement.

In 2004, the countries bordering the EU will include Russia, Belarus, Ukraine, Bulgaria, Romania, Serbia and Croatia. Only a stone's throw beyond these new borders lie Moldova, Macedonia, Bosnia-Herzegovina, Albania, Georgia and Armenia.

The new neighbours have different perspectives about entering the EU. While Croatia, Serbia, Albania, Bosnia-Herzegovina, Macedonia and Montenegro need to be pushed for stronger reforms and democratic stability in order to be considered for EU-accession in the medium term, Romania and Bulgaria in particular should be held to a tight schedule. These are the countries most at risk in any slow-down of EU-enlargement. They need to follow closely the roadmap spelt out at the Copenhagen Summit so that no excuses can be made to keep them out and so that their elites take a more radical approach to reform.

While enlargement has been successful in prompting and sustaining a revolutionary transformation of eight formerly communist countries, the picture is rather different for the rest of the post-communist world. Those states that failed to enact deep and wide-ranging reforms are plagued by metastasizing corruption; their societies inadvertently export organized crime, illegal immigrants and little else. The new neighbours, especially those with few prospects at this time for EU membership, have advanced little since the collapse of communism.

The challenge is to prevent that border line from becoming an economic, social and political dividing line, constructed, bolstered and maintained by EU policies, resulting in what Toomas Hendrik Ilves has called a 'Great Wall of Europe' (see his essay 'The Grand Enlargement and the Great Wall of Europe').[1]

If Europe is unwilling to entertain the idea of a Ukraine or a Belarus as EU members, then it is necessary to develop a new, alternative strategy, and also make it clear that membership during the next quarter century is not possible.

The European Union could seriously consider other forms of relations with its new neighbours, a form of association less than membership but considerably more substantial than what is currently offered by the Partnership and Cooperation Agreements, or the even more substantial Association agreements. A new, expanded Association agreement would have to offer far more generous economic support and market access, as well as access to various EU programmes from e-Europe to Sapard (Special Accession Programme for Agricultural and Rural Development) and ISPA (Instrument for Structural Policies for Pre-Accession) – but without an accession perspective. Such an approach would make it clear to the new neighbours that membership is possible in the distant future, but until then serious reforms are expected.

As for Turkey, at the Summit in Copenhagen in December 2002 the EU decided not to offer a concrete date for the beginning of accession talks and merely promised that if Turkey fulfilled the so-called Copenhagen criteria on human rights and democracy by December 2004, these talks could then begin 'without further delay'. Going forward, the EU needs to encourage Turkey to pursue its reform process in order to enhance its chances to start accession negotiations by 2004.

Turkey knows that it can only become a member if it shows greater respect for human rights and a reduced role in government affairs for Turkey's military. Ankara must also demonstrate sustained economic growth to minimize the flood of Turkish emigration that many Europeans fear will result from its admission to the EU.

If Turkey fulfils all the requirements necessary, the fact that it is a Muslim country should not be a used as an argument against accession. On the contrary, the EU should apply a geo-strategic perspective and see Turkey's immediate closeness to the Islamic world as a major advantage. With Turkey as a member, the EU would be much better positioned to establish sustainable relationships with the greater Middle East.

Turkey's Foreign Minister Yasar Yakis is right in the long-term when he claims that the EU needs Turkey to become a truly global player influencing world affairs meaningfully. Turkey is stabilizing the Black Sea region as a counterweight to Russia. It controls the passage between Black Sea and the Mediterranean, and it plays an important role on the Balkans. In addition, 60 per cent of Europe's gas and oil imports come from countries that border Turkey.

The US puts special emphasis on its geo-strategic partnership with Turkey. Cooperating with countries in the conflict regions of the Middle East, and building bridges with the Islamic world, are among the prime goals of European foreign policy. Fostering the integration of this region will be much easier when Turkey is admitted and given the role of serving as a European–Muslim bridge, thereby helping to prevent Samuel Huntington's 'Clash of Civilizations' from expanding into Europe.

(2) Completion of the Constitution of the European Union – more Monnet, less Metternich

The Presidency of the European Convention has just presented the first draft of the first 16 articles of the first Constitution of the European Union, which can be expected to be completed soon. Greece, home of the world's earliest democracy, is holding the EU presidency in this defining moment of the Union and might see the finalization of the European Constitution. Should it happen within Greece's term, the signing-ceremony of this epochal moment can only take place at the true cradle of democracy – the Acropolis.

For centuries a constitution has served as a nucleus around which institutions of democratic decision-making processes are built. And, as Carl Bildt pointed out at Humboldt University in his lecture 'Is Europe Ready for the Future', a federation of nations-states is necessary 'since this is the way in which we can ensure that the powers of the regions and of the nations are preserved and protected, thus furthering the diversity in cultures, traditions and experiences that gives Europe a richness others can only envy'. This process today is a unique moment in history – a union of independent national states voluntarily committing themselves in writing to further unity, a unity that might one day become a truly supranational European power.

The EU should strive for 'more Monnet and less Metternich' (to quote Elmar Brok), for more European integration and less nationalistic behaviour, because single national states are ill-equipped to meet the new challenges and threats of globalization.

With regard to foreign policy, the Iraq crisis has shown that Europe is still characterized by national interests. The rules laid down more than ten years ago on a Common Foreign and Security Policy in the Treaty of Maastricht are often openly infringed upon or ignored. Europe does not speak with one voice in the world – because there is no common voice.

The creation of the European Convention is a tremendous opportunity to make a decisive step forward towards a united foreign policy for the European Union.

The draft articles on external action in the Constitutional Treaty of 23 April 2003 already demand that the members of the European Union need to define the common interest in all foreign and security policy matters and develop an institutional process for streamlined consultation and decision-making. In particular, it suggests the creation of a European Minister for Foreign Affairs, who speaks and represents the entire EU when it comes to foreign affairs.

Also, Qualified Majority Voting (QMV) is suggested. Here, it should be added that QMV would apply in all matters of foreign and security policy with the exception of subjects with military implications, in which case member states that are willing to cooperate more closely may do so – on the clear premise to do so without excluding other members.

The draft of the European Constitution also suggests that the diplomatic missions of the member states and the delegations of the

Union shall cooperate in third countries and in international organizations. To enhance the efficiency of European foreign and security policy, the pooling of diplomatic staff could be furthered, and most national representations could be easily transformed into 'EU Embassies' staffed by EU representatives and diplomats from the member countries.

As for a future president of the European Union, the President of the European Convention, Valéry Giscard d'Estaing, has recently proposed that the European Council elects its president for two and a half years, following the suggestion of larger member countries such as France and Germany. This provoked immediate resistance from both the EU Commission and from smaller member countries. The fear is that EU policy will be dominated by the national interests of larger countries and will pursue a less integrative approach.

While Giscard's suggestion allows for better coordination of the Council's decision-making process by ending the 6-month rotating presidency, and might be implemented into the Constitution, it does not address the problem of double structures between Council and Commission.

The positions of Javier Solana, the High Representative, and of Chris Patten, the Commissioner for External Relations, will rightly be brought together in order to create greater coherence of EU action and clarity in EU representation. The EU has drawn lessons from the problem of over-representation in the field of Foreign and Security Policy. One has to ask, then, if a 'double hat' would not make sense at the presidential level as well.

The European Union might consider electing *one*, not *two* presidents in order to overcome the inefficiencies in its decision-making process. As a suggestion, the leaders of the European Union should consider combining the functions of the president of the Commission and the president of the European Council. The president of the Commission should also act as a chair of the European Council and coordinate and lead its meetings, without having a voting right.

Such a model would bring the same advantages as a permanent president of the Council: The decision-making process could be streamlined here as well since the six-month rotating presidency would end in this case, too, and with it the accompanying nationally-driven priority settings, thus creating stronger cohesion and continuity in the EU's policies.

Another added value of such a solution would be that the president of the Council would already have his or her own secretariat and staffers who would be capable of coordinating the policy-making process of the Council without having to create an extra administration. In contrast, a separate permanent president or chair would need to build up this capacity first, leading to the creation of another bureaucratic body within the EU.

The future president of the European Union, who would need to be approved by the European Parliament, could act as neutral voice and mediator in conflict situations within the Council. And with the inauguration of a president of the 'United States of Europe', the EU will be closer to equal partnership with the United States of America as well as also closer to Jean Monnet's vision.

(3) Establishing an EU seat at the UN Security Council and reform of international law

As a result of a stronger European approach in the conduct of foreign and security policy, the EU should find it easier to commit its member states to first find a common position and to forestall in the future a multi-voiced nationally driven diplomacy. The recent crisis over Iraq at the United Nations, specifically within the UN Security Council, undermined Europes' unity and demonstrated the need to reform UN decision-making structures and current international law. If no adaptation to the realities of a post 9/11 world order takes place, both institutions otherwise run the risk of losing their world-political relevance.

The EU Seat at the UN Security Council

A common European position would need support from a qualified majority of the EU members. It must also allow members to abstain if they cannot be convinced to follow the EU-wide position. Such an agreement could serve as a prerequisite for a new initiative to establish an EU Seat at the UN Security Council so that Europe might speak with one voice to the world community. However, given that the reform of the UN Security Council has been postponed for years now, the EU should make use of the seats of Great Britain and France. Both countries are understandably not willing to permanently give up their seats. They could however, forego their seat every other year to the benefit of the EU. For example, in 2005 Great Britain would offer its seat to the EU; in 2006 Great Britain regains its seat and France steps back in favour of the EU.

Such a bold step would demonstrate urgently-needed European leadership and set examples. As a permanent member, the European Union could push for the urgently required UN reforms.

Reform of international law

The 11 September 2001 terrorist attacks, as well as the Iraq crisis, made current international law obsolete, which means that it needs to be changed substantially.

The United Nations were once again unable to see the consequences of their own decisions when they failed to do what United Nations Security Council Resolution 1441 had threatened as the consequence of Iraq's non-compliance with weapons inspectors. As a result no one should expect that an American administration will turn to the UN again as long as the United States believes it is at war. This, however, is the view in Washington since 9/11.

But the issues at stake go beyond the UN. They aim at some of the fundamentals of international law. One question raised by this crisis is whether an international order that treats democracies as the equals of tyrannies, and which therefore offers the same degree of protection against intervention to both of them, is the order of the twenty-first century. Another issue to be debated is whether the extant definition of self-defence is good enough in a world in which weapons of mass destruction (WMD) are spreading. There are no answers at this time, but to cling to an order which was born in the seventeenth century and then heavily influenced by the outcome of the Second World War and the defeat of colonialism is definitely no answer as well.

Clearly, after the Iraq crisis the attempt to impose binding international law on the use of force has failed, and the structure and rules of the UN Security Council reflect the hopes of its founders rather than the realities of the twenty-first century.

Article 51 of the charter permits the use of force only in self-defence, and only 'if an armed attack occurs against a Member of the United Nations'.

September 11th made clear that this rule alone is no longer sufficient to guide an international system based on the assumption of attacks from states – not from non-state actors such as totalitarian terror groups that cannot be classically deterred.

The US, after the crushing of the World Trade Center, concluded that under certain circumstances it must be allowed to defend itself before an 'armed attack' occurs. Or, as the American National Security Strategy of 2002 put it, Americans 'cannot let our enemies strike first'. Therefore, 'to forestall or prevent ... hostile acts by our adversaries, the United States will, if necessary, act pre-emptively'.

Key in this regard is the definition of when an attack would be of 'immediate imminence'. Jospeh Nye argues pre-emptive strikes should be backed up multilaterally, and he suggests defining the conditions in which such a strike would be legitimized in Article 7 of the UN Charter, which defines cases of threat to peace.

The difficulty is that such definition of conditions needs to be an ongoing process, as it will be difficult to anticipate future challenges and then strive to regulate in advance, before problems, which we cannot anticipate, develop.

In times of major uncertainty and earthmoving shifts in the international political system, it makes more sense to continuously develop international law.

The legitimacy of pre-emptive strikes is debatable, but before portraying the United States as warmongering Rambos, one needs to consider that the American President – George W. Bush or any other president – feels first and foremost committed to defending the American people. The US administration considered the danger arising from the combination of a mass-murderer and a dictator who has produced and used WMD, and from terrorist groups with ambitions to acquire such WMD, a grave enough danger to legitimize self-defence. It feared that the price of waiting – perhaps thousands more Americans killed – was too high.

Those who blame a new American unilateralism for undermining international law should consider the following sentence: 'We have to keep defending our vital interests just as before; we can say no, alone, to anything that may be unacceptable.' It may come as a surprise that those were not the words of administration hawks such as Paul Wolfowitz or Donald Rumsfeld. In fact, they were written in 2001 by Hubert Vedrine, then France's foreign minister. Similarly, critics of American 'hyperpower' might guess that the statement, 'I do not feel obliged to other governments,' must surely have been uttered by an American. It was in fact made by German Chancellor Gerhard Schröder on 10 February 2003. The first and lasting geopolitical truth is that states pursue security by pursuing power. After all, would China, France, or Russia – or any other country – voluntarily abandon pre-eminent power if it found itself in the position of the United States?

The greater danger after the second Iraq War is not that the United States will use force when it should not, but that, chastened by the war's horror, the public's opposition, and the economy's gyrations, it might not use force when it should.

With all the unpredictable disorder and elements of anarchy in the world, Europe and the United States cannot afford to be at the brink of divorce over such overarching topics like International Law.

There are no two societies so close to each other, sharing the same history, values and culture. The West has to take the initiative for the reform of international law. A joint commission of American and European legal experts should be asked to make suggestions that will be presented at the United Nations and discussed in the UN General Assembly.

(4) Creation of a Transatlantic Free Trade Area – TAFTA

Economically, Europe and the United States are the two most closely bound regions in the world. Globalization is happening faster and reaching deeper between Europe and the United States than between any other two regions. This high degree of transatlantic interdependence shows strong potential for future cooperation.

Europe and America could probably not find a better moment to turn the severe crisis in their relationship into a promising economic success story. What is needed now is a relaunch of TAFTA, an idea that was brought forward for the first time in 1994: a Transatlantic Free Trade Area.

The then Commission-Vice-President Sir Leon Brittan and former German Foreign Minister Klaus Kinkel were the strongest supporters of this idea, which found its first expression in the 'New Transatlantic Agenda' (NTA), signed in December 1995 at the EU–US Summit in Madrid, and which commits the EU and the US to 'progressively reducing or eliminating barriers that hinder the flow of goods, services and capital between us'. Much of this work has since then been carried out within the 'Transatlantic Business Dialogue' (TABD), pursuing a step-by-step approach of harmonizing regulations and standards. However, initiatives like the NTA or the 'Transatlantic Economic Partnership' (TEP) have been of limited success. A new, more ambitious approach, a single comprehensive agreement, is needed.

The creation of a Transatlantic Free Trade Area (TAFTA), linking the United States and the European Union together and establishing the world's largest free trade zone, would not only guarantee the free movement of goods, capital, services and persons, but would also bring a new dynamism in both transatlantic relations and global trade, a dynamism that is urgently needed in the EU–US relationship.

Foreign direct investment – not trade – is the backbone of the transatlantic economy. Although transatlantic trade disputes steal the headlines, trade itself accounts for less than 20 per cent of transatlantic commerce, and US–EU trade disputes account for less than 1 per cent of transatlantic commerce.

The total output of US foreign affiliates in Europe ($333 billion in 2000) and of European affiliates in the US ($301 billion) is greater than the total gross domestic output of most nations. In 2001, and throughout most of the 1990s, Europe accounted for *half* of the total global earnings of US companies, as measured by US foreign affiliate income. Vice versa, the United States is the world's most important market in terms of earnings for European multinationals. United States affiliate income of European companies rose more than fivefold in the 1990s to nearly $26 billion.

Corporate America's foreign assets totalled over $5.2 trillion in 2000. The bulk of these assets – roughly 58 per cent – were located in Europe. America's asset base in the United Kingdom is almost equivalent to the combined overseas affiliate asset base of Asia, Latin America, Africa and the Middle East. American assets in Germany alone – $300 billion in 2000 – were greater than total US assets in all of South America.

Europe's investment stake in the US, on an historical-cost basis, grew to a whopping $835 billion in 2000, which is nearly one-quarter larger than America's stake in Europe. European firms have never been as exposed to the US economy as they are in the first decade of the twenty-first century.

In addition, Europe profits strongly from the fact that two-thirds of US corporate research and development conducted outside the United States is conducted in Europe.

In sum, the years since the fall of the Berlin Wall have witnessed one of the greatest periods of transatlantic economic integration in history. Our mutual stake in each other's prosperity has grown dramatically since the end of the Cold War – and the importance of Europe for the American economy is greater than ever.

As an economic giant the EU is taken seriously by the US and seen as an equal partner. In contrast to international security issues, it is in this area that the EU can take the lead in further developing the transatlantic relationship – especially after enlargement.

Given the data mentioned above, it seems logical that American and European leaders of world trade could work together to resolve their remaining trade problems, and in the process set powerful precedents for the rest of the world to follow. In so doing, they would accelerate progress towards the ultimate goal of global free trade.

Already, a large proportion of bilateral trade takes place free of any restrictions, but major exceptions, such as non-tariff trade barriers, remain. To overcome this a powerful new initiative, such as TAFTA, is needed.

The EU should set up a timetable for TAFTA's implementation. Since the majority of the US leadership recognizes that it benefits from fair and healthy relationships with the EU in trade questions, it should be possible to find support in Washington.

Ideas like TAFTA have been raised several times over the last years. Maybe they would have been discussed more sincerely had there been more frequent and stronger institutionalized discussions between European and American political and business leaders on how to improve EU–US relations in practical terms. Let's make TAFTA an economic transatlantic imperative, now, by developing NAFTA and EMU into a new Transatlantic Free Trade Area.

(5) Establishment of an 'European Academy' for scholars and artists in Washington, DC

Apart from efforts to strengthen transatlantic ties politically, economically and diplomatically, the intellectual exchange between the United States and Europe needs to be enhanced in a time when many European scholars, writers and artists are at odds with the United States and its policies.

The creation of an institution in the United States that would allow both America-critical and America-appreciative artists and scholars to live and work for a year in the United States could help to overcome some stereotypes about America in the minds of opinion-makers and could serve as intellectual bridges over the Atlantic.

The goal of a 'European Academy' in Washington DC would be to foster the exchange of leading European intellectuals and their American counterparts, and to expose visiting Europeans to a broader American audience outside academia. Selected fellows from all EU member countries would be given an opportunity to stay and work for a significant amount of time in the US, receiving a vibrant picture of the diversity and dynamism of American political thought and culture, thereby fostering an appreciation of the wide and sophisticated spectrum of American society, science and arts. At the same time, the presence of the fellows would help ensure that many facets of European history, cultures and values are present in the US capital, as well.

For example, fellows could be scholars and artists engaged in history, philosophy, literary criticism, economics, public policy, painting or classical and modern music. The 'European Academy' would provide a home and work environment for the fellows, giving them the opportunity to work on their individual projects. While in Washington, each fellow would engage in a significant scholarly or artistic project – be it a biography or novel, a philosophical analysis, a painting or the composition of a concerto.

While a residential environment would offer the fellows valuable opportunities for cross-disciplinary discussion amongst themselves, one of the main goals would be interaction with Americans in Washington DC and elsewhere. Public lectures, seminars, debates and performances would typically involve the fellows and the US capital's cultural, political, academic and corporate communities. Also, the Academy would help arrange affiliations for the fellows with universities, ministries, agencies, think tanks, museums, libraries and other professional organizations in Washington.

The fellows would receive a monthly stipend, room and board and other support for their work. Funding would need to come from both private and public sources within the EU and would require significant fundraising efforts.

The amount of money needed will be a small price to pay when one considers the quality of exchange that would be enabled by the 'European Academy' and the fact that the fellows would become ambassadors from Washington and the US when they return to Europe, thus deepening and broadening the transatlantic ties. The Academy would be a symbol to remind America that it is also a European power and that Americans should never forget their roots.

(6) Make a Common European Foreign and Security Policy a strategic reality

To be a strong partner and a serious player in the transatlantic security partnership with the United States, and to be strategically relevant in a new global security environment, the European Union not only needs to speak with one voice, but also to fulfil its pledges to build up military capabilities, strengthen its intervention and crisis management capabilities and commit its forces to more power projection in order to meet the security challenges of the twenty-first century: fundamentalism, ethnic strife, the spread of WMD, and new and old forms of terrorism.

After the embarrassing performance of EU troops in the management of the Balkan crisis and in particular in Kosovo, the EU initiated the European Security and Defence Policy (ESDP) at the Helsinki Summit in 1999. EU member states committed themselves to 'Headline Goals'. It was agreed that by 2003 they would be able to deploy forces of up to 60,000 military personnel capable of the full range of the Petersburg tasks.

These forces were to be militarily self-sustaining, with the necessary command, control and intelligence capabilities, logistics, other combat-support services and air and naval elements. Member states were to be able to deploy at this level within 60 days, and to provide smaller rapid-response elements more quickly than this. They were to be able to sustain such a deployment for at least one year.

The reality looks darker: Even after 9/11 and the Iraq crisis, the sum of military resources committed to the Headline Goals will probably not be met by late 2003. This means that the EU's first serious attempt to reduce the growing capability gap towards the United States has failed.

The gap between words and deeds concerning the ESDP led Washington to repeatedly ask Europeans to back up their new strategic claims with financial and military resources. Unless specific and binding convergence-criteria and fiscal discipline, similar to those imposed on the European Monetary Union, are put into effect, Europe will never be able to manage crises without heavy dependence on the United States.

Another key to the fulfilment of the EU Headline Goals will be the establishment of an 'Agency for Armaments and Strategic Research', as suggested in the draft articles for the European Convention, in order to encourage the improvement of military capability. Such an effort can build on experiences made in already existing defence cooperation forums such as the Organization for Joint Armaments Cooperation (OCCAR), whose participants Britain, France, Germany and Italy account for 80 per cent of EU spending on research, development and procurement already. The Netherlands, Spain and Belgium have applied to join, and Sweden has expressed serious interest, which would bring most of the EU's defence industry within the ambit of OCCAR.

There is also need for closer cooperation of defence industries across the Atlantic. The policy should not be to *buy American* or *buy European* but to *buy transatlantic*, procuring the most advanced systems at the lowest cost. Political will in Washington to share US technology with European Allies is a precondition for transatlantic defence consolidation. There is only one way to gain influence on the United States, and that is to acquire capabilities that really matter. Sectors where the United States could need European contributions to sustain operations or be able to operate in more than one theatre include ground surveillance, air-to-air refuelling and air transport. European willingness to launch such a modernization programme should be matched by increased American preparedness to share technology. Close industrial and military transatlantic cooperation can become a strategic component of both a Common European Foreign and Security Policy (CFSP) and ESDP – in particular after EU-enlargement.

To make a Common European Foreign and Security Policy a strategic reality, the EU could develop a coherent foreign policy strategy towards the major countries and regions in the world. Such thinking is unfamiliar to most European countries, with the exception of Great Britain and France.

Furthermore, the EU should project a united image to the outside world. European disunity during the Iraq crisis harmed Europe's interests, damaged relations with the United States and paralysed NATO. This is all the more a reason to speak sooner rather than later with *one* and not with *two* voices to the outside world.

In most EU countries, geo-strategic planning has been replaced by extensive multilateralism. This applies in particular to Germany. However, dialogues, multilateral discussion-groups and frameworks for cooperation with other countries will not position the EU as a strategic player on the world stage. For CFSP and ESDP to be acknowledged as a driving force in the world, the leaders of the European Union need to set clear priorities as to what kind of relationship they want to maintain with the most important countries, and what the European Unions' interests in that relationship should be.

Of course, political dialogue is maintained with all key countries and regions of the world, and these efforts have resulted in progress in both the development of the respective countries and in their relationships towards the EU. However, the EU policies towards these countries are mainly based on trade and business and efforts to integrate these countries multilaterally. But who could name clear interests and goals the EU pursues in China or India – two of the largest countries in the world?

If the EU does not want to leave global strategic-alliance-making to the US, a precise strategy combined with a precise message to the outside world is imperative. A common EU approach on politically restructuring Iraq would be a beginning.

A Marshall Plan for the Greater Middle East

A common set of driving forces from Northern Africa to Pakistan is contributing to a toxic combination of radical anti-Western ideologies, terrorism, rogue states, failed states, and the drive to acquire weapons of mass destruction.

A common goal, shared by the UN and safeguarded by NATO, should be an American–European initiative 'to make the Middle East safe for democracy'. A Marshall Plan against the 'Talibanization' of the Middle East is necessary to dry up support for Islamic terror.

In the medium term, such a strategy must aim to provide work, dignity and livelihoods for the people of the region. Societies in the Middle East need to come to grips with modernity and create new civil societies that allow them to compete and integrate in the modern world. Fighting against illiteracy and youth unemployment are the most important steps to be taken. The drivers for such a process are democratization, free market economics, rule of law and progressive education.

In this respect, the countries of Central and Eastern Europe could provide special expertise. A fresh voice of a new member of the European Union, former Polish Minister of Finance and former Deputy Prime Minister, Leszek Balcerowitz suggests: 'Iraq's present condition is no more difficult than that of the Central European countries twelve years ago. Iraq has high inflation, variable rates of exchange (official versus unofficial), one dominant economic sector, rationing of foodstuffs, and a large percentage of young people. All of this is similar to what the first post-communist Polish government inherited in 1989. Central European and Baltic countries could share these experiences with the Iraqis, especially with regard to the privatization of small and medium-sized enterprises.'

An agenda for NATO to remain politically and militarily relevant

After the end of the Cold War, NATO did not fall apart, but rather adapted to new requirements. NATO has a success story to tell. NATO expansion happened twice: In March 1999 the Czech Republic, Hungary and Poland joined the Alliance at the Washington Summit. And now we were witnessing the second NATO enlargement with the recent accession of seven new member states. Bulgaria, Estonia, Latvia, Lithuania, Romania, Slovakia and Slovenia were invited last November in Prague to become members of NATO. The Alliance has achieved a historical triumph: Europe united in peace, democracy and common values from the Baltics to the Balkans, from the Atlantic to the Black Sea.

From the beginning, the purpose of NATO enlargement was, as Ron Asmus points out in his book *Opening NATO's Door*,[2] to help lock in a new peace in Europe following communism's collapse and the end of the Cold War. The goal was to promote a process of pan-European integration and reconciliation that would make the prospect of armed conflict as inconceivable in the eastern half of the continent as it had become in the western half.

From an American perspective, the imperative was to ensure that America never again had to fight another major war in Europe. The US used the window that had opened after 1990 to lock in a durable peace in Europe. Most importantly, the Americans wanted to be able to face future security threats elsewhere in the world, knowing that security in Europe was assured.

The purpose of NATO enlargement was and is to strengthen Europe's security within its own borders and not to worry about conflict with Russia or ethnic strife in their backyard. At the same time, NATO gained new allies who joined the West in addressing the new threats of the post-Cold War era. 'The new Allies from Central and Eastern Europe, having fought hard to regain their freedom and independence,' stresses the former Deputy Defence Minister of Hungary, István Gyarmati, 'bring also fresh blood, ideas and enthusiasm to NATO.'

But NATO also went through troubled waters. After the fall of the Berlin wall, at their July 1990 meeting in London, NATO's Heads of State and Government recognized in the 'Strategic Concept' that risks to their security would be less likely to result from calculated aggression against the territory of the NATO members, but rather from 'adverse consequences of instabilities that may arise from the serious economic, social and political difficulties'. The war in Kosovo was a bitter example which proved NATO right.

Also, NATO's new 'Strategic Concept' of April 1999 explicitly reflects the fact that 'Alliance security interests can be affected by risks of a wider nature, including acts of terrorism, sabotage and organized crime, and by the disruption of the flow of vital resources.' It took only two years to prove the relevance of this farsighted mission statement. The ruthless attack by totalitarian Islamic terrorists on the United States of America on 11 September 2001 reminded us of the enduring requirement for transatlantic cooperation and made it clear that the new strategic challenges are global in nature and need a collective response. Only in a common effort, institutionalized in NATO, will Europeans and Americans will be able to meet the challenges of the twenty-first century.

In decades of Cold War and dangerous political and military confrontations, it was never necessary to invoke Article 5 of the

Washington Treaty. But in September 2001 NATO was able to show that the key to peace and security is decisiveness and solidarity, and that Europe is willing to fulfil its NATO commitments in supporting the United States. By invoking Article 5 NATO made it clear to the outside world that the Alliance is faced with challenges of historical magnitude.

Even the most NATO-sceptic officials at the Pentagon acknowledge today that their failure to respond to the immediate post-September 11 offer from Europe to use the Alliance in the war in Afghanistan was a mistake. They now see the opportunity NATO presents in post-conflict conditions.

The Iraq crisis damaged NATO, too, since three nations refused to allow precautionary planning for the defence of a member nation (Turkey). 'This really means', as Klaus Naumann said, 'to put the axe at the very roots of any defensive alliance since it destroys the credibility of NATO's central promise, collective defence. If no corrective action were taken, nations will inevitably look at coalitions of the willing. Increased reliance on such coalitions will turn out to be divisive at the end of the day.'

The war in Iraq was also the moment of truth for the Atlantic alliance, whose future depends on a twofold strategy: It must be able to respond militarily to global security threats, and it must be allowed politically to do so.

The following issues must be addressed in order for NATO to remain relevant.

(1) Military lessons of the Iraq war

There is a lot to do since Saddam Hussein succeeded in severely damaging the UN, NATO and the EU and, as long as the existence of WMD remains to be proven, the credibility of the US.

The EU is possibly the organization which was most severely damaged. Europe no longer speaks with one voice. The majority of nations clearly signalled that they are not prepared to accept domination by any other nation or nations. Europe must eventually understand that it will only have influence if it speaks with one voice and if that voice is backed by capabilities. This means that all efforts which do not include the United Kingdom are doomed to fail. This week's meeting [the informal EU–Foreign Ministers' Meeting of 2–4 May 2003, Greece] of four European nations who wish to enforce more and closer defence cooperation will therefore fail, as did the French attempt to prevent an invasion of Iraq during the most recent crisis.

The political repair work can succeed only if the European NATO allies demonstrate that they understand the main military lesson: They need to acquire some twenty-first century capabilities.

The war in Iraq saw the quick defeat of a twentieth-century army by an armed force of the twenty-first century, which was able to conquer a country of the size of France with some three army divisions. It was indeed an asymmetric war.

One can follow retired General Klaus Naumann, former Chairman of the Military Committee of NATO, when he describes the lessons learnt from the war in Iraq:

What were the ingredients of success?

1. The US achieved operational surprise in an announced war because they began the war by joint and combined operations and not, as many had assumed, by an air campaign. This was complemented by tactical surprises achieved through operations by Special Forces. Some of them had been in Iraq for quite some time.
2. The US paralysed the Iraqi C3 and air defence through surgical strikes within a couple of days which led to unchallenged air superiority.
3. The US applied for the first time ever Network Centric Warfare (NCW) by taking advantage of their incredible ISR (Intelligence, Surveillance, Reconnaissance) capabilities which were linked to excellent C4 ISR (Command, Control, Communications, Computers, Intelligence, Surveillance, Reconnaissance) and connected to shooters of all kind. They thus reduced the response time to strike strategic targets to less than one hour.
4. The US forces availed themselves of a firepower which was superior to any they had fielded in previous post-Cold War conflicts in terms of precision, effectiveness, flexibility and mobility to support ground forces which were more mobile, flexible and agile than any force employed since the Second World War.
5. The US commanders operated in a daring and flexible way which took many observers by surprise.

The truly new dimension was the degree to which the US forces were able to conduct network centric operations against an enemy who initially offered a stiffer resistance than expected.

Network Centric Warfare (NCW) had seen its real and first time baptism of fire and had proven that it will allow numerically inferior twenty-first-century forces to defeat numerically superior twentieth century forces. Consequently, American efforts to transform their armed forces will accelerate and, as a consequence of the failure to win Turkey's support, the US will make additional efforts to secure additional over-flight rights in the region within the next ten years or so.

What does this mean for future conflicts and for force planning?

European nations are well advised to review their force planning carefully as most of them have armed forces that are stranded in the twentieth century. Industry should also look carefully into the lessons learned in the Iraq war. They may wish to widen the range of products they offer and to phase out or modify hardware left over from the Cold War.

The key to modernization and transformation is C4ISR. The main emphasis should be on systems which provide forces with actionable target information. For the immediate future this will require the involvement of live soldiers. For example, the C4 needs manned carriers to link the three levels of operations: ISR, C4 and precision engagement. UAVs (unmanned aerial vehicles) and increasingly UCAVs (unmanned combat air vehicles) will play an important supplementary role provided they have access to GPS (global positioning systems) or possibly one day Galileo information.

C4ISR is followed by all-weather precision strike as the next key element of transformation.

The European defence industry has much to offer in this area. It could well create incentives for American companies to cooperate and to exchange information. European industry might wish to consider concentrating research on nano and biotechnology and on supersonic cruise missiles. The capabilities are there, which is one reason why we Europeans should be optimistic about the future of the European defence industry. Most of the precision strike weapons will be air or sea-launched long range weapons. Helicopter-launched weapons in particular often provide vital to support special forces who will undoubtedly play a key role in any NCW operation. Special forces are one of the best instruments to paralyse an opponent's C4, fulfilling the tactical aim of all NCW. High energy weapons that disable enemy communications, which the US obviously did not use this time, might be another area of interest for both European defence industries and their clients in European defence ministries.

Last but not least, the European industry is well positioned to provide armed forces with air mobility, which remains a badly needed capability. All assets should in principle be equipped for air-to-air refuelling and should be equipped with stealth technology wherever possible. They should be designed for multiple purposes. For example, it should be possible to use them as transport assets and to equip them as gun ships if required.

Obviously, these twenty-first century forces will need protection as well, and one of the areas for which European defence industries can provide solutions is missile defence – both for expeditionary forces as well as for the homelands. All solutions in this area will require transatlantic cooperation as the critical element is not so much the weaponry but the battle management system.

These observations are not much more than a very preliminary analysis. However, it is clear that the European defence industry is well positioned to provide the armed forces of EU nations with some and possibly most of the equipment they will need to transform themselves into twenty-first century forces. The European industry might even be able to more fully penetrate the American market through cooperative and joint ventures. The weak elements in this forecast are the European customers, the ministries of defence, as none of them is very likely to get big increases in their defence budgets.

(2) Completion of Pragues' capabilities agenda

Prague became the summit for the transformation of NATO into a global alliance. Global challenges require global security, and thus a global NATO.

NATO must extend its reach globally or it will become irrelevant. And the ESDP has to become an equal pillar in the transatlantic security alliance. This means first and foremost that European nations must acquire new military capabilities in order to maintain interoperability between US and European NATO forces.

DCI

In 1998 then Secretary of State Madeleine Albright realized after it had become clear in Kosovo that the Alliance faces an increasing capability gap. Consequently she launched the Defence Capabilities Initiative (DCI), which was adopted at the 1999 NATO Summit in Washington.

The objective of the 58 capability items was and is to ensure that the Alliance can effectively carry out operations across the entire spectrum of its present and possible future missions – from responding to humanitarian disasters, to carrying out peace-enforcement operations, to conducting high-intensity warfare in defence of Alliance territory.

After it became clear that not even half of the NATO members were prepared to comply with the DCI-NATO improvement measures, the

2002 NATO-Summit in Prague launched the Prague Capabilities Commitment (PCC) which reduced the 58 DCI items to four core areas:

1. Enhanced rapid deployment and self-sufficiency, to ensure NATO's forces are able to arrive quickly where and when they are needed, and to maintain operations over distance and time.
2. Improvement of interoperability between NATO forces. As a vital aspect of combat effectiveness, the growing technology gap between the United States and other member states must be halted.
3. Enhancement of command, control and information systems to maintain information superiority. This will allow NATO to respond quickly to new and changing threats and will optimize the application of military capabilities.
4. Improvement of NATO's ability to defend against chemical, biological, radiological and nuclear attacks, to reflect the heightened threat posed by these weapons.

But these are all on-paper commitments. If Europe does not stop its pattern of announcing defence reform measures without sticking to its promises, the United States will have little choice but to act alone.

This would strengthen the already evident trend of the United States assembling 'coalitions of the willing', and Europe's ability to influence US decisions and policy will further decline. This in turn will create even greater frustration and resentment in Europe, as Europe finds itself increasingly unable to affect decisions that impact on its own security.

Creation of a NATO Response-Force

Another key issue at the Prague Summit was the launching of a new NATO Response Force (NRF), which was initiated by the US to strengthen transatlantic capabilities.

The idea is that NATO needs a multilateral joint force for primarily out-of-area operations, with immediate readiness (5–30 days), thus capable to move quickly to wherever needed, as decided by the NATO Council. The NRF will bring together elite forces from both sides of the Atlantic and will be technologically advanced and highly flexible. It will have initial operating capability at the latest by October 2004, and full operating capability no later than October 2006. It will be capable of fighting in an NBC (nuclear, biological, chemical) environment and self-sustainable for a certain period of time.

Tasks are similar to those of the European Reaction Force described in the Helsinki headline goals, and include non-combatant evacuation operations, force projection and serving as an initial entry force for a large scale operation.

The NRF, however, is essentially a strike force for use in high-intensity combat operations beyond Europe, whereas the European Union's Reaction Force is primarily designed for peace and stability operations in and around Europe. Thus, the forces are basically complementary.

In essence it will be a NATO force that allows European and US forces to fight together whenever and wherever the Alliance political authorities decide. The force will be able to react very quickly to crises in or beyond Alliance territory. This will set a standard for all NATO forces in the medium and long term.

The NRF will also set a new standard for European military capabilities. The need for strategic airlift, air refuelling, secure command and control, and precision guided munitions for the European elements of the NRF will become unavoidably clear. European governments will be challenged to set necessary priorities.

The NRF has a chance to become a new US–European project with increased military cooperation and interoperability. The great advantage for Europe is that it requires interoperability with US-forces, specifically: precision-guided munitions; stealth for greater power projection; advanced intelligence, surveillance and reconnaissance systems; and advanced command, control, communications and computing systems.

The German ministry of defence emphasized this integrative potential of the NRF by announcing that capabilities and troops for the European Reaction Force will also be provided to the NRF. These troops will be under the command of either NATO or the EU, depending on which organization takes the lead in a given operation.

(3) Addition, not duplication, of EU defence capabilities to NATO's set of forces

The EU and NATO need to work together as partners, not rivals, on the EU Security and Defence Policy. Independent European military planning capabilities are currently duplicating already existing structures such as SHAPE (NATO's military headquarters).

NATO's defence capabilities initiative, the EU headline goal and the EU's collective capability goals should complement each other. And the 3D policy – no duplication, no de-coupling, no discrimination – should also still apply for both sides.

To be clear, NATO and the EU have only one set of forces available to handle crises when needed. The Defence Capabilities Initiative and the ESDP are meant to enhance the capabilities of this common NATO and EU set of forces, in order to make NATO's global role militarily credible.

France, Germany, Belgium and Luxembourg sent the wrong signal in this regard in Brussels on 29 April 2003, when they suggested independent military planning among EU members and in particular discussed the creation of a NATO-independent EU headquarters. The realization of such plans would ultimately rival NATO and lead to a clash with the American ally. Colin Powell made that clear when he commented on what he called 'some kind of plan' and said what was needed was 'more military capability, not more headquarters'.

Europe in the twenty-first century deserves better options than these. It can only be taken seriously as a partner of the US if at least London, Berlin and Paris agree. In terms of military power, all efforts that do not include the United Kingdom are doomed to fail.

(4) A lead function for NATO in Afghanistan and Iraq

In the Balkans NATO has proven itself effective. NATO handles post-conflict conditions professionally. It provides practical support in securing and stabilizing a volatile environment and gives a veneer of respectable multilateralism to the process.

Most of the 19 NATO allies have had forces directly involved in operation 'Enduring Freedom', the ongoing US-led military operation against terrorist targets in Afghanistan.

The International Security Assistance Force (ISAF) has been under the command of NATO members since its deployment in January 2002: United Kingdom, Turkey and, at the moment, Germany and the Netherlands. NATO Allies currently provide 95 per cent of the more than 5,000 personnel in ISAF III. NATO, as an organization, provides essential operational planning, intelligence and other support to ISAF III, and may assume an even greater role in the future.

NATO could and should play an equally important role in securing post-war Iraq. No organization is as suitable as NATO, with its range and its capacities, to provide and guarantee peace, order and stability in post-war situations.

1. Protection from Weapons of Mass Destruction

NATO's deployable weapons labs can find ABC (Atomic, Biological, Chemical) weapons, analyse their content and secure the contaminated area. NATO can also provide soldiers with protective gear. NATO countries can provide response teams trained in the environmentally-friendly disposal of NBC weapons. This includes incineration, neutralization or destruction. The Czech chemical and biological brigade, with 400 troops, is said by NATO officials to be one of the best. The Poles, Germans, Hungarians, Britons and Americans also have teams well-trained in detection and removal of weapons of mass destruction. In addition, NATO countries have explosive ordinance teams who are trained to get rid of and detect exploded and unexploded ordinances.

2. Communications

NATO countries can provide satellite communications, intelligence and secure communications systems during a post-war reconstruction period. These would be coordinated from the military headquarters in SHAPE.

3. Command and control system

Unlike the UN, NATO has a military headquarter and an organized command and control system that ensures communication equipment, gear, infrastructure and equipment from different countries are interoperable. This system makes it much easier to coordinate a NATO peacekeeping force in a post-war Iraq than it would be with a UN force. However, NATO's command and control structure could also make it possible for NATO to coordinate humanitarian help together with the United Nations. It could allow NATO to coordinate assistance for Iraq from non-NATO countries. Assistance from Arab countries such as Algeria, Egypt, Morocco, Mauritania, Tunisia and Jordan could also be coordinated by NATO.

4. Civil emergency planning

NATO organizes national assets such as ships, airplanes, trains, medical facilities and communications in cases of war or other national disasters. It also coordinates the repair and rebuilding of streets, airports, bridges and water systems. These assets are brought together under the Senior Civil Emergency Planning Committee (SCEPC), which reports directly to the North Atlantic Council. The Senior Civil Emergency Planning Committee coordinates planning in the categories of European inland surface transport, ocean shipping, civil aviation, food and agriculture, industrial production and supply, post and telecommunications, medical matters, civil protection, and petroleum production and supply. After a meeting of all NATO nations' ambassadors and following their approval, NATO can immediately put into action any assistance that is needed in a civil emergency. For civil emergency planning to be functional in Iraq, heavy lift transport would be needed, as would a large number of engineering battalions. The US is in the position to provide the airlift, and since the Prague summit, many European countries have the capability to make their engineering battalions available.

5. Policing

NATO countries provided training to local police and also provided policing in crisis areas throughout the Balkans. NATO also has around 200 military police who could be used for the protection of the non-combatant population in Iraq.

NATO's capabilities can contribute to peace and stability in Iraq.

(5) Strengthening NATO's dialogue in the Mediterranean and developing a relationship with the Middle East

The Mediterranean remains a fragmented and highly unstable region. Terrorism, religious extremism and the proliferation of weapons of mass destruction constitute a threat as much to the southern Mediterranean countries as they do to members of the EU and NATO. In the next decade all capitals of Southern Europe could be in the range of missiles launched from North Africa and the Middle East.

Profound changes to the European security environment that resulted from the end of the Cold War led NATO to recognize the interdependence of European and Mediterranean security. NATO's Mediterranean dialogue was launched 1994 and involves Algeria, Egypt, Israel, Jordan, Mauritania, Morocco and Tunisia. It aims to achieve better mutual understanding between NATO members and the countries of the region.

The overall aim of NATO's Mediterranean dialogue is to contribute to regional security and stability, and to achieve better mutual understanding between NATO and its Mediterranean partners. The Alliance also intends to correct any misperceptions that may have arisen with regard to NATO activities. In particular, it wants to dismantle the myth that NATO is in search of new, artificial enemies. And it seeks to dissipate fears that the emerging European security architecture may exclude its southern neighbours.

The tragic events of 9/11 have turned NATO's dialogue with its Mediterranean partners into a key element of its relationship with the region. The strengthening and deepening of relations between NATO and the Mediterranean dialogue countries is now considered among the highest priorities for the Alliance, as confirmed at the Prague summit. So far the dialogue initiative has accomplished significant achievements:

- It became an important vehicle for information-sharing across the Mediterranean, and it has developed into a useful confidence-building forum, especially after the creation of the Mediterranean Contact Group.
- It has provided a context for practical cooperation, and it has greatly increased the interest for the understanding of Mediterranean security within the Alliance.
- The dialogue also created 'contact' structures both inside NATO and in the dialogue countries that allow for the accumulation of knowledge, information and experience and also on-job training for officials on non-traditional issues in a multinational environment.

However, the following measures are recommended to strengthen dialogue in the region. NATO should:

1. Increase the number of educational courses.
2. Focus on civil emergency planning.
3. Increase the participation of dialogue countries in activities related to disaster management.
4. Further enhance 'low cost' confidence-building and transparency measures, such as alerting countries in the region to future military activities, discussing a code of conduct for military activities, and exchanging information among military staff.
5. Invite dialogue countries to send observers to large-scale NATO exercises.
6. Sponsor fellowships and exchanges for researchers from dialogue countries at major institutes in NATO countries dealing with defence and security matters.
7. Increase support for visits to NATO by key opinion-makers from the dialogue countries, especially journalists, academics and parliamentarians.
8. Encourage greater participation in courses, especially peacekeeping courses, offered by the NATO School in Oberammergau.
9. Reinforce the nongovernmental dimension and consider establishing a NATO Mediterranean defence studies network.

10. Consider establishing a crisis prevention and confidence-building network for the Mediterranean.

Looking beyond the Mediterranean dialogue, NATO needs to develop a long-term strategy for the broader region. The dialogue could eventually evolve into a 'Mediterranean Partnership for Peace' programme, drawing inspiration from the 'PfP' programmes in Central and Eastern Europe. Such a programme could be applied to countries of the greater Middle East to foster their transformation and democratization.

NATO should also look to broaden its dialogue with Mediterranean countries to nations in the Middle East. The Alliance should engage young intellectuals, officers, parliamentarians, government and NGO-officials, and journalists to influence future decision-makers.

(6) Prepare NATO for global missions

Does the Alliance want to play a real military role in the war against terrorism and the proliferation of WMD or will it become an armed version of the Organization for Security and Cooperation in Europe – irrelevant in projecting power on a global scale?

Europeans will have to give an answer, not only to the ongoing demands of NATO Secretary-General George Robertson, but also to themselves. Are they interested and willing to keep NATO militarily relevant, which means making not only another general political commitment to increase expenditures, but a genuine, precise, timed commitment to acquire missing defence capabilities?

And Americans will have to give an answer as well, not only to George Robertson, but also to themselves: Are they interested in keeping NATO militarily relevant for future crises, or is the Pentagon doctrine of 'keeping the illusion alive' already the new policy of the Bush administration?

On 11 September 2001, the world did not really change. The attacks simply reminded us in a brutal way that the new strategic challenges are global in nature and need a collective response. Almost overnight the 11th of September persuaded the European allies to accept the key-lesson of a new NATO, a lesson that had already been discussed since the end of the Cold War: either NATO goes out of area or out of business. NATO's prompt reaction on 12 September 2001, when it invoked Article 5, made clear that the organization had become a de facto global alliance and that its pledge to support the United States had no geographical limits.

The problem is that some Europeans still see NATO as a collective defence and crisis management organization, while its most powerful and indeed indispensable member country, the US, no longer see NATO as an instrument they would wish to use in conflict and war. They regard NATO as a useful political instrument and a collective security arrangement with the task of stabilizing and protecting Europe. This was NATO's mandate when it was founded in 1949. The United States wishes to keep it intact.

However, if NATO becomes so political that its defence guarantee appears hollow and it cannot be used in crises, it would soon lose support and then disappear. This would be a disaster for Europe, and it would be a severe blow to American national interests as well. The US would run the risk of losing control of one of its opposing coastlines and it would give away one of its most powerful instruments of political influence on Europe. It is quite obvious that this must never happen as it is neither in the interest of the US nor of the Europeans.

Both the US and its allies must find ways to revitalize NATO. That means much more than further enlargement and a new agreement with Russia. It also means more than adaptation or the acquisition a few more numerous and more modern capabilities. NATO must no longer remain the regional defensive alliance it used to be. NATO must become a global alliance, ready to defend its member countries' interests wherever they are at risk. Global challenges require global security – and global security requires a global NATO.

The following guidelines should be under consideration:

First: There is only one way to gain influence on the US, and that is to possess capabilities which really matter. This means that the Europeans have to take an American approach: They should concentrate on those capabilities which the US need to run and sustain one or more operations, such as in Afghanistan, and which at the same time will improve the ability of the EU to conduct operations on its own in areas the Americans do not wish to be involved. To this end NATO should take a new approach to force planning: The issue is no longer to acquire capabilities which more or less copy American capabilities, albeit on a much smaller scale. The goal must be to identify American shortfalls and weaknesses and to plan for capabilities which reduce these weaknesses through the provision of non-US NATO forces. Examples of deficiencies for which the US would need European contributions in order to sustain operations or to be able to operate in more than one theatre include: ground surveillance; air-to-air-refuelling and air transport; and also effective engagement assets. Such instruments in the hands of US allies will not be inexpensive, but Europe can afford the cost. America's European allies would become indispensable for the US, and their influence would grow.

Such an approach would kill two birds with one stone: It would foster the irreplaceable transatlantic link, and it would at the same time strengthen the capabilities of the EU since, after all, we still talk about one set of forces. In addition, such steps could narrow the gap which exists today and which is growing minute by minute. The best evidence for this assertion is that the US defence budget foresees 140 billion $US for capital investment, i.e. 37 per cent, whereas most Europeans spend some 20 per cent or so to modernize their forces. If the European allies spend a similar percentage upgrading their armed forces as to the Americans, the Americans would simultaneously look at the other, truly substantial European political contributions from a different angle. They would no longer be seen as a compensation for the inability to contribute militarily but as a genuine contribution of its own value. Thus the Europeans could gain more political influence as well. It goes without saying that the willingness on the side of the Europeans to launch such a modernization programme should be met by an increased American preparedness to share technology.

Second: Closer cooperation is required in infrastructure, logistics and defence industries across the Atlantic, including the creation of transatlantic synergies in procurement policies. Our policy should not be 'buy American' or 'buy European'. Rather, we must create conditions to 'buy transatlantic', i.e., procuring the most advanced systems at the lowest costs. Neither the Americans nor the Europeans can be interested in prolonging the two-class society as it has evolved in the wake of the Revolution in Military Affairs (RMA). A serious political willin Washington to share US-technology with European allies is the precondition fortransatlantic defence consolidation, which is indispensable to ensure NATO interoperability and thus guarantee the future military cohesion of the Alliance.

Third: The military action-plan adopted at the Prague Summit – the Prague Capabilities Commitment (PCC) and the Creation of a NATO Response Force (NRF) – should be the first step of a European defence improvement programme which could solve two problems at once. It would allow NATO to acquire the needed new capabilities, and it would enable the EU to implement the Helsinki 'headline goal'. The allies need to understand as well that they have to enter binding commitments this time. Otherwise they cannot expect the US to agree on the transfer of technology which is so badly needed. To this end,

NATO and the EU could and should establish a monitoring and sanctions regime. The successful establishment of the European Monetary Union (EMU) only worked because of strict criteria which had to be fulfilled and, iron fiscal discipline. There should be no doubt that NATO and EU-countries could apply similar strict criteria to their security policy in order to enhance their defence capabilities within NATO and the EU, if the political will is there.

Fourth: All these good intentions will be in vain if Washington, instead of capitalizing on the momentum of a serious European commitment in the war against terror and a willingness to do more in terms of military burden-sharing – continues to carry out future military campaigns with a 'coalition of the willing' that might include some NATO allies but involves no formal sanction.

Today, as a result, we are witnessing something akin to a beauty contest in Europe as individual nations seek close and sometimes exclusive bilateral security ties with Washington. This might endanger not only European unity, but also the relevance of NATO as the core of transatlantic security. To be certain, the American preference for coalition-building within NATO is not least a response to the present lack of European defence capabilities, logistically understandable, but symbolically unfortunate. Even with the next US defence budget envisioned at $US 415 billion, America will not be able to handle new crises and security challenges alone. It will still need a strong and reliable partner such as NATO, and Europe should still be the first and relevant choice. No one in Washington should forget that not only capabilities matter in the war against terrorism, but also shared convictions and values. No one else in the world can offer this combination to the US but Europe.

Fifth: 'To make the world safe for democracy in the twenty-first century' Washington will need European allies. Meeting the new challenges of the twenty-first century, Europe will also need a new credible and courageous policy if it wants to become a mature partner of the United States and a global player. The Iraq crisis and 9/11 made clear that the political will to exercise a role as a global player is the prerequisite for a competitive Europe in political, economic and military terms, and for a Europe that cares to preserve together with its American friends its cultural identity vis-à-vis any attacks from totalitarian Islamic terrorists on Western civilization. It is also the prerequisite for an equal partnership with the United States and a strong and balanced European–Atlantic alliance, able to meet new challenges anytime and anywhere.

3. Conclusion: initiation of an EU–US strategic dialogue

The Papandreou/Powell-Report for a New Transatlantic Charta

The aim of this paper is to contribute some ideas about reshaping European–American relations.

The issues raised in our paper could only be touched briefly here, and a more devoted and concrete effort is advisable. Our recommendation would be to initiate a 'New Transatlantic Charta' to revitalize the European–American partnership. Such an effort should take place under the leadership of a senior European and a senior American politician in order to give it the adequate weight and depth.

Ideally, such a 'New Transatlantic Charta' would not only be an agenda listing the deficits and assets of the EU–US relationship but would include a comprehensive strategy on how to overcome the transatlantic rift. Applicable measures would be particular helpful, addressing all levels of transatlantic exchange: political, economic, military, academic and cultural.

The initiation of such a 'New Transatlantic Charta' would require the leadership of highly regarded politicians on both sides of the Ocean. Given its very successful EU presidency – crowned by the signing of the Accession Treaties in Athens – Greece is very well positioned to lead the endeavor for crafting this Charta and Foreign Minister George Papandreou is one of its most distinguished and liked personalities in Europe as well as in the United States. Given his unbiased position within Europe and the transatlantic community, he would be an ideal candidate to co-chair a committee consisting of leading policy-makers and scholars from both sides of the Atlantic that shall gather regularly in order to craft a New Transatlantic Charta within the next six to eight months.

As his American counterpart we suggest US Secretary of State Colin Powell, as he is a strong defender of the interests of the transatlantic community and would give the initiative gravitas as well as public attention in the United States.

The *Papandreou/Powell-Report* for a 'New Transatlantic Charta' could become the founding document for a renewed partnership between Europe and the United States in which both sides will reflect and remember their common roots, values and interests, which have been covered recently under political differences. To overcome these differences is imperative for both Europe and America.

The Potsdam Centre for Transatlantic Security and Military Affairs would be honoured if the dialogue on a 'New Transatlantic Charta' would be held in our institute.

Brief overview on EU-members' foreign policy: prepared for the informal EU-Foreign Ministers' meeting in Greece 2–4 May 2003

Prof. Dr **Margarita Mathiopoulos**, Professor of US-Foreign Policy and International Security at the University of Potsdam; Founding and Executive Director of the Potsdam Centre for Transatlantic Security and Military Affairs; (contributions by Jan Friedrich Kallmorgen, Research Fellow at the Potsdam Centre and Salim Abu-Abed, Project Manager at the Potsdam Centre). http://www.mathiopoulos.deinfo @aspide.de

Notes

1. Toomas Hendrik Ilves, 'The Grand Enlargement and the Great Wall of Europe', *Estonian Foreign Policy Yearbook 2003*, Tallinn 2003, 181–205.
2. Ronald D. Asmus, *Opening NATO's Door: How the Alliance Remade Itself for a New Era*, Foreword by Lord Robertson, Secretary General of NATO (New York: Columbia University Press, 2002).

Table 33.1: EU member countries

	Foreign policy/goals	Regional and bilateral cooperation
Austria	• 'neutrality' • gateway to Central and Eastern Europe • host of international organizations and conferences	• cultivating good relations with its eastern neighbours based on close historical and cultural affinity • enhancement of so-called strategic partnership with Poland, the Czech Republic, the Slovak Republic, Hungary and Slovenia
Belgium	• closer coordination within the Benelux framework • strong support for ESDP • strong cooperation in the field of justice and home affairs with the EU • especially focused on respect for human rights, the principles of democracy and the rule of law, environmental protection, sustainable development and regional conflict containment	• a former colonial power in the Democratic Republic of Congo, Rwanda and Burundi, Belgium has assumed a leadership role in treating the problems of Central Africa and the Great Lakes. • advocates an active mediating role of the European Union in the Congo conflict, which depends on still missing progress in the inter-Congolese dialogue
Denmark	• strong international commitment to development assistance, human rights policy and military peace-keeping, particularly under UN auspices • acts as a kind of a pioneer in providing operations-ready staff elements for potential peace missions • prominent donor of development aid, giving 1% of its GNP each year, which is considerably higher than the United Nations target	• strong tradition of participation in Nordic cooperation • no participation in military operations under EU leadership

Table 33.1: EU member countries – *continued*

Foreign policy/goals	Regional and bilateral cooperation
Finland • traditional neutrality was replaced by an active Western-oriented policy • continuation to a policy of military non-alignment combined with credible self-defence in the foreseeable future • taking pragmatic steps to draw closer to the Western defence organizations, such as participating in the Partnership for Peace (PfP), the PfP Planning and Review Process (PARP) and KFOR	• cultivating good relations based on mutual trust with Russia • regional cooperation with neighbouring countries in the Nordic Council, the Council of the Baltic Sea States and the Barents Euro–Arctic Council
France • preservation of national independence • autonomous power over its military, in particular its nuclear potential • active role in Europe and the world; emphasizes need for independent European security and defence policy • privileged relations with Third World countries as well as worldwide campaigns for freedom and human rights • permanent member of the Security Council • making the EU a political, economic and cultural heavyweight in a multipolar global order while maintaining the cultural diversity within Europe and the European social model	• close political, economic and technological cooperation with Central and Eastern Europe, to bolster the democratic and market-oriented restructuring process • policy towards Russia geared to economic and political partnership, also within international organizations • active player in the Balkans, displaying both diplomatic and military commitment (large French contingent in the SFOR in Bosnia and Herzegovina and the KFOR in Kosovo) • criticism of the US in world politics, particularly since the terrorist attacks of 11 September 2001 • preserving traditional ties to Francophone Africa and the Middle East

Table 33.1: EU member countries – *continued*

	Foreign policy/goals	Regional and bilateral cooperation
Germany	• deepening of integration among current members of the EU • expansion of European Union membership • support of the United Nations and of the Organization for Security and Cooperation in Europe (OSCE) • strong emphasis on multilateral foreign policy • strong focus on civilian crisis management • strong focus on rule of law in international relations	• once upon a time had good relations with the US • vehement criticism of the US policy towards Iraq • close post-war relationship with France • strong relations with Central Europe / CIS-States • particular emphasis on relationship with Poland • strives for particular close relations with Israel due to history • seeks to foster Middle East peace process • strongly involved in peacekeeping efforts in the Balkans (SFOR, KFOR) • participating (co-lead) in peacekeeping efforts in Afghanistan (ISAF) • seeks to integrate Russia closer into Europe
Ireland	• maintaining military neutrality • favouring EU integration • promoting disarmament • strong consideration for the concerns of the Third World	• Ireland and Great Britain have together been seeking a solution to the Northern Ireland question. Among other things, the reunification mandate enshrined in the constitution was abrogated under that agreement. • close political and economic relations with the United States of America, where more than 40 million Irish Americans and temporary Irish residents live

Table 33.1: EU member countries – *continued*

Foreign policy/goals	Regional and bilateral cooperation
Italy <ul><li>particularly high commitment to international peace missions with more than 10,000 Italian soldiers engaged in missions all over the world</li><li>backing of ESDP with its own military and non-military capabilities</li><li>emphasis on arms control, arms export regimes for goods relevant for military purposes, non-proliferation of weapons of mass destruction, destruction of conventional weapons</li></ul>	<ul><li>particular attention on the Middle East conflict building on traditionally good relations with Arab states</li><li>traditional focus on the countries of Southeast Europe (particularly the former Yugoslavia and Albania), the Horn of Africa (Ethiopia/Eritrea, Sudan), but also on South American countries with high numbers of Italian emigrants and their descendants (Uruguay, Argentina)</li><li>Berlusconi government attaches importance to the fact that Italy is a strategic partner of both the US and Russia.</li></ul>
Luxembourg <ul><li>notable contribution in the field of humanitarian assistance and development aid</li><li>increased defence spending expected over the coming years.</li></ul>	<ul><li>maintaining close relations with the countries of Central and Eastern Europe, in particular Romania, which is home to many descendants of Luxembourg emigrants</li></ul>
Netherlands <ul><li>focus on development cooperation and generous development assistance (0.8% of GDP). The population is extremely supportive of this practice.</li><li>promotion and hosting of the Permanent Court of Arbitration, the International Court of Justice/ the International Tribunal for the Former Yugoslavia disarmament secretariats and the chemical weapons</li></ul>	<ul><li>multilateral cooperation of great importance, with focus on implementing human rights and peace-keeping</li></ul>

Table 33.1: EU member countries – *continued*

	Foreign policy/goals	Regional and bilateral cooperation
Portugal	• close relationships with Spain and Germany (main trading partners) and traditionally with Great Britain and France • strong diplomatic role in Africa, member of the so-called Troika (along with the US and Russia) for the peace process in Angola • relations with the Portuguese-speaking African countries (PALOP countries) and with Brazil are given high priority. • support for the process of democratization and reconstruction in East Timor as well as the stabilization of the country's independence	• very close security relationship with US within NATO • traditionally close political relations with Great Britain and France • intensifying relations with Asia, particularly China and Japan
Spain	• strong focus on development cooperation mainly in Latin and South America • bringing influence and initiatives to bear on the development of the EU's international relations with North Africa • cooperation in the Mediterranean region based on the Barcelona Dialogue • combating human trafficking and the increasing number of illegal immigrants across the 14 km wide Straits of Gibraltar	• special significance to bilateral relations with France, cooperation to combat ETA terrorism • close relations with the US since the mid-20th century • particularly close intellectual, cultural and social ties with Latin America

Table 33.1: EU member countries – *continued*

Foreign policy/goals	Regional and bilateral cooperation
Sweden • government is keen for Sweden to renounce its commitment to neutrality but adhere to its policy of non-participation in any military alliance • strong emphasis placed on participation in international peace missions • United Nations seen as 'very important' in ensuring respect for human rights and building a more democratic and equitable world	• priority on developing its bilateral relations with the countries of the eastern seaboard – Russia, the Baltic states and Poland • strong interest in the consolidation of Estonia, Latvia and Lithuania as stable sovereign states
United Kingdom • strong Atlantic orientation and the central importance accorded to NATO • providing strong momentum on EU reform of economic structures (single market, deregulation), on the Common European Foreign and Security Policy as well as justice and home affairs • pursuing active Third-World-policy focusing on poverty eradication and advocating debt relief • UK government is keen to join European Monetary Union.	• special relationship based on shared cultural and historical roots with United States, especially after 11 September 2001 • relations with the countries of the Commonwealth of special importance • regional focus on the Near and Middle East, anglophone sub-Saharan Africa (in particular South Africa), the Indian subcontinent and the Far East • in China and in Asia as a whole, the UK is the largest source of European direct investment. • improved relationship with Russia

Table 33.2: Prospective EU-member countries

Foreign policy/goals	Regional and bilateral cooperation
Bulgaria aims for membership in EU 2007 NATO membership expected May 2004	• accession to EU is priority of its foreign policy, with a clear Euro-Atlantic orientation. • sees itself as a stabilizing force in Southeast Europe following crises in the region • transit country (transport, sources of energy) • seeks active cooperation in the Stability Pact for South-Eastern Europe • comprehensive reform of the armed forces to be completed by the year 2010	• relations with Romania have been intensified, not least through enhanced cooperation within the framework of the Stability Pact • developments in the Federal Republic of Yugoslavia have opened good prospects for Bulgarian regional policy • developing equal and mutually beneficial relations with Russia and other successor states to the former Soviet Union are further key goals
Cyprus Accession treaty with EU, membership expected May 2004	• swift accession to the European Union (EU) • follows historically a non-aligned foreign policy • Since the 1974 Turkish invasion, Cyprus has sought the withdrawal of Turkish forces from the North and the most favourable constitutional and territorial settlement possible. • pursues solution of the Cyprus problem along the lines of the latest proposal of the UN Secretary-General	• close relations with Greece • expanding relations with Russia, Israel, Egypt, and Syria, from which it purchases most of its oil

Table 33.2: Prospective EU-member countries – *continued*

Foreign policy/goals	Regional and bilateral cooperation
Czech Republic Accession treaty with EU, membership expected May 2004 NATO member since 1999	• swift accession to the European Union (EU) • strong involvement in international peace missions (Kosovo, Kuwait, Afghanistan)	• close cooperation with Visegrad neighbours Slovakia, Poland and Hungary • Germany and the US are its most important partners. Austria continues to be an important partner due to the historical ties. • Russia is important because it supplies natural gas and because of marked increase in the number of Russian nationals permanently resident in the Czech Republic
Estonia Accession treaty with EU, membership expected May 2004 NATO membership expected May 2004	• swift accession to the European Union (EU) • enhancement of regional cooperation in the Baltic Sea region through the Baltic Council • improvement of relations with Russia • deepening of relations with Ukraine and Belarus	• close relations with Germany and Finland • much sympathy towards the USA, with a strong emphasis on security policy issues • relations with Russia are marked by different perspectives on the question of the integration of the Russian-speaking minority

Table 33.2: Prospective EU-member countries – *continued*

Foreign policy/goals	Regional and bilateral cooperation
Hungary Accession treaty with EU, membership expected May 2004 NATO membership expected May 2004	• swift accession to the European Union (EU) • safeguarding the interests of Hungarian minorities in neighbouring countries • promotion of cooperation on the fight against organized crime and corruption	• developing fast expanding economic relations and infrastructure with new neighbours • strengthening of a Central European identity within the framework of the Visegrad cooperation • active role in the Stability Pact for South-Eastern Europe with various initiatives of its own • signed a free trade agreement, mutual investment protection and double taxation agreement with Federal Republic of Yugoslavia
Latvia Accession treaty with EU, membership expected May 2004 NATO membership expected May 2004	• swift accession to the European Union (EU) • seeks increasingly to speak with one voice with other Baltic states through Baltic Council	• relations with Russia marked by differing views on NATO accession, issues concerning the Russian-speaking minority and history. Trade relations are important for both sides, mainly due to Latvia's role as a transit country particularly for crude oil and gas • Charter of Partnership with the United States, which actively supports Latvia's transformation process

Table 33.2: Prospective EU-member countries – *continued*

Foreign policy/goals	Regional and bilateral cooperation
Lithuania Accession treaty with EU, membership expected May 2004 NATO membership expected May 2004	• swift accession to the European Union (EU) • cooperation between the Baltic States • aiming for strategic partnership with Poland	• excellent relations with US • relations with Russia hampered disagreements over energy supplies (oil, gas) and border treaty • Kaliningrad: Russia has accepted a special regime (visa-free access to the Kaliningrad region) and hopes to use this as a basis for closer contacts • relations to Belarus marked by problems – payment for energy, border demarcation, no withdrawal agreement yet • cooperation with Denmark, Sweden and Finland developing satisfactorily
Malta Accession treaty with EU, membership expected May 2004	• focuses on the Mediterranean basin • since 1987 constitutionally committed to neutrality, enshrined in the guarantee treaty concluded with Italy in 1980	• relations with Britain and its neighbour Italy, as well as with the US, are particularly close • relations with Libya are important especially in economic terms

Table 33.2: Prospective EU-member countries – *continued*

Foreign policy/goals	Regional and bilateral cooperation
Poland Accession treaty with EU, membership expected May 2004 NATO member since 1999	• swift accession to the European Union (EU) • further development of bilateral relations with most important Western European and transatlantic partners (the United States, Germany, France, the United Kingdom and Italy) • strengthening of Central Europe within the framework of the Visegrad cooperation. • support for the independent development and strengthening of its eastern neighbours, above all Ukraine and Lithuania, but also Belarus • smooth relations with the Russian Federation	• close bilateral relations with US • especially close bilateral relationship with Lithuania; problems involving their respective minorities are now handled in a dispassionate manner • relations with Russia have improved considerably
Romania aims for membership in EU 2007 NATO membership expected May 2004	• accession to the EU is a priority of Romania's foreign policy, which has a clear Euro-Atlantic orientation • active support of regional-cooperation initiatives, particularly the Stability Pact for South-Eastern Europe	• particular importance to developing bilateral relations with Germany • traditionally good relations with France • relations with the US of great importance • OSCE chairmanship 2001 regarded as a success internationally

Table 33.2: Prospective EU-member countries – *continued*

Foreign policy/goals	Regional and bilateral cooperation
Slovakia Accession treaty with EU, membership expected May 2004 NATO membership expected May 2004	• swift accession to the European Union (EU) • Slovak government seeks strong relationship with Germany • restructuring of armed forces by 2010: reduction in size, professionalization, an increase in mobility and operational capability, and greater international participation in UN missions and the fight against terrorism	• strives to improve relations with its Visegrad neighbours after tensions in relations with Hungary and the Czech Republic have been resolved
Slovenia Accession treaty with EU, membership expected May 2004 NATO membership expected May 2004	• swift accession to the European Union (EU) • commitment to regional cooperation and bilateral and multilateral free trade given the highly dependence on exports. • maintaining security policy and military cooperation with the US • stepping up relations with Russia	• relations with Croatia improving; relations with Bosnia and Herzegovina and Macedonia traditionally friendly; normalization of relations with the Federal Republic of Yugoslavia and Serbia [Serbia is part of Yugoslavia, or what is now 'Serbia and Montenegro'] • Italy has been lending strong support to Slovenia's accession to the EU and NATO • relations with Hungary: intensive efforts to extend the transport corridors linking the two countries • relations with Austria characterized by an intensive exchange of visitors

Table 33.2: Prospective EU-member countries – *continued*

Foreign policy/goals	Regional and bilateral cooperation
Turkey aims for EU membership NATO member • Western integration (NATO, EU) is key feature of national policy • urging for an intensification of international cooperation in the fight against terrorism after 11 September underlined Turkey's strategic importance as the only Western democracy in the Muslim world located in the 'crisis triangle' Balkan–Caucasus–Middle East • other priority is the resolvment of the Cyprus conflict • support in principle for the development of a European Security and Defense Policy and cooperation in its practical implementation • strengthening role as transit country for natural gas and oil from the Caspian Sea aiming to build a number of pipelines	• US supports Turkey on central issues such as EU accession and the fight against PKK terrorism; Turkey trusts that America appreciates the country's foreign policy and strategic importance • Turkey and Greece, for decades entangled in a clash of interests, have been able to palpably defuse their relations after the earthquakes 1999 and due to the 'good-neighbour-policy' of the Simitis / Papandreou Government relations improved • vying with Russia and Iran for political and economic influence in the Caucasus and Central Asia, especially over the question which corridors are to be used for transporting Caspian and Central Asian oil and natural gas to Turkey and Europe • sees itself as the natural partner of the new Turkic Republics in this region, bound to them by religious (Islam) or ethnic (Turkic peoples) ties; trying to prevent the establishment of an independent Kurdish state in northern Iraq • bilateral relations with its neighbours Syria, Iraq and Iran focus on the fight against the PKK and the Kurdish question; relations with Syria in particular are overshadowed by the 'water issue'

34

European Attitudes towards Transatlantic Relations 2000–2003: an Analytical Survey

Prepared for the informal meeting of EU Foreign Ministers, Rhodes and Kastellorizo, 2–4 May 2003

The Centre for European Studies, Birmingham: Anand Menon and Jonathan Lipkin

Executive summary

- *The European see-saw of hope and frustration.* Part 1 of the study looks broadly at transatlantic relations during the first two years of the George W. Bush administration. It recalls how the concern about the likely foreign policy direction taken by Bush was confirmed by his stance on the Kyoto Protocol and the decision to push ahead with the missile defence project. Hopes that the 11 September attacks could be an opportunity to cajole the United States in a more multilateralist direction were soon frustrated by the increasingly hawkish line on Iraq, confirmed in the State of the Union address of January 2002. Signs of relative European unity rapidly disappeared as the showdown with Iraq moved closer.

- *Analysing recent developments in Europe.* Part 2 observes that responses from European states – both current and prospective EU members – to the imminent war with Iraq showed a re-emergence of the classic Europeanist–Atlanticist division on the shape of the transatlantic security architecture. Nonetheless, it also points out that on many non-military foreign policy issues, the EU is able to foster relatively united and effective positions.

- *The nature of EU–US divisions.* Part 3 engages with the notion that the future of EU–US relations is being determined by deep divisions in political values between Europe and the United States which help to shape their relative international power. At public opinion level, we find little evidence to back assertions of fundamentally different world-views, and much hostility aimed at the Bush administration rather than America or Americans in general. While at government level, there are major transatlantic divisions over how to achieve international objectives, the nature of those international objectives is not radically different. We further suggest that the measurement of power in terms of military strength is an inadequate way of gauging European potential on the international stage, as a number of recent European figures have pointed out.

- *Recommendations*. Our final recommendations centre less on immediate means to reduce transatlantic tensions – for example, the need for a calming in rhetoric on both sides – than on issues of longer-term institutional behaviour and the need for clearer strategic thinking and positioning:

1. The EU must as far as possible practice internally in Common Foreign and Security Policy (CFSP) what it preaches externally about multilateral and collective decision-making. A more closely-defined series of EU foreign policy ambitions may facilitate this.
2. Care must be taken in designing an institutional foreign policy framework that allows enough flexibility to avoid instances of unilateral action or action by small groups being seen as a failure for CFSP.
3. In order to help the EU to define its ambitions and roles in the foreign policy domain, a high-level working group should be created with the aim of surveying views within the Union and considering the possibility of an EU security plan.

Introduction

Transatlantic relations have endured a turbulent few months. Among the numerous questions confronting European states as a consequence are:

- How divided are Europeans in terms of their approach to international relations in general and the United States in particular?
- How deep are transatlantic divisions and to what extent do they reflect longer-term processes of drift on the two sides of the Atlantic?

- What can and should Europeans do to address the current divisions both between themselves and between them and the United States?

We were requested to provide a survey of European attitudes towards transatlantic relations, the way these have altered in recent months, and the various visions of the future of US–European relations that such attitudes have spawned. What follows is in no way meant to be exhaustive, nor does it cover the positions of all the member states in equal detail. Rather, it presents a broad overview of European attitudes, focusing in particular on the larger EU member states, these having been most prominent in recent controversies surrounding Europe's relationship with the United States.

Through an exploration of the first two years of the Bush administration and the specific context of the Iraq crisis, the paper illustrates that while there is considerable common ground between European states on many aspects of foreign, environmental and commercial policy, familiar divisions among European states over the appropriate form of relationship with the United States have tended to re-emerge as the former grapple with the challenge of adjusting to the threat – and actual use – of US military power. Thus while the United Kingdom and France (which have long epitomized the Atlanticist–Europeanist split in thinking over Europe's security architecture) have been able to work effectively since St Malo in 1998 to promote the development of the EU's European Security and Defence Policy, the Iraq crisis has seen a reversion to type that many had hoped would no longer occur as the ESDP evolved. Certainly, these renewed divisions may, to an extent, be conjectural. However, they are no less real and threaten to have an adverse effect on the Union's ability to act together on the international stage.

As far as the issue of broader US–European relations are concerned, we attempt to demonstrate that at both public opinion and elite level, the currently dominant hypothesis about fundamental differences between the world-views of Europeans and Atlanticists is at best an incomplete characterization of the way in which Europeans see the world. We reject the notion of a fundamental clash or divergence in values across the Atlantic. Such a view both oversimplifies what 'Europe' is, and the divisions within it, and misunderstands the nature of transatlantic disagreements. Rather, we conclude that Europe and the United States are not so much separated by conflicting values as by different views of the most appropriate means to achieve their international objectives, objectives which are far from incompatible.

Nonetheless, alongside the question of intra-European divisions and current European–US tensions, one should also note an additional dimension: the fact that the United States has still not itself worked out what its international role should be in the early twenty-first century. While a detailed examination of this issue is beyond the scope of this paper, it adds a further complication to calculations about the future of the transatlantic relationship on both sides of the Atlantic.

Anand Menon
Professor of European Politics, and Director of the
European Research Institute, University of Birmingham.

Jonathan Lipkin
Western Europe Analyst at Oxford Analytica,
writing in a personal capacity.

1. The European see-saw of hope and frustration

Arguably, there had been clear signs of increasingly unilateralist tendencies on the part of the United States over the past decade. However, the accession to power of George W. Bush heightened unease in Western Europe. Most EU capitals reacted with caution and in some cases alarm to a number of key emerging policy stances, notably the intention to pursue the missile defence programme to protect against so-called 'states of concern'[1] – with the ensuing implications for the Anti-Ballistic Missile (ABM) Treaty[2] – and not to submit the Kyoto Protocol for ratification.[3] There was also considerable criticism of US–UK military strikes on Iraq in 2001, with the kind of doubts about UK commitments to the nascent European Security and Defence Policy (ESDP), and indeed to the EU itself, that have again been seen in the context of the Iraq crisis.[4]

Immediate tensions with the United States were to a limited extent assuaged by the summer of 2001:

- A high-level diplomatic campaign by the Bush administration succeeded in muting the most outspoken criticism of missile defence – for example by playing down the 'national' element of what was originally termed 'NMD' (European states were in any case somewhat divided in the level of their hostility).[5]
- While American opposition remained constant (although a softening of tone on the global warming issue was evident in June), the

Kyoto Protocol was saved at the Bonn Conference in July 2001, with almost 180 countries reaching a broad political agreement on the operational rulebook for the Protocol.

Indeed, initial concerns about the Bush administration notwithstanding, bilateral relations between the United States and individual European capitals remained relatively cordial. German Chancellor Gerhard Schroeder, for example, paid a visit to Washington in March 2001 during which he and President George Bush issued a joint statement on a 'Transatlantic Vision for the 21st Century' (29 March 2001).

However, even among the most supportive of European allies, initial concerns regarding the general attitude towards international relations being adopted by Washington intensified and elite opinion was mirrored by public attitudes: A Pew Research Center survey in August 2001 showed considerable hostility to Bush's international policy in certain parts of Western Europe: 59% of those questioned in France disapproved, compared to 65% in Germany, 49% in the United Kingdom and 46% in Italy. At the same time, however, it is notable that a solid majority disagreed with the view that Europe and the United States were growing apart.[6]

From 'We are all Americans' ...

That the multiple terrorist attacks of 11 September 2001 momentarily changed attitudes towards the United States has become something of a cliché. The *Le Monde* headline 'We are all Americans' was indicative of a sharp increase in positive French opinion of the United States[7] which was, at least initially, widely mirrored across the continent. Furthermore, opinion polls revealed strong support for European participation in military action against terrorists.[8] Given current public misgivings in much of Europe about the Iraq war, it is notable though not only that the same polls revealed distinct unease concerning the prospect of attacking those countries where the terrorists might be based, but also that French opinion was significantly more favourable to the idea than was British.[9]

At governmental level, as speculation mounted about the form any US military response might take, sympathy was mixed with the hope of being able to steer the Bush administration in a direction desired by all EU states: action through multilateral institutions in line with the structures of international law. Thus when the UK Prime Minister offered to stand 'shoulder to shoulder' with Bush,[10] as well as being a simple declaration of solidarity, the phrase was taken by some to imply a desire to draw on longstanding US–UK ties and act both as an influence and a restraining force.

Certainly, the range of European military contributions to the campaign against the Taliban regime and al-Qaeda in Afghanistan mirrored the professions of support.[11] Given recent rhetoric on both sides of the Atlantic (and indeed the Channel) concerning Franco-US relations, it is perhaps worth emphasizing the scale of the French contribution in particular: France's carrier battle group, headed by the *Charles de Gaulle*, supported combat operations for Operation Enduring Freedom from the North Arabian Sea; air resources were deployed in Tajikistan and Kyrgyzstan, with Mirage fighters and tanker aircraft in action to support Operation Anaconda; an infantry company was deployed to Mazar-e-Sharif to provide security; special forces were used in a variety of operations. In addition, Paris provided a range of ongoing logistical and intelligence support.[12] In a real sense, the scale of French involvement – both in military terms and diplomatically symbolized by French President Jacques Chirac's trip to express solidarity with Bush in Washington following the events of September 11 – was in keeping with the tradition of the Fifth Republic. It has long been a French claim to be the closest ally of the United States in times of real crisis – hence rapid and overt support for Washington at the time of both the Cuban missile and Euro missile crises.

Nonetheless, although the invocation of NATO Article 5 was initially seen as a step in a multilateralist direction, it is notable that non-US contributions to the Afghan campaign were essentially offered on a bilateral basis, to be accepted or rejected by Washington. Mindful perhaps of the experience in Kosovo, the Bush administration was keen to avoid the kind of 'decision-making by committee' that it felt had undermined the efficiency of the campaign in the Balkans.[13] However understandable this approach may have been in operational terms, it appeared to many in Europe much more like an ad hoc 'coalition of the willing' than a serious attempt to mobilize through multilateral institutions – an impression merely reinforced by Donald Rumsfeld's comment that the 'mission determines the coalition and the coalition must not be permitted to determine the mission'.[14]

The 'cherry picking' approach adopted by the Bush administration certainly did little to foster EU unity in its response to 11 September. Indeed, a striking feature of US policies towards Europe has been the willingness of the administration to promote divisions amongst Europeans on issues ranging from the ICC (International Criminal Court) (where the administration placed heavy pressure on European states to sign bilateral agreements exempting US personnel from the jurisdiction of the court) to Iraq.[15] Despite this, there were signs of a growing understanding among the three most powerful West European nations

– France, Germany and the United Kingdom. An Anglo-Franco-German conclave at the Ghent European Council in October 2001 (and subsequent mini-summit in London) unleashed controversy within the Union (with smaller member states enraged at what appeared to be large state domination), but suggested a growing desire to advance ESDP in the context of changed global security issues and to present a more unified front to Washington, and on the world stage, as the 'war on terror' moved forward.[16] This appeared all the more timely in the late autumn/early winter of 2001, as hawks within the Bush administration began to talk once again of taking on Saddam Hussein in a subsequent wave of the 'war on terror', and international controversy began to build over the status and treatment of, and the possible use of the death penalty for, prisoners at the 'Camp X-Ray' facility at the US Naval Station in Guantanamo Bay, Cuba.

... to 'simplistic' US foreign policy

By the end of January 2002, when President George Bush delivered the State of the Union address that included the famous reference to Iraq, Iran and North Korea as the 'axis of evil', European alarm about the potential for a military conflict with Iraq had increased substantially. Not only was the language disturbingly aggressive, but the choice of targets conflicted with European analyses which almost unanimously would have ranked Yemen, Pakistan and Chechnya above the three 'axis' states as sponsors of terrorism. Moreover, Bush further exacerbated European concerns about possible US unilateralism with his statement that 'some governments will be timid in the face of terror. And make no mistake about it: If they do not act, America will.'[17] While nobody was surprised that Iraq should be singled out,[18] the toughness of the rhetoric – signalling to both allies and enemies that WMD proliferation would not be tolerated – spawned a highly negative reaction Europe. In early February, with EU foreign ministers attempting to advance their plan for the Middle East peace process (an area where there is substantial consensus within the EU), then French Foreign Minister Hubert Védrine received broad support when he condemned US foreign policy as being 'simplistic'.[19]

With relations between Washington and a number of capitals – particularly Paris – beginning to spiral downwards, London was once again placed in a difficult situation, torn between its preferred European policy (engaging on the ESDP) and compromising continental credibility and relationships by backing the Bush administration. However, it was clear which way the United Kingdom was turning. While London had previously suggested that action against Iraq should not be contemplated until clear evidence of a link between Saddam Hussein's regime and the attacks of 11 September could be produced, the emphasis began to shift onto showing that Saddam's regime did indeed pose a threat to international security.

Given the 'axis of evil' speech, and underlying European suspicions of Bush's intentions, when US tariffs were announced in early March 2002 on the vast majority of steel products, the angry reaction from European member states and the EU was symptomatic not just of periodic transatlantic trade tensions (which are relatively frequent and have so far been fairly successfully contained), but of a growing conviction that the United States was becoming more unilateralist. This was an issue which saw unanimity of condemnation and which cut across the European cleavages that often develop on security issues (see Part 2).[20] EU Trade Commissioner Pascal Lamy captured the mood in an address to the European Parliament: 'Despite the initial hopes for a re-launch of American interest in engaging with the international community after the events of 11 September, we are at the moment faced with what seem to be increasingly unilateralist US tendencies. This can be seen in different policies and the list is continuing to grow: the International Criminal Court, the ABM Treaty, Kyoto and the steel market are the most striking.'[21]

... and further European divisions

In the summer of 2002, although the positions of the three most powerful European players differed markedly over Iraq, there was as yet little sign of the Franco-German axis that would emerge so clearly in January 2003:[22]

- Against a background of strong misgivings within the ruling Labour Party and little public appetite for war, the United Kingdom was taking the most consistent line of support for the United States. While London made it clear that it wanted all possible avenues explored to address the Iraq WMD issue (particularly a return to the UN), there seemed little doubt that it would support the United States, both politically and militarily, if force were used against the regime of Saddam Hussein.

- At the other end of the spectrum, Germany (both at political and public opinion level) was opposed to the prospect of military action against Iraq. However this opposition was reinforced by the anti-US tone taken by Chancellor Gerhard Schroeder in an election that the SPD won only narrowly. Where the former French 'plural left' government of Prime Minister Lionel Jospin and Foreign Minister

Védrine had left off, Schroeder picked up, accusing the Bush administration of 'adventurism', while his justice minister, Herta Daeubler-Gmelin, was alleged in a newspaper article to have compared Bush's methods to those of Hitler. Whatever the truth of this particular allegation, the Schroeder election campaign marked a mile-stone in US–German relations. Outright opposition to a major US foreign policy priority was a new departure for a German government.[23]

- While essentially substantively unchanged, French policy over Iraq was initially expressed with a degree of diplomatic restraint under the re-elected conservative President Jacques Chirac, who had attempted to mend fences with Washington after the victory of a conservative-led coalition in the parliamentary elections of June. However Paris began to make it increasingly clear that it was not prepared to be pushed into a diplomatic and/or military line decided in Washington. Situated some way between the London and Berlin line, the French position was – and remains – essentially that the UN must be pre-eminent in dealing with Iraq and that force would only be justified once a full new weapons inspections process had been exhausted.

2. Analysing recent developments in Europe

The striking feature of the first few months of 2003 has been the very public re-emergence of classic Europeanist–Atlanticist divisions over the nature of the transatlantic security and defence relationship. In the past, the Europeanist–Atlanticist dichotomy has best been epitomized by the contrast between French and UK approaches to the European security and defence architecture. While the EU's commitment to the creation of the ESDP has clearly shifted the parameters of the debate – not least as a function of the British conversion, following the Amsterdam summit, to the cause of endowing the EU with a defence capability – the two terms are still apposite descriptive terms in pointing to national/common European security and defence aspirations that lean more towards balance and/or independence, or towards complementarity and/or relative dependence.

Europeanist axis?

The establishment of an apparent foreign policy alliance between France and Germany opposing the US strategy in the run-up to war was symbolized in comments made at the 40th anniversary celebrations of the Elysée Treaty on January 22, with both French President

Jacques Chirac and German Chancellor Gerhard Schroeder emphasizing that the UN must be pre-eminent in dealing with Iraq and that they were opposed to precipitate military action. Their comments followed blunt remarks by French Foreign Minister Dominique de Villepin to the UN Security Council suggesting that war on Iraq was so far unjustifiable.

This alliance was unusual in several respects:

- While the French stance appeared to owe much to a longstanding view of international relations, the German approach was not in keeping with Germany foreign policy traditions. As we suggest in Part 1, it had its origins in the election strategy adopted by Schroeder in September 2002 as well as in a gradual reassessment of that country's position in the international order. Nonetheless, there is no equivalent in Germany of the French Gaullist tradition that has consistently emphasized the desirability of a multipolar geo-political order.
- Despite statements suggesting a common approach to the Iraq crisis,[24] it was evident that there were still differences between France and Germany on the issue of the eventual use of force should the UN process fail, reflecting very different traditions of post-war military development and deployment. While Berlin appeared implacably opposed to the notion of taking military action (reflecting a strong pacifist and anti-militarist tradition), the French position was – and remained – that force would only be justified once a full new weapons inspections process had been exhausted.[25]
- While the French political class was fairly unified in its hostility to the line taken by the Bush administration over Iraq, there was far more disagreement between (and, to some extent, within) the Schroeder administration and the CDU/CSU opposition. In this respect, it should be emphasized that the tone taken by Schroeder would not have been mirrored in the event of a CDU/CSU victory in September 2002.

Nonetheless, the Franco-German understanding over Iraq was cemented further by their refusal in early February, together with Belgium, to countenance formal approval for NATO contingency planning for the provision of military support to Turkey in the event of an attack by Iraq. The three countries broke their silence on the issue on 10 February. While the question was eventually resolved, the initial decision caused near apoplexy in the United States and deep concern in a number of other European capitals.

Transatlantic comment

Over the past few months, there have been a number of pronouncements from France, Germany and Belgium on the future of transatlantic relations. The three countries are together with Luxembourg, due to hold a defence summit at the end of April, 2003. Although the emphases of public discourse have sometimes differed somewhat, there is a clearly expressed desire to bolster the European security and defence capability in order to work towards a world order with greater balance, in which international law and international institutions determine the scope of political and military intervention in global trouble-spots:

- French Foreign Minister Dominique de Villepin's keynote IISS speech last month, 'Law, Force and Justice' concentrated on the notion of complementary 'regional poles' in a new world order. Strikingly, NATO was mentioned just once in the speech (and only in the context of EU involvement in Bosnia[26]): 'To be truly stable, this new world must be based on a number of regional poles, structured to face current threats. These poles should not compete against one another, but complete each other. They are the cornerstones of an international community built on solidarity and unity in the face of new challenges. The determination of European countries to develop a common foreign and security policy must reflect that. This determination shows our will to bring about a true European identity.'[27] A further hardening in the French position regarding the relationship between Europeanism and Atlanticism was evident in President Chirac's reported remarks to Latvian President Vaira Vike-Freiberga that NATO was no longer relevant in the modern world.[28] Interestingly, and perhaps dangerously, this again mirrors comments made by some US conservatives.[29]
- A speech by Belgian Prime Minister Guy Verhofstadt in February emphasized 'a new Atlanticism',[30] in which NATO could be reinvigorated by a stronger and more unified European presence within it: the final objective being that 'NATO no longer remains an organization grouping a superpower and a series of states ... We have to look for an alliance of partners, of two partners, not necessarily equal but strongly linked.' This, according to Verhofstadt, should take place in a multipolar world in which, notwithstanding the common values shared with the United States, Europe should continue to develop its own views and standpoints. The 'new Atlanticist' theme can in part be attributed to the conjuncture – NATO was in the throes of

the Turkey protection crisis. A lecture on transatlantic relations in January by Belgian Foreign Minister Louis Michel appeared more similar to French public discourse, devoting little time to the future of NATO and concentrating on the need for the EU to develop as a serious foreign policy actor.[31]

- Remarks by German Foreign Minister Joschka Fischer have lamented the lack of real transatlantic debate over the issue of how to tackle new security threats, and more generally, over the shape of a future international order.[32] However, he has been very specific about German support for a strengthened ESDP: 'If Europe stands for multi-lateralism, for a cooperative new world order, Europe must also have the political will and the full palette of options, institutions and capabilities to meet the demands of such multilateralism. A strong United Nations presupposes that the Europeans unite and do their part to ensure that a multilateral world order built on a cooperative security foundation becomes reality.' At the same time, recent state-ments by Chancellor Schroeder have underlined Germany's contin-ued commitment to ensuring developments within the EU occur within a NATO framework (not least given Germany's insistence that NATO take over the ISAF mission in Kabul). Thus in a recent inter-view, whilst acknowledging that there is not 'too much America but too little Europe' and that the CFSP should be built faster, he noted that 'this should happen inside the frame of NATO and not against it'.[33]

Schroeder's recent comments seem to indicate a desire to repair rela-tions with Washington after an exceptionally difficult period since last summer. They also confirm the somewhat conjunctural Europeanism that cemented the Franco-German alliance over Iraq earlier this year. Recent French comments about the need immediately to suspend UN sanctions against Iraq may also be read as an attempt to ease trans-atlantic tensions, further to a phone call by Chirac to Bush. However, further evidence of France's intentions may become clear at the defence summit at the end of April 2003.

Playing an Atlanticist card – the gang of eight

The January 30 newspaper letter signed by the leaders of five existing EU members and three applicant states (followed by a statement from the 'Vilnius group' a short time later) provided highly public and explicit evidence of intra-European tensions over the conduct of Euro-pean policy towards the United States, and over the disputed nature of leadership in the EU. Indeed, the Franco-German behaviour on the occasion of the 40th anniversary of the Elysée Treaty celebrations, and a number of subsequent pronouncements, had caused considerable resentment in a number of existing member states and applicant states, worried about both the question of 'who speaks for Europe on international affairs' and the implications for the longer-term balance of power within the Union.

Addressed as much to other European states as to the United States, the letter was a powerful statement of the common ground between Europe and the United States, formulated in the context of deteriorating transatlantic relations, particularly in the aftermath of the Elysée Treaty celebrations and the 'old Europe / new Europe' distinction subsequently coined by US Secretary of Defence Donald Rumsfeld, which had provoked a deeply hostile response from those supposed pillars of the 'old Europe'. Two things are particularly striking about the letter. First, it reveals the degree to which the debate sparked by Robert Kagan on the possibility of a clash of values between the United States and Europe has shaped subsequent debates. The first sentence of the letter reads simply that the 'real bond between the United States and Europe is the values we share'.[34]

Perhaps more importantly, apart from the implicit warning to France over its UN 'responsibilities', the statement of solidarity contains little that other EU member states – including France and Germany – could not have signed up to themselves.[35] In this regard, the fact that there was only a partial set of EU member state signatories for such a statement probably contributed further to the negative diplomatic atmosphere developing between Washington and Paris and Berlin in particular – an atmosphere not helped by allegations that the letter had originated in mischief-making by journalists from the *Wall Street Journal*.[36]

Nonetheless, it is notable that all the signatories shared a broadly 'Atlanticist' perspective. Three broad groups can be identified:

1. Traditional Atlanticists

The United Kingdom, Denmark and Portugal have been traditionally among the most solidly Atlanticist states in the EU.

- While British official discourse has for obvious reasons focused mainly on immediate matters relating to the major UK military involvement in the Iraq war, Prime Minister Tony Blair used a newspaper interview at the end of April to spell out his vision of transatlantic relations. In contrast to remarks made by De Villepin and Chirac, Blair notes that: '[s]ome want a so-called multi-polar world where you have different centres of power ... others believe, and this is my notion, that we need one polar power which encompasses a strategic partnership between Europe and America.' This, according to Blair, means a stronger Europe, but not a rival power which would be 'the quickest way' to get unilateralism in America.[37]

- Recent remarks from Danish and Portuguese ministers have emphasized the importance of the US partnership and of NATO as the main guarantor of security for all EU member states.[38] Indeed, a staunchly Atlanticist tone has been taken by the new right-wing Portuguese government under Prime Minister Jose Manuel Barroso. Although the decision announced earlier this year to pull out of purchasing A-400M military transport planes (and perhaps to buy new capacity from Lockheed Martin) was justified on cost grounds, it has nonetheless been interpreted symbolically in some quarters given the current international environment.

- Given the defence and security stance traditionally adopted by the Netherlands, it would hardly have been surprising had the government been a signatory to the letter. Concern about the potential effects on European relations (particularly relations with Germany) of such a public EU division, together with the uncertainty associated with the absence of a new government after the general election, were key factors in persuading the caretaker Dutch government not to sign.

2. 'Reflex Atlanticism' in Central and Eastern Europe

Comments by Polish Foreign Minister Wlodzimierz Cimoszewicz that NATO is today the only structure which can guarantee Poland's security,[39] reflect broader views shared by Poland, the Czech Republic and Hungary (and other East European states) influenced by Cold War and post-Cold War history. The first wave of NATO expansion in 1999 has long preceded any enlargement eastwards of the EU, which (for now) offers no security guarantee of the kind still provided by NATO. The close ties between Poland and the United States were underlined recently with the signing of an agreement under which Poland will purchase 48 US F-16 fighter jets from Lockheed Martin.

The Central and East European applicants are also generally less than enthusiastic about the prospect of an EU potentially dominated by a resurgent Franco-German axis, a suspicion reinforced by comments made by French President Jacques Chirac after the European Council meeting of 17 March 2003 in which he (now famously) described their behaviour as 'childish' and suggested that they had 'missed a good opportunity to remain quiet'.

3. *Conjunctural Atlanticism*

Neither Spain nor Italy are usually thought of as defining their strategic outlook in more Atlanticist terms and their stance over Iraq owes much to the position of the current government incumbents:

- The strong pro-US position adopted by the José-Maria Aznar government in Spain has only really been evident in the last couple of years, since its position was strengthened by winning an outright parliamentary majority. Previously, Madrid seemed to be identifying far more closely with the pro-integrationist dynamic in the EU than with US interests. Recently, Spain – currently a member of the UN Security Council – has been playing a leading role, alongside the United States and United Kingdom, in the diplomatic manoeuvring which surrounded the immediate pre-war period. For José-Maria Aznar, the stakes are less high personally than for his party, given his pre-standing decision not to run for re-election in the next parliamentary elections.
- Similar to the situation in Spain, the Italian government's pro-US stance owes much to the influence of Prime Minister Silvio Berlusconi. Italy has traditionally adopted a position which prioritized multilateral institutions / agreement (e.g. EU, NATO), while maintaining strong ties with Washington. However, Berlusconi's signature of the 'gang of eight' letter symbolizes a far more explicit commitment to supporting elements of US foreign policy.

It should be noted though that in many of the so-called 'Atlanticist' states, there has been considerable public opposition to the stance taken by the governments over the Iraq war, and also intense political debate. This has in some cases seen divisions between the political class in general and the public (Poland), deep divisions within the ruling party alongside initial public hostility (United Kingdom) or shifts in the parliamentary handling of foreign policy issues:

- Danish participation in the Iraq conflict (in the form of modest naval support for surveillance and logistics) saw parliamentary backing, but not the tradition of a broad (cross-party) majority when Danish soldiers are sent to war (the broad majority was in favour of participation only under explicit UN mandate).
- In Portugal, the cross-party consensus on foreign policy that has existed since the democratic transition in 1974–5 has been broken. While the Socialists made support for the war conditional on expli-

cit UN backing, the PSD-led coalition government under Prime Minister José Manuel Durao Barroso aligned itself with the United States.

The neutrals/non-aligned (Austria, Ireland, Finland, Sweden)

While the relationship with ESDP and NATO is more complex in the four member states who have traditions of neutrality or non-alignment, the general tenor of deep concern about the war on Iraq and the absence of a second UN resolution explicitly authorizing the use of force also characterizes their approach. The Swedish government explicitly pointed out that it did not believe that the action was in line with international law.[40] The Irish, Finnish and Austrian governments also made it clear that in their judgement explicit new UN authorization for military action should have been received.

How deep are European divisions?

Fundamentally, the European preoccupation is about how to deal with a United States itself still coming to terms with its hegemonic status in international security terms. In the three largest member states, so divided over war in Iraq, the concern about unilateralism and its potentially negative effects on the wider international institutional, economic and security environment, is generally shared. Paris, Berlin and London would all like to steer the Bush administration towards a stance in the ongoing 'war on terror' more accommodative of a multilateral environment. However, in addition to differences over the shape of that multilateral environment (particularly with respect to security institutions as we have noted) the means of doing this and, to some extent, the interpretation of the nature of US power, vary:

- For the current governments in Paris and Berlin, the need actively to oppose or at least present an alternative approach, has become increasingly important, not least because of a growing conviction that unchecked US power may not necessarily be motivated by ideological convictions to which many in Europe can subscribe.
- For London, due to a number of reasons related both to historic transatlantic ties and to Blair's evolving relationship with Bush, the 'shoulder to shoulder' strategy of hoping to exercise restraint through solidarity remains paramount.[41] The United Kingdom is generally less suspicious of US motives and international action than France, and Blair sees this strategy as being as much about gaining influence though supporting US policies as about restraining the

unwanted and irresponsible exercise of US power. Indeed, the show of Atlanticism in the 'gang of eight' letter can also be interpreted generally in the context of increasing concern about the potential for miscommunication at a time when there is great uncertainty within Europe about where the United States is heading strategically.

Clearly though, the UK position on European security policy is far more complicated than the label 'Traditional Atlanticist' suggests and is far from irreconcilable with the kind of 'new Atlanticist' rhetoric used by Verhofstadt earlier in the year. While the current Labour government in the United Kingdom may be committed to ESDP more through pragmatic strategic thinking than through a visceral commitment to European unity, this does not imply that a workable solution for ESDP cannot be found. To some extent, the outcome of the Franco-British Le Touquet summit demonstrates this, and it is clear that to be militarily viable any EU military capacity requires UK involvement. In this respect, it will be difficult for the meeting between France, Germany, Belgium and Luxembourg to achieve any substantial reorientation of ESDP.

We would re-emphasize that it is primarily in the security/defence domain involving specific military action/military strategies by the United States that this aspect of divisions is evident. In areas of foreign policy more generally, the pattern of European unity and disunity is very different.

- As we point out in Part 1, the EU has been fairly united on key questions of international economic and environmental policy, demonstrated most notably in the condemnation of Bush's rejection of the Kyoto Protocol and of the imposition of steel tariffs last year.[42]
- The EU has been fairly consistent in its message regarding the response to international terrorism and in its approach to the Middle East peace process, offering a plausible solution to the current impasse.[43]
- The EU has taken over policing in Bosnia and peacekeeping in Macedonia, with the hope of eventually taking over from the NATO-led force in Bosnia. Despite the public furore over Iraq that engulfed its genesis, discussion between the EU and NATO on putting this Berlin Plus mission in the field were rapid and effective.[44] Similarly, agreement has now been reached on allowing NATO to take over the ISAF mission in Kabul.[45]
- The EU is agreed that a diplomatic – rather than confrontational – engagement with Iran, the other Middle Eastern member of the 'axis

of evil', offers for now the most promising way of achieving political change.

- Post-Iraq, the EU agreed at the Athens European Council on 17April that the 'UN must play a central role' including the process leading towards self-government for the Iraq people.[46] While the press was quick to comment that the expression 'a central role' was ill-defined and ambiguous, and certainly not synonymous with 'the central role', it is clear that the EU, the United Kingdom included (even if Blair's scope to express this is constrained), is at odds with the way in which more hawkish elements of the Bush administration wish to conduct the physical and political reconstruction process.

The risks of cultivated division

While it is certainly true that European member states on occasion need no encouragement from outside to split into rival or disputing factions, we have already noted that the United States has shown signs of encouraging such division. The cherry-picking of military partners certainly has the potential to undermine common EU action/positioning. At the annual Wehrkunde meeting in the spring of this year, Donald Rumsfeld made a point of insisting that there were more differences among Europeans on Iraq than between the US and Europe.[47] Beyond exacerbating existing long-standing strategic divisions, there is the additional danger that the conjunctural Atlanticism of Italy and Spain, linked so clearly by a very specific pair of political leaders, may be replicated if individual countries perceive that they can obtain advantages by attempting to do deals directly with the United States. As the EU strengthens its own foreign and security policy machinery, the incentives for opportunist bilateralism may diminish, but they will only do so if Washington can be persuaded that it is in its best interests to deal with the Union as an actor as opposed to national capitals. The past few months have provided clear evidence of how far from that point the EU still is.

Illustrating the problem

Some of these differences in approach to foreign policy and security/defence policy questions are illustrated in Figure 34. The four charts are intended to reinforce the key observation made in this part of the study that the Europeanist–Atlanticist division still forms a fundamental source of division that may emerge from within the dynamic of intra-state and intra-EU tensions, or be encouraged from outside.[48]

Figure 34 (a): Missile defence (early summer 2001)

Figure 34 (b): Decision not to ratify Kyoto (2001)
Steel tariffs (2002)

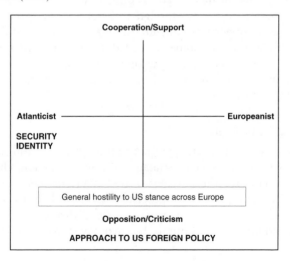

Figure 34 (c): Post 9/11 – war in Afghanistan

Figure 34 (d): Iraq war

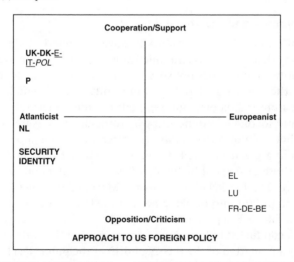

3. The nature of EU–US divisions

Although most press and analytical attention in recent months have focused on the immediate ramifications of the Iraq conflict, there has been considerable discussion of the proposition that there is a basic strategic divide opening up between Europeans and Americans. Indeed, Robert Kagan's convenient catchphrase 'Americans are from Mars, Europeans are from Venus', and the accompanying claim that US and European values are increasingly divergent, have in some respects dominated discussion on both sides of the Atlantic.[49] That debate has also been strongly coloured by the diplomatic fall-out from events earlier this year (particularly the NATO crisis), with a vitriolic reaction from US conservatives.[50] From the European perspective, a strong response to Kagan has come in the form of a speech by High Representative for the CFSP Javier Solana at Harvard in early April,[51] and in a number of addresses by European Commissioner for External Relations Chris Patten.[52] A significant contribution, emphasizing the close nature of EU–US economic relations, has been made in a paper by Joseph Quinlan.[53]

Public opinion and shared values?

A central proposition put forward by Kagan is that 'it is time to stop pretending that Europeans and Americans share a common view of the world'. Although he does not specify whether he means the public at large or the government policy community, we present here some evidence from well-known opinion polls in order to test this assertion. Values and ideologies are notoriously difficult to measure and large-scale public opinion surveys can only offer a snapshot approximation of views at a given moment. However, a number of major studies – notably those carried out by the Pew Research Center and the Chicago Council on Foreign Relations / George Marshall Fund (CCFR-GMF) – do offer an insight into thinking both in the United States and Europe.

The CCFR-GMF report of last year (*Worldviews 2002*), based on fieldwork conducted in June–July,[54] provides what the authors describe as 'partly a refutation of the theory of drift at the public level':[55]

- *Mutual goodwill.* There is a considerable amount of mutual goodwill, with warm feelings towards the United States clearly in evidence not just in the United Kingdom, but also in Germany, France and Italy (60–68 degrees in the four countries, according to a 'thermometer scale' of 0–100).

- *Unilateralism.* Americans are as supportive as Europeans of involvement in international institutions, such as the United Nations (77% of Americans thought that the UN should be strengthened, against 75% of Europeans), NATO (61% of Americans for strengthening and 63% of Europeans) and the WTO (63% and 59% respectively).
- *Use of force.* Europeans are as supportive as Americans (sometimes more so) of using troops in certain circumstances (for example, 80% of Europeans would approve if it was to uphold international law, against 76% of Americans).
- *Iraq policy.* 65% of Americans thought that the United States should only invade Iraq 'with the approval of the United Nations and its allies' (against 60% of Europeans). Only 26% of Europeans (against 13% of Americans) thought that the United States should not invade Iraq.[56]

However, there are of course significant divergences:

- US public opinion is far more favourable, for example, to using troops to guarantee oil supplies (65% against 49% of Europeans) than to using it to contain a civil war (48% against 72% of Europeans). This had already been evident in attitudes towards intervention in the Balkans. A Pew study in August 2001 found that only 47% of Americans favoured keeping troops in Bosnia and Kosovo, compared to 57–64% of those in the United Kingdom, France, Germany and Italy.[57]
- Threat perceptions differ considerably, sometimes for quite obvious reasons. Americans worry far more about international terrorism (91% view it as extremely important against only 64% of Europeans), Iraq developing weapons of mass destruction (86% to 57%), Islamic fundamentalism (61% to 47%), war between Israel and its neighbours (67% to 42%), and the development of China as a world power (56% to 18%).
- Europeans tend to be more sympathetic to Palestinian statehood – 72% favoured the establishment of an independent state on the West Bank and Gaza against 40% of Americans (although the latter were markedly more enthusiastic in supporting this option when it was presented as part of official Bush policy – which is perhaps cause for hope in the context of the much vaunted 'roadmap'*).

In sum, on international affairs issues, the divisions look less about values in the most basic sense – e.g. support of military force – than about perceptions of international affairs and national priorities. Caution should also be exercised about sweeping judgements regarding value questions such as the death penalty, a source of periodic tension between Europe and the United States. While there is an certainly an obvious problem at elite level, it not completely clear that there is a fundamental divide between US (shifting steadily downwards in support) and European public opinion (itself not unified) on this question.[58]

Anti-Americanism or anti-Bush-ism?

The most recent European survey data from the Pew Research Center (carried out during March 2003)[59] shows a marked deterioration in perceptions of the United States since the CCFR-GMF study was carried out and from a previous Pew survey mid last year:

- Only 48% of those questioned in Britain held a favourable view of the United States (from 75% in 2002). The figure was marginally higher in Poland at 50% (from 79%). In France, only 31% held a favourable view (from 63% in 2002), 25% in Germany (from 61%), 34% in Italy (from 70%) and just 14% in Spain (no figure given for 2002).
- There was higher European support for greater independence, although the change was less marked over the year. 48% of those questioned in Britain favoured more independence (from 47% in 2002). The figure was 67% (from 60%) in France, 52% (from 51%) in Germany and 63% in Italy (from 59%).
- Interestingly though, when asked whether the problem was 'mostly Bush' or 'America in general', 76% of those in France and 68% in Germany answered 'mostly Bush' compared to 56% in the United Kingdom, where one might have expected greater general affinity with the United States. On the contrary, 31% of Britons blamed 'America in general' compared to just 15% in France.
- In connection to the 'Bush or America' question, partisan divisions within the United States on the question of Bush's foreign policy are also increasingly evident: 44% of Democrat voters were totally opposed to military action against Iraq, while 59% of Republicans supported unilateral action.

Public opinion moving forward

The results of the latest surveys contain mixed messages for the European political class as it seeks to stabilize and reinforce EU–US relations:

- The negative is that the Bush administration is seen as a major problem and the Iraq crisis has severely and dramatically damaged European popular perceptions of the United States (even if many of those questioned believe that Iraq will be better off as a result – 76% of those questioned in Britain; 73% in France; 71% in Germany; and 61% in Italy).[60] The 'mud slinging' or 'trading insults' matches since January between Washington and certain European capitals have probably further contributed to this.

- The positive is clearly that such distrust and unfavourable views may be more temporary and conjunctural than necessarily structural. The data does not suggest that, at public opinion level at least, the doom-laden scenario of a 'parting of the ways' or deep division is an immediate reality.

Further detailed survey data will be needed to confirm such conclusions, and public perception may in any case evolve if, for example, it is perceived that US unilateralism may be more bi-partisan than many had realized.

Elite opinion and EU–US divisions

Whatever the faults of generalization that Kagan's work may contain, he puts his finger on a salient and crucial point in relation to the policy communities in Europe and the United States. While in Washington there is a sizeable, and apparently growing, group which believes in the unilateral exercise of power, acting with allies as and when it is convenient to do so, Europe on both right and left is dominated by multilateralists who do not wish to see the United States acting without recourse to international law and institutions. The EU's recent compromise Athens statement on the Iraq crisis (in a period where there is a majority of conservative governments in Western Europe) is a powerful demonstration of this.

An interesting point of debate is the extent to which the current European insistence on the importance of the United Nations and international law is merely instrumental: Does it represent a genuine attachment to these facets of the international order, or is it rather motivated solely by a desire to use these as methods to constrain a United States that is unrivalled militarily (the ropes that the Lilliputians use to restrain Gulliver, to employ an oft-used current metaphor). One only has to look at the intervention in Kosovo, broadly supported by most Europeans, to see an example of a regional crisis dealt with without the UN. Some have even claimed that there is an element of opportunism in EU opposition to the United States even in areas where the Europeans seem to find it the easiest to agree on such a line.[61]

However, it remains generally true that the EU as an economic and political construction is a symbol of the importance placed upon broadly-accepted rules and norms, and that it has played a significant part in taming member states and prompting them to act multilaterally. This does not mean that those (many) critics, including Kagan, who point to the relatively low level of military spending and of the coordination of procurement and research and development are wrong. As Javier Solana acknowledged in his recent address in Harvard, more needs to be done. Nonetheless, as Solana himself and other key figures and commentators have pointed out, simply spending more money is not a sensible solution.[62]

Different power for different powers

One of the great weaknesses of Kagan's book is his one-dimensional appreciation of power.[63] The EU is seen as weak because it does not choose to develop and exercise conventional military power in the way that the United States has chosen to do so. However, there are a number of responses to this:

- First, such an approach represents a huge oversimplification. Europeans have not eschewed the use of military force. Their troops made a significant contribution to the war in Afghanistan, and to peacekeeping missions such as those in Kabul or Macedonia. These lattermost, while small scale, have the potential to escalate into something more militarily serious. And all this is, of course without mentioning the significant UK contribution to the war in the Gulf.
- Second, it is far from clear what the most appropriate way of dealing with the threat posed by international terrorism and the new security threat posed by potential WMD proliferation by states of concern/failed states actually is. Indeed, Bush's attempt to link these two issues inextricably in the 2002 State of the Union Address alarmed many observers in Europe. The power to defend national interests may come as much from a top class intelligence network and police force as from laser-guided missiles.
- Third, power is often exercised through influence, and influence can be developed through a number of 'soft' tools such as aid conditionality or preferential access to markets. With the EU rapidly becoming the most important trading block in the world, soft power has considerable potential, as is becoming increasingly evident in areas such as Palestine and Iran.[64]

- Finally, Europe and the United States are not so much separated by conflicting values as by different views of the most appropriate means to achieve their international objectives.

Recommendations

Clearly, the Union itself is not fully in control of the current situation or of its possible future development.

- Much will depend on the attitude of the United States, not only towards areas of concern highlighted by Europeans – notably the Israeli-Palestinian conflict – but also towards the European allies themselves. Talk of 'punishing' states that obstructed the path towards war in the Gulf is hardly helpful in terms of the imperative of rebuilding transatlantic relations.
- Second, the Union is crucially dependent upon consensus between its member states in order to function effectively. One fundamental and obvious consequence of the Iraq crisis has been the rift between Europe's two major military powers, the United Kingdom and France. It is not our place to suggest, amongst our recommendations, that this relationship be repaired as soon as possible. However, there is something incongruous about discussions in the Convention and elsewhere concerning institutional proposals for enhancing the effectiveness of CFSP and ESDP at a time when the two states whose active participation is crucial to the effectiveness of either are at loggerheads.

Nonetheless, three general recommendations can be made regarding what Europeans could and should do to promote CFSP / ESDP revival:

(1) Multilateralism in practice

What emerges clearly from the above analysis is the fact that, whatever their differences over specific issues, all the EU member states share the objective of attempting to ensure that the US works through multilateral institutions rather than pursuing unilateralist foreign policy initiatives. In order to do this more effectively, they themselves must endeavour to work collectively through such organizations in their own dealings. Both the 'gang of eight' letter and the mini summit on defence planned for late April serve to undermine European solidarity. In so doing they both eased the path for those Americans keen to maintain a posture of divide and rule vis-à-vis the 'Old Continent', and undermined their own case in arguing for the need for multilateralism in contemporary international affairs. As Philip Stephens has put it recently: 'The presumption by France and Germany that they could speak for Europe followed by the public retaliation led by Spain and Britain brought only smiles to the faces of Washington's unilateralists.'[65]

One possible means of addressing the tendency of unilateralist or small group initiatives to undermine Union solidarity would be to define more closely the scope of the Union's external policy ambitions. The EU, and EC before it, have had a marked tendency to define themselves in somewhat aspirational terms. Thus, the stipulations concerning not only the mechanics of the CFSP in the Maastricht Treaty, but also the aspiration to go further, and eventually build – should the European Council agree – a common defence. The problem with such an approach is that it has a tendency to raise expectations unrealistically. Whilst this is relatively unproblematic in the sphere of domestic policies of the Union, the dangers of such an approach to external affairs have been all too evident in the myriad pieces bemoaning the death of the CFSP that have followed the recent Iraq crisis. Clearly identifying those issues on which the Union will act and those that will be left primarily to member states (perhaps in the context of the wise men's study we propose below) could be one way of avoiding such disenchantment.

(2) EU institutions and CFSP

It is not the purpose of this paper to produce detailed recommendations for EU institutional change based on our analysis. The current state of these relations, however, does give pause for thought concerning at least two aspects of the Union's institutional architecture.

- The creation of a European foreign minister/Council chair with a foreign policy remit. Clearly there are divisions between the European member states over one of the most important strands of foreign policy – relations with the United States. Clearly, too, these will not simply disappear with the final resolution of the Iraq crisis. Thus claiming, or seeming to claim, that Europe will create institutions to allow it to speak with a single voice is something to be treated with caution for the reasons alluded to in our discussion of the need to define the range of the CFSP. It is inconceivable that particularly the larger member states will defer to a European Council Chair or EU foreign minister, whoever these individuals might be. Thus care must be taken, in both presentational and institutional design terms to allow enough flexibility in the overall European foreign policy system that each instance of unilateral action (and these will continue) is not viewed as a failure of the new institution.

- The EU presidency should not be bypassed if it is not held by one of the larger member states. This happened both in the preparations for the letter by the 'gang of eight' – where the presidency was not consulted (although the signatories purported to speak for 'Europe') – and the recent Athens summit, where the declaration was reportedly drafted in advance by France, the United Kingdom, Spain and Germany. Institutions created to ease the task of pursuing multilateral policies should be involved in the formulation of these policies both in order to prevent resentment on the part of the smaller member states, and in order that Europe can be seen to be practising what it is preaching to the United States.

(3) Be clearer about strategic objectives: towards an 'EU Security Plan'?

In order that the EU is able to act more effectively both towards the United States and in international relations more generally, a more sustained effort must be made to identify the Union's position on the major global issues. One particular criticism of the EU that has been made in this respect – particularly from the United States – is that it is too preoccupied with its own internal development, which has bred a degree of introspection. This, it is claimed, prevents the Union from being clear about how it is positioned strategically in the current geopolitical environment.[66]

We would recommend that steps be taken to identify both key global security issues, and the degree of consensus that exists between member states on appropriate measures to be taken in connection with them. The recent meeting about WMD represented an interesting and important first step in the right direction, but the task needs to be carried out in a far more wide-ranging and systematic way. The EU should appoint a group of senior experts capable of carrying out such a survey and considering the possibility of developing a US-style 'Security Plan' for the Union. This would try to identify the provenance and nature of potential threats to European security, together with recommendations as to how best to tackle them. This would represent a concerted attempt on the part of the Union to look beyond immediate responses to international crises. It is only within the context of such a strategic assessment that plans for the development of either CFSP or ESDP can be effectively put into place.

Of course, sceptics might point out that the very nature of the EU means that a security plan would be unnecessary and that, certainly in the case of terrorism, specific member states – notably now the United Kingdom, Spain and Italy – may be far more likely targets and would need to undertake the appropriate security assessment at national level. Of course, we are not suggesting that national level planning should cease or be supplanted. On the contrary, it should feed into the overall EU assessment. However, as the struggle against the perpetrators of 11 September has demonstrated, there are many areas where European member states need to cooperate to be effective. Indeed, terrorism is only one area that the security plan would touch on. There is a far broader set of security questions, concerning the shape of the broader international political, economic, military and technological environment that are worthy of consideration.

Notes

1. 'States of concern', three of whom later famously become part of the 'axis of evil', had previously been known as 'rogue states'. The change in nomenclature occurred before the Bush administration came to power (in June 2000).
2. In contrast to the Clinton administration's early plans for what was originally known as the National Missile Defence project, which foresaw renegotiation of the 1972 ABM Treaty, the Bush administration saw it as too restrictive and therefore wanted to abandon it.
3. Although there was recognition that Kyoto was unlikely to have been ratified by the Senate even under President Clinton, the language used by Bush was initially more hard-line. In mid-March, the president wrote a letter to senators noting the 'clear consensus that the Kyoto Protocol is an unfair and ineffective means of addressing global climate change concerns', and effectively stating that any measures would be subordinate to concerns about US economic growth at a time of what the president described as 'a serious energy shortage' in the United States – i.e. that a unilateral approach to the question would be adopted. 'Letter from the President to Senators Hagel, Helms, Craig, and Roberts', 13 March 2001.
4. Perhaps these doubts have been somewhat naïve in that the United Kingdom has not been slow to underline its close relationship with Washington throughout the development of the ESDP: for example, launching with the United States a short bombing campaign against Iraq barely two weeks after the Saint Malo summit in 1998, and insisting on statements guaranteeing the primacy of the Atlantic Alliance throughout the development of ESDP.
5. For reasons elaborated in Part 2, Spain, Italy, Poland and Hungary had moved to a position of public support by the summer of 2001, with the United Kingdom and Denmark quietly supportive.

6. Pew Research Center, 'Bush unpopular in Europe, seen as unilateralist', 15 August 2001.
7. An opinion poll carried out for *Le Nouvel Observateur* on 2–3November 2001 showed 65% of those questioned in France expressing a favourable attitude towards the United States. This had risen from around 35–40% in 1996–2000.
8. A poll taken by GALLUP on 14–15 September 2001 showed that 73% of those questioned in France favoured participation with the United States in military action against terrorists. With the exception of the United Kingdom (79%), this was the highest level of support among the larger EU states.
9. The GALLUP poll of 14–15 September showed that only 29% of those questioned in France favoured attacking 'the country or countries where the terrorists are based'. Moreover, the figure was only 21% in Italy, 17% in Germany, 12% in Spain and, perhaps surprisingly, 18% in the United Kingdom.
10. Statement by Prime Minister Tony Blair on 11 September attacks, 11 September 2001.
11. European support for any attack was not unequivocal even in the immediate post-11 September period. The Dutch government repeatedly insisted – even during the North Atlantic Council meeting of 2 October 2002 – that the United States should provide sufficient evidence against Bin Laden and his network. See Monica Den Boer and Joerg Monar, '11 September and the Challenge of Global Terrorism to the EU as a Security Actor', *Journal of Common Market Studies* 40 (2002), p. 13.
12. For more on the French contribution to the war on terror, see Jeremy Shapiro, 'The Role of France in the War on Terrorism', Brookings Institute, May 2002.
13. Interestingly, however, the man who was SACEUR (Supreme Allied Commander Europe) at the time of that conflict, General Wesley Clark, has been outspoken in pleading for the United States to adopt a multilateralist approach to international security issues. See Clark, 'An army of one', *Washington Monthly*, September 2002.
14. Remarks made at a press briefing by Rumsfeld, 23 September 2001 in response to a question speculating about tension between Rumsfeld and Secretary of State Colin Powell over this issue of coalition building.
15. Certain right-wing US commentators have explicitly propounded cherry picking as an approach destined to maximize American influence whilst minimizing the constraints upon it. See, for example, Charles Krauthammer, 'American unilateralism', speech given at the third annual Hillsdale College Churchill Dinner, Washington, DC, 4 December 2002 (http://www.hillsdale.edu/newimprimis/2003/january/default.htm)
16. See for example, Philip Stephens' article, 'Europe discovers a single voice ...' in the *Financial Times*, 5 October 2001.
17. State of the Nation address, 29 January 2002.
18. The issue of what the United States might do with respect to 'states of concern' such as Iraq had been simmering for some time. Indeed, as early as 1998, a number of figures, including Dick Cheney, Richard Perle, Donald Rumsfeld, Robert Zoellick and Robert Kagan, had written to President Bill

Clinton urging him to 'act decisively' against Iraq in order 'to end the threat of weapons of mass destruction against the US or its allies'. Letter to President Clinton, 26 January 1998.

19. In an interview on France Inter on 6 February 2002, Védrine commented that: 'We're threatened by a new simplistic approach, which is reducing all the world's problems to the fight against terrorism ...'

20. UK Prime Minister Tony Blair told Parliament on 6 March 2002 that the steel tariffs were 'unacceptable and wrong'. In a BBC interview, Trade and Industry Secretary Patricia Hewitt commented that '[w]e won't stand by and simply let [the United States] dump their problems onto us'. However, subsequent attempts to obtain special exemptions for the United Kingdom created some tension with EU partners.

21. Pascal Lamy, 'Etat et perspective des relations transatlantiques', European Parliament, Strasbourg, 13 March 2002.

22. Franco-German relations were still at a relatively low ebb, having earlier been described by Hubert Védrine as 'clinically dead'. It was only once a series of difficult internal EU institutional and budgetary differences were overcome that the Franco-German relationship could begin to look more solid again.

23. However, this was not just a case of electioneering in order to rally the SPD vote. Since 11 September, German foreign policy-makers had wanted to avoid the battle against terrorism being superimposed on the debate over the appropriate policy response to states trying to acquire or boost their WMD capacity. There was an emerging consensus that, while pre-emption and prevention were necessary in the case of terrorism, containment was the more appropriate strategy for dealing with WMD.

24. Jacques Chirac commented after the Elysée Treaty celebrations on 22 January that: 'Germany and France have the same view on [the Iraq] crisis, which is essentially based on two ideas: the first is that all decisions lie with the Security Council, and it alone, pronouncing its verdict after having heard the inspectors' report, and in accordance with the relevant resolutions adopted by the Council. And the second reality is that for us, war is always a symbol of failure and the worst solution.'

25. Comments made by Jacques Chirac in an interview on CBS news (16 March 2003) are representative of the French line: 'France is not pacifist. We are not anti-American either. We are not just going to use our veto to nag and annoy the US. But we just feel that there is another option, another way, another more normal way, a less dramatic way than war, and that we have to go through that path. And we should pursue it until we've come [to] a dead end, but that isn't the case.'

26. In some respects, therefore, the speech was a mirror image of that given by Rumsfeld at the Wehrkunde in 2001; the Secretary of Defence failed to mention the EU once in his substantive comments, even in a section of the speech specifically on ESDP.

27. Dominique de Villepin, 'Law, Force and Justice', IISS, 27 March 2003.

28. *Financial Times*, 16 April 2003.

29. See, for example, an interview with Richard Perle in *Berliner Zeitung* on 26 March which is dismissive about the future importance of the UN and NATO.

30. Guy Verhofstadt, 'A call for a new Atlanticism', The Hague, 19 February 2003.
31. Louis Michel, 'Transatlantic relations', Conference at the University of Liege, 24 January 2003.
32. Joschka Fischer address to the Bundestag, 20 March 2003.
33. *EU Observer*, 27 March 2003.
34. Article in *Wall Street Journal Europe* and a number of European newspapers, 30 January 2003.
35. See, for example, the interview given by Chirac to the *New York Times* on 8 September 2002. 'It's true that when the tragedy took place, my first reaction was to say: "We are all Americans". And I want to say today that those feelings have not disappeared; on the contrary, they've grown even stronger with the anniversary ... Something inside the French people was touched, and that hasn't changed ... It demonstrates once again that when the chips are down, the French and Americans have always stood together and have never failed to be there for one another. That's been the case since Yorktown and it still holds true today. That's the reality.'
36. For a refutation of such allegations, see the *Wall Street Journal Europe*, 3 February 2003. Relations between Belgium and the *Wall Street Journal* were considerably worsened by an article on EU defence budgets on 13 February, which singled out Belgium as an offender and provoked an outspoken protest from Belgian Defence Minister Andre Flahaut, who accused the paper of 'prostituting itself' ('Letter to the Editor, an Insult to My Country and Its Military', 26 February 2003).
37. Tony Blair interview in the *Financial Times*, 28 April 2003.
38. Svend Aage Jensby, 10 April 2003, Danmarks Radio P1. Source: BBC Monitoring European. Antonio Martins da Cruz, 5 March 2003, Radio Slovenia. Source: BBC Monitoring European.
39. Interview published in French newspaper, *Libération*, 21 March 2003.
40. Foreign Ministry statement on the conflict in Iraq, 21 March 2003.
41. See, for example, Quentin Peel, 'An understanding lost in translation', *Financial Times*, 3 March 2003.
42. Maintaining unity of action in the steel crisis was admittedly difficult. While the UK backed the EU's stances on the tariffs, London also lobbied the Bush administration for special exemptions for UK companies.
43. See, for example, Steven Everts, 'The EU and the Middle East: a call for action', Centre for European Reform Working Paper, January 2003.
44. However, rumours that the Pentagon did its best to block the deployment of the EU force, despite the supportive stance of the State Department, will hardly have helped transatlantic relations. See *Financial Times*, 31 March 2003.
45. NATO may thus be taking on the kind of global role foreseen by Thomas Friedman, though not in the way – with Russia and without France – that he foresaw, which can only be good for Europe; for Friedman, see the *New York Times* 30 March 2003.
46. EU presidency statement on Iraq, 17 April 2003.
47. *Financial Times*, 10 February 2003.
48. The charts are intended to be broadly illustrative, rather than precise or comprehensive calibrations of EU member state and applicant state

positions. For that reason, we do not include all member states or all candidates, rather we seek to point out the most evident differences and tensions.

49. Robert Kagan, 'Power and Weakness', *Policy Review* 113, 2002; *Paradise and Power: America and Europe in the New World Order* (2003: Atlantic Books). One should not forget how ideologically engaged Kagan is. He was, for example, one of those to sign the 1998 letter to Clinton on Iraq. See note 18.

50. For an interesting discussion of American anti-Europeanism, see Timothy Garton Ash, 'Anti-Europeanism in America, *New York Review of Books*, 13 February 2003.

51. Javier Solana, 'Mars and Venus reconciled: a new era for transatlantic relations', 7 April 2003, Kennedy School of Government, Harvard University.

52. See notably, 'America and Europe: an essential partnership', speech to the Chicago Council on Foreign Relations, 3 October 2002. Also Chris Patten and Pascal Lamy, 'Let's put away the megaphones: a trans-Atlantic appeal', *New York Times*, 9 April 2003. It is not clear to what extent the symbolism of the latter – penned by a Brit and a Frenchman, was picked up in the United States.

53. Joseph Quinlan, 'Drifting Apart or Growing Together? The Primacy of the Transatlantic Economy', Center for Transatlantic Relations, Johns Hopkins University, 2003.

54. The data is based on MORI fieldwork in France, Germany, Italy, the Netherlands, Italy, Poland and the United Kingdom in June–July 2002.

55. CCFR-WMF, *WorldViews 2002*, p. 3.

56. Although public opinion in the United States clearly moved once the UN route seemed to reach an impasse, a point made by Kagan to justify his standpoint. See 'Repairing the rift: the United States and Europe after Iraq', transcript of the roundtable at the Brookings Institution, 3 April 2003.

57. Pew Research Center, 'Bush unpopular in Europe, seen as unilateralist', 15 August 2001.

* (References to the 'roadmap' are fairly dated by November 2003.)

58. See, for example, Anthony Blinken, 'The False Crisis Over the Atlantic', *Foreign Affairs* 80/3 (May/June 2001), pp. 36–8.

59. Pew Research Center, 'America's image further erodes, European want weaker ties', 18 March 2003.

60. Pew Research Center, 'America's image further erodes, European want weaker ties', p. 4.

61. 'On environmental matters the EU pushed on regardless of the US position, and indeed because of it. Conviction mixed with the knowledge that here was an issue, like GM foods, where European opinion was firmly opposed to any significant move towards the Bush policy, and indeed where some relatively cheap political points could be scored. It is convenient for the Europeans to be able to show their unity on a question where the US seems to be behaving selfishly and short-sightedly, and where, of course, European interests – on energy, welfare and business – differ markedly'. Chris Hill, 'EU Foreign Policy since 11 September 2001: Renationalising or Regrouping?', First annual guest lecture Europe in the World Centre, University of Liverpool, 24 October 2002.

62. '[A]s far as contemporary security is concerned, there is no standard "unit of account". How much additional security does an aircraft carrier bring? Is it more or less than spending the equivalent amount of money on peacekeeping or the reconstruction of failed states?', Solana, 'Mars and Venus reconciled: a new era for transatlantic relations', 7 April 2003, Kennedy School of Government, Harvard University.
63. This is a point well made in a review of Kagan's *Paradise and Power* by Mark Leonard in *New Statesman and Society*, 17 March 2003.
64. See Everts, op. cit. and Andrew Rathmell et al., A New Persian Gulf Security System, RAND Issue Paper, 2003.
65. 'Capital E', E! Sharp, April 2003.
66. As Richard Haass, Director of Policy Planning at the US State Department put it: 'We have strong relationships and alliances around the world, but there is no "concert" of like-minded powers with the consensus, institutions, and capabilities to ensure the orderly functioning of the international system ... Instead, today's Europe is occupied with completing its own internal development' ('From Reluctant to Resolute: American Foreign Policy after September 11', Address to the Chicago Council on Foreign Relations, 26 June 2002).

Selected references

Speeches and discussions

Bush, George W., 'A Distinctly American Internationalism', Ronald Reagan Presidential Library, Simi Valley, California, 19 November 1999
Bush, George W., State of the Union Address, 29 January 2002
Cimoszewicz, Wlodzimierz, 'The future of the Common Foreign and Security Policy', lecture at the Friedrich Ebert Foundation, Berlin, 12 March 2003
De Villepin, Dominique, 'Law, Force and Justice', Alastair Buchan address to the International Institute of Stategic Studies, London, 27 March 2003
Fischer, Joschka, Speech in the German Bundestag, 20 March 2003
Haas, Richard, 'From Reluctant to Resolute: American Foreign Policy after September 11', speech at the Chicago Council on Foreign Relations, 26 June 2002
Krauthammer, Charles, 'American unilateralism', speech given at the third annual Hillsdale College Churchill Dinner, December 2002
Michel, Louis, 'Transatlantic relations', speech at the University of Liège, 24 January 2003
Patten, Chris, 'America and Europe: an essential partnership', speech at the Chicago Council on Foreign Relations, 3 October 2002
'Repairing the rift: the United States and Europe after Iraq', transcript of the roundtable at the Brookings Institution, 3 April 2003
Solana, Javier, 'Mars and Venus reconciled: a new era for transatlantic relations', speech at the Kennedy School of Government, Harvard University, 7 April 2003
Verhofstadt, Guy, 'A call for a new Atlanticism', speech in The Hague, 19 February 2003

Books, journal articles and pamphlets

Blinken, Anthony J., 'The False Crisis over the Atlantic', *Foreign Affairs* 80/3 (2001).

Clark, Wesley, 'An Army of One', *The Washington Monthly*, September 2002.

Everts, Steven, 'Managing divergence in transatlantic foreign policy', Centre for European Reform working paper, February 2001.

Everts, Steven, 'The EU and the Middle East: a call for action', Centre for European Reform working paper, January 2003.

Garton Ash, Timothy, 'Anti-Europeanism in America', *New York Review of Books*, 13 February 2003.

Grant, Charles and François Heisbourg, 'How should Europe respond to the new America?', *Prospect,* March 2003.

Hassner, Pierre, 'The United States: the empire of force or the force of empire', Chaillot Paper 54 (2002).

Judt, Tony, 'America and the World', review essay, *New York Review of Books*, 10 April 2003.

Kagan, Robert, 'Power and Weakness', *Policy Review* 113 (2002). Extended into *Paradise and Power: America and Europe in the New World Order* (Atlantic Books, 2003).

Malone, David and Yuen Foon Khong (eds), *Unilateralism and US Foreign Policy: International Perspectives* (Lynne Rienner, 2002).

Nye, Joseph, *The Paradox of American Power: Why the World's Only Superpower Can't Go It Alone* (Oxford University Press, 2002).

Quinlan, Joseph, 'Drifting apart or growing together? The primacy of the transatlantic economy', Center for Transatlantic Relations, Washington (2003).

Rathmell, Andrew, Karasik Theodore and David Gompert, 'A New Persian Gulf Security System', RAND issue paper, 2003.

Rice, Condoleezza, 'Promoting the national interest, *Foreign Affairs* 79/1 (2000).

Wallace, William, 'Europe, the necessary partner', *Foreign Affairs* 80/3 (2001).

Index